Journal Of An Expedition To Explore The Course And Termination Of The Niger

Harpers' Fam Liby

JOURNAL

OF

AN EXPEDITION TO EXPLORE THE COURSE AND TERMINATION

OF

THE NIGER.

WITH A

NARRATIVE OF A VOYAGE DOWN THAT RIVER TO ITS TERMINATION.

BY

RICHARD AND JOHN LANDER.

ILLUSTRATED WITH ENGRAVINGS AND MAPS

IN TWO VOLUMES.

VOL. II.

NEW YORK:

HARPER & BROTHERS, PUBLISHERS.

1838.

CONTENTS

OF

THE SECOND VOLUME.

A 2

CHAPTER XXI.

APPENDIX.

No. I.

No. II.

No. III.

JOURNAL

CHAPTER XIII.

The King and Midīki take leave of the Travellers—They embark on the River, and depart from Boossà—Island Melálie—Inguázhilligee—Island Patáshie—The Chief of Teáh—Messengers from the King of Wowow—Perplexity of the Travellers respecting their Route—Terror of the Natives at their Appearance—An Invalid—Diseases of the Natives—Their Medicines—Richard Lander goes to Wowow—Superstition of the Natives—Charms—Return of Richard Lander to Patáshie—His Interview with the King of Wowow—House of Correction at Patáshie—Native Pagan Priest—Departure from Patáshie—Ráah—Arrive at Lever—An officious Friend in the Priest Ducoo—Disappointment of the Travellers.

Monday, September 20th.—As may be supposed, our hearts beat high this morning with the anticipation of at length leaving Boossà, and of proceeding on our journey; and we were all on the *qui vive* at a very early hour, ransacking our lumber, packing it up, and turning it all out into the yard, from whence it was conveyed to the water-side. About breakfast-time the king and queen arrived at our hut, to pay us a farewell visit, and bestow upon us their last blessing. They brought with them two pots of honey and a large quantity of goora-nuts, strongly recommending us to present the latter to the Rabba chieftain, for that nothing we might have in our possession could so effectually conciliate his favour, procure us his friendship, and command his confidence. When mutual compliments were passed, we expressed our acknowledgments to both of them with sincerity and earnestness, for the benevolence,

II.—B

hospitality, and attention with which they had uniformly treated us; for their kindness to us; for their zeal in every thing that regarded our welfare; and for the protection they had afforded us during a period little short of two months, in which we had enjoyed the utmost security, and as much of happiness and gayety as it had been in their power to bestow. And we assured them, that should we be so fortunate as to return to England, it would be our first care to acquaint our countrymen of all their kindness to us, which we would remember as long as we lived. We then shook hands heartily, and concluded by wishing them a continuation of the simple blessings and the felicity they enjoyed; that they might ever be loved by their subjects, and feared and honoured by the neighbouring nations; that they might live to a good old age, and die in peace with all mankind. They were both touched with sorrow at our words, for they were the last which they would hear us utter; tears were glistening in the eyes of each as they were making an affecting and suitable answer; and the good couple walked out of our hut with heavy and mournful countenances, and immediately repaired to their own abode in order to make a powerful spell for our preservation and success.

When we ourselves quitted the hut, which was shortly after their departure, we found our yard filled with neighbours, friends, and acquaintances, who all fell down on their knees to bid us good-by. They blessed us earnestly with uplifted hands, and those among them that were of the Mohammedan religion fervently implored for us the favour and protection of Allah and their prophet. The eyes of many of them were streaming with tears, and all were more or less affected. As we passed by these poor creatures, we spoke to them all, and thanked them again and again for their good wishes. Our hearts must have been of marble if we could have beheld such a scene without some slight emotion. On our way towards the river, also, the path was lined with people, some of whom saluted us on one knee, and some on both, and we received their benedictions as we walked along.

It was exactly half-past nine in the morning when we arrived at the river-side, where we found two canoes lying to receive our goods, which we quickly loaded. But with that indolence and indifference which distinguish all ranks of people here, the canoemen did not make their appearance till nearly two hours after, though we had sent messengers repeatedly to them to hasten their coming; the head of them is the "sullikin zhilligee" (king of the canoe) that conveyed us from Kagogie to Yàoorie. When our people were all embarked on the Niger and ourselves, we humbly thanked the Almighty for past deliverances, and fervently prayed that he would always be with us, and crown our enterprise with success.

We had been but a short time on the water when we discovered that the smaller canoe, in which were six individuals and a number of sheep belonging to the Nouffie messengers, was overladen and in danger of sinking, and that both were very leaky, insomuch that it required three men to be constantly employed in baling out the water to keep them afloat. To lighten the smaller canoe, we took a man from her into our own, and afterward we proceeded more safely and with less apprehension; yet at one o'clock in the afternoon we were obliged to put into a small island called *Melàlie*, to get it repaired, for we were afraid to proceed any farther with the small canoe on account of the rocks and the velocity of the current.

The chief of the village, a decent-looking, elderly man, came down to salute us at the water-side; and would not suffer us to depart till he had prevailed on us to drink beer with him and fire off our guns, when he compelled us to accept of a fine kid, which we were too polite to reject. He was dressed in a tobe made of a mixture of country cloth and Manchester cotton, &c. After we had remained on the island about half an hour, which was occupied in making the necessary repairs to the canoe, we launched her out into the water, expressed our thanks to the chief, and took our leave. Melàlie is tolerably cultivated, and is inhabited solely by Borgoo men. It lies on the western side of the river. Between this island and Boossà the river is full of small islands, with channels of deep water between them. The banks on both sides are very fertile, as well as the islands themselves, which are mostly inhabited and well cultivated.

The current, according to our estimation, was here running at the rate of five or six miles in an hour; and the bed of the river was full of rocks, some of which were only a few inches below the surface of the water, which occasioned it to make a loud rushing noise, and forewarn the canoeman of his danger. Owing to the skilfulness of ours, we succeeded in crossing one or two sunken reefs, which, in the dry season more especially, must be extremely dangerous; even as it was, we experienced considerable difficulty in getting over them. At two o'clock we passed the boundaries of Boossà on the eastern side of the river, and entered the dominions of the King of Nouffie. A town belonging to the former power, on the eastern bank of the river, marks the spot; but we were unable to ascertain its name. We then travelled along by the side of an island, very woody, called " Any Man's Land," which, though fertile, is uninhabited, in consequence of the vast number of wild horses which it is said to contain.

At five P. M. we came to Inguâzhilligée, having passed, just before, a very large and pleasant, but

straggling town called *Cengie.** Inguâzhilligee† is
the first town on the Wowow ground; all above, on
the western bank of the Niger, belonging to Boossà.
Journeying along for a quarter of an hour without
stopping here, we put into a market-town, on a large
and beautiful island called *Patàshie*, just in time to
save ourselves from a heavy shower; and here we
shall be obliged to remain till the return of a messenger whom we landed in the middle of the day,
and sent to Wowow for the purpose of informing
the king of our departure from Boossà, and of our
intention to abide at Patàshie till he chooses to send
us the large canoe that we have purchased of him.
We are now out of the protection of the friendly
monarch of Boossà, who will have nothing further
to do with us.

About twenty or thirty paces from the river's
side, we discovered a great quantity of huge bones
and sculls of hippopotami, piled up on a high platform which has been erected for the purpose. These,
we understand, are preserved as trophies by the natives, on much the same principle as foxes' tails are
kept by many country gentlemen in England. From
the decayed appearance of some of the sculls, we
are inclined to believe that most of the animals must
have been destroyed very many years ago. We
were speedily introduced to the chief, who gave us
a hearty welcome, and whom we found to be a little,
round, fat, jolly-looking old man; and as soon as
was convenient we were conducted to an excellent
hut, received a quantity of provisions from the chief,

---

* This is most probably the Songa of Clapperton, he having passed
through it on his way to Comie from Boossà; and his name, therefore,
has been adopted in the map.

† This place has three names. Clapperton calls it *Comie*, " or more
properly *Wonjerque*," and Lander *Ingudzhilligee*. It appears to be the
first place below Boossà, where the river is entirely clear of rocks, and
is therefore adopted as the ferry, and called the "King's Ferry." It is
the general thoroughfare for merchants passing and repassing from
Nouffie and the countries to the north-east of Borgoo.

and then lay down to rest.   Thermometer 76°, 86°, 88°, during the day.

Tuesday, September 21*st.*—Patàshie, as we have said, is a large, rich island, unspeakàbly beautiful, and is embellished with various groves of palm and other noble trees.   Its distance from Boossà, as nearly as we can guess, may be between forty and fifty miles.   It abounds with horses, asses, bullocks, sheep, goats, poultry, &c., and produces abundance of corn and yams; in fact, the soil is so exceedingly fertile, and its inhabitants so industrious, that not an acre of ground in the whole island, it is said, is left without cultivation.   Patàshie is tributary to Wo-wow, though it is inhabited solely by Nouffie people, who are considered honest, active, laborious, and wealthy.   We find the river very much swollen, the banks are of a shelving nature, and the water is now nearly on a level with the highest part of them. We observed several small villages on the Nouffie side.

Our hut has this day exhibited a scene of revelry and mirth more becoming a native inn than a private dwelling.

The chief of the island, accompanied by our four messengers from Boossà and Nouffie, our canoemen, and several of his own people, all dressed " in their holyday best," paid us a visit in the earlier part of the morning, and out of compliment, I fancy, re-mained with us till evening, with the exception of a short absence in the middle of the day; during all which time they were employed in swallowing palm-wine, which is procured in the island in great plenty, and in telling nonsensical stories.   We were glad when they said it was time to depart, and having shaken hands with the ardour of drunkards, they took their leave, staggered out of the hut, and all went laughing away.

It is rather singular that though the chief is a sooty black, he has bright blue eyes.   We received from him about noon a fine goat, and messes of pounded yam and meat stewed in palm-oil These were brought in well-carved wooden dishes of huge dimensions; and we subsequently received a ewe sheep and similar dressed dishes from the chief of an island belonging to Nouffie, which lies abreast of this, and whom we have not yet seen.

The magīa's son (whose name is Mohammed), and whom we find to be a very intelligent youth, informs us, that if the prince of Wowow be unable to furnish us with a canoe sufficiently large for our purpose, it would be well to demand the restoration of our horses, which we could dispose of advantageously in Nouffie, and purchase a quantity of beads and other trifles with the money, as presents to the various chiefs along the banks of the river. Instead of purchasing a canoe ourselves, which would be very expensive, the young man promised, in the name of his father, to obtain one of commodious size, which should answer all purposes, and take us to *Tagra*, with men whom it should be his business likewise to get. Tagra, we believe, is very near Benin. In our own opinion, this would certainly be the safest and best means of journeying down the Niger, as the protection of all the chiefs would thereby be ensured to us. But we are apprehensive that we have gone too far towards adopting a different scheme, and we see very little likelihood, indeed, that we shall be able to embrace the plan suggested, and so strongly recommended by Mohammed, unless the Wowow ruler be not in a condition to perform his engagement, and is willing to return our horses, which does not appear to us at all probable under existing circumstances. The messenger we sent to him is not yet returned. Thermometer 74°, 83°, 85°, during the day.

Wednesday, Sept. 22d.—This morning we were visited by the revellers of yesterday, who brought with them several gallons of palm-wine, which they swallowed in a very short time, and to every appearance we were threatened with a renewal of yesterday's debauch; but, luckily for us, they went out for a few minutes to procure more liquor, when we embraced the opportunity of closing the door of our hut against them, and thus prevented their reentering it.

In the morning we were favoured with a visit from the Chief of Teah, the Nouffie island alluded to yesterday. He is a venerable-looking old man, of advantageous stature, and exceedingly corpulent. He expressed the utmost delight and satisfaction on seeing white men before he died, and declared it was a pleasure which neither his father, mother, nor uncle had ever enjoyed, and a gratification which his ancestors had never hoped for; he should therefore cherish the remembrance of it as long as he lived. We have with us a quarto edition of natural history with plates; these, though incomprehensible to the natives of Yarriba, appear to be extremely well understood here, and have excited in the minds of those that have seen them the highest degree of admiration, rapture, and wonderment. The old Chief of Teàh gazed upon them in silent astonishment; but when we took out a watch and mariner's compass for his inspection, and their uses were explained to him, he became at first very uneasy, and afterward perfectly wild with amazement. No one in the world could express more naturally or forcibly the emotion of wonder, or the passion of fear, which the countenance of this old man displayed as he looked at the watch; nor could he be persuaded for a long time but that it was in possession of life and being, and had the power of moving. After a long and friendly chat the good old chief saluted us, and took his leave.

Teàh lies very near the island of Patàshie, from which it is divided only by a very narrow channel. Of the two Teàh is said to be the larger and more popu-

lous, but with regard to agreeableness of appearance,
amazing fecundity of soil, and natural productions,
they are pretty much alike, both being beyond
description fertile and beautiful. In both provisions are reasonable, and in the greatest plenty;
they are both inhabited by individuals of the same
nation, who enrich the islands by their industry and
labour; and both have been equally exempt from
those intestine broils and commotions which have
for so long a time agitated and impoverished the na
tives of the mainland.

In the evening a messenger arrived from the King
of Wowow, with news not at all to our liking. He
informs us that we were anxiously expected in that
city from Boossà at the time of the holydays; and
because we did not come agreeably to our promise,
the prince could not conceal his chagrin, and was exceedingly angry, not only with the King of Boossà,
who was the cause of our absence, but with us likewise. The messenger continued, that his sovereign
had most certainly procured for us a canoe, which is
laid up at *Lever;* but that if we wished, or rather if
we were determined to have our horses back again,
the king would send them to us in compliance with
our wishes, " for who," said he, with much emphasis, " would presume to assert that the monarch of
Wowow would keep the property of others ?" It
would not be paying him that respect, he continued,
which his rank and situation demanded, were the
white men to leave his dominions, and the country
altogether, without first coming to pay him their respects, and he would therefore entreat us to pay a
visit to Wowow immediately for that purpose, or if
both of us could not leave Patàshie, he requested
that I would come and bid him adieu, because I had
not done so when my illness compelled me to leave
his city.

The man finished his message by complaining bitterly of the conduct of the King of Boossà, who, he

said, had acted towards his sovereign deceitfully
unhandsomely, and inconsistently, throughout all the
transactions in which we have been principally concerned. We ourselves are confident that the King
of Wowow will strongly object to the arrangement
of his relative, regarding our being sent either to the
magia or to the chief of the Falátahs at Rabba, if
not endeavour to frustrate it; because he is at enmity
with the one, and both fears and hates the other.
But how he can positively prevent this scheme from
being carried into effect, seeing we shall have the
magia's son and a Nouffie messenger in the same
canoe with us, we cannot imagine.

The monarchs of Boossà and Wowow seem to
have very opposite opinions regarding our journey.
The former insists on the necessity of our proceeding down the Niger on the eastern, or Nouffie side,
which would certainly be the most interesting and
desirable; whereas the other makes use of strong
language to persuade us that the Yarriba side of the
river would be the most convenient, the most agreeable, and the safest; and that if we would make up
our minds not to attend to the King of Boossà's advice, he would send a messenger with us, who should
protect us even to the sea. This difference of opinion,
we are apprehensive, will involve us in a thousand
perplexities; yet we must be guided in our choice
entirely by circumstances. Interest, present or remote, and prejudice and passion, seem to sway the
minds of both these rulers, though each of them
avows his disinterestedness. The King of Boossà,
a good man, but of an humble, yielding, peaceful,
enduring temper, and of a timorous, wavering disposition, requests us earnestly to visit the magia and
the Falátahs, because he knows it would gratify
their vanity, and make them his friends for ever;—
the King of Wowow, of a firm, sagacious, and un-
bending mind, scorns the friendship and defies the
power of either, and is inveterate in his dislike both

of the very name of Falátah, and that of the brother
of Ederesa; he is aware that our visiting their territories in person would not only be paying them a
very high compliment, but would likewise, in some
measure, be advantageous to them, and is guided by
this decided partiality in doing all in his power to
bring us over to his own views and sentiments.
From the treatment I experienced at Soccatoo, I
must say that I entertain a very great aversion to
the whole Falátah nation; and am of opinion, that if
we put into Rabba, according to the suggestions of
the King of Boossà, we shall be detained there till
Bello be informed of the fact, and his intentions with
regard to us be communicated to the chief. I am
therefore inclined to adopt the advice of the King of
Wowow, rather than to comply with the wishes of
his august relative, though there is no just or reasonable ground to fear either ill-treatment or detention at the hands of the Falátahs, more especially
since we have received ample and satisfactory assurances from the powerful Chief of Rabba himself
of their favourable disposition towards us, that we
shall be received as friends, and meet with every encouragement and support as far as their power and
interests extend, and as far as their name is known
and respected. Yet we cannot follow the bent of
our own inclinations; we are involved in difficulty;
and though every thing appears propitious to our enterprise, yet we are not masters of our own actions;
we must follow where others lead, and we are still
in doubt as to what we shall do. At all events, we
shall be guided in our choice entirely by circumstances; "we shall trust our fortune to the powers
above," and can only pray that an indulgent Providence will succour, befriend, and protect us in all
circumstances, as it has heretofore done.

The Wowow ambassador will rest with us to
morrow; and on the day following I intend accom
panying him to that city, not only to pay my re-

spects to the sovereign, but likewise to have a final
and decisive answer from him regarding the canoe,
without further subterfuge or procrastination. Thermometer 76, 87, 89, during the day.

Thursday, Sept. 23d.—At Boossà, latterly, we had
the greatest difficulty and trouble in procuring the
bare necessaries of life ; but here, in this flourishing
Patàshie, provisions have been sent us from the
chiefs of the two islands, in such abundance that
half of them, we regret to say, have been uncon-
sumed by our people, and thrown to the dogs: we
have received from each of them, daily, as mucn
as a strong man could carry, consisting of the
usual gigantic bowl of pounded yam and meat,
stewed in palm-oil. People here, of all ages, display the most anxious, though perhaps natural, curiosity to see us ; and large crowds of them assem-
ble every day, and wait from morning till night patiently, till they have gained the object of their visit.
However, they are all as timid as hares, and if we
happen to look fixedly in their faces for a moment,
most of them, more especially the females, and the
junior classes of both sexes, start back with terror,
as if they had seen a serpent in the grass ; and when
we attempt to walk near any of them, they run away
screaming, as though they had been pursued by a
lion, or were in danger of falling into the jaws of a
crocodile, so horrified are these poor people at the
bare sight of a white man, and so frightful do their
imaginations picture him to be.

In the evening, long after the sun had gone down,
the chief brought a youth for us to pass our opinion
on, whom he introduced as a near relative. He has
been ill for the last fourteen months, and the chief
prayed that we would endeavour to cure him of his
complaint. He is a tall, lank young man, of humble,
modest, and reserved manners. From a state of ro-
bust health and vigour, which it appears he formerly
enjoyed, he is wasted away almost to a skeleton

and his temper, once pleasant, cheerful, and sprightly has lost its elasticity, and he is become thoughtful, dejected, and melancholy: however, though the invalid rarely enjoys sound and refreshing sleep, yet he has a wonderful appetite, and he eats with voracity. We sincerely regret our ignorance of the nature of his disorder, and therefore our utter inability to do him the slightest benefit; nevertheless, the old chief solicited us so warmly for medicine, and with such pressing importunity, that, rather than give offence, and because the young man complained of a sore throat and neck, which seemed to annoy him at present more than any thing else, we chafed those parts with a little spirits of hartshorn, and wrapped round them several folds of warm flannel. It was all that we could do to relieve his pain, and it seemed to give complete satisfaction. Poor people! how happy did this little service make them!

The natives are subject to very few diseases, and those, generally speaking, are not of a dangerous or malignant tendency. As far as we are able to judge from the symptoms he describes, the complaint under which the old chief's *protégé* labours approaches nearer to the nature of consumption than to any other disease with which we are acquainted. Small-pox is very-prevalent, but we do not hear that it often terminates fatally. The Guinea-worm is frequently met with; ulcers of that frightful description which prevails on the coast are unknown; but agues and slight fevers are by no means uncommon; and of all complaints, sore eyes and affections of the bowels are by far the most general. Properly speaking, the natives have no active medicine of their own, though they boast an acquaintance with a variety of medicinal plants, which, as far as our observation extends, are wholly inefficacious; they likewise ascribe the most wonderful healing properties to a quantity of roots and fibres of trees, which are sought after and vended by a number of idle.

lazy fellows, who pretend to be Mohammedan priests: however, from our experience, these do neither good nor harm, being perfectly innocent in their effects, and altogether useless. The root of a large and scarce tree holds so high a reputation for the astonishing properties which it is supposed to possess, that it has obtained, by way of distinction, the name of the "mother of roots." Besides its other virtues, the credulous people believe, that while they have the smallest portion of this celebrated "mother of roots" about their persons, they can assuage every sorrow, alleviate every misfortune; banish care from their minds and want from their dwellings, avert pain, and secure happiness. From the Arabs, however, the natives obtain great quantities of *trona*, which is a fossil alkali, and is found on the borders of the desert. It is a strong and active aperient, and possesses other medicinal properties, which are understood by the people. It is taken by all ranks in every complaint, of whatsoever nature it may be. Trona is likewise beat to a powder and mixed with snuff, to which it imparts a great degree of pungency. And lastly, it is given to horses, sheep, and other animals, which eat large lumps of it with the greatest avidity. Thermometer 78, 89, 91, during the day.

Friday, Sept. 24th.—The Boossà canoe-men, who have been intoxicated every day since they have been here, returned to their homes this morning in a state of ebriety, having received a shilling each and a few needles as a reward for their labour. Shortly after their departure, I landed for the purpose of proceeding to Wowow, and took possession of a house on the bank of the river, which had been prepared for me. The King of Wowow's messenger accompanied me, and having got every thing ready as soon as we could, we commenced our journey towards his city. It was the intention of the man from Boossà to have taken his leave of us here.

and return to his sovereign; but when he heard the extraordinary communication and insinuations of the prince of Wowow, he changed his mind, and resolved to accompany me as above related. I left my brother on the island to take care of our things, and the following remarks were made by him in my absence.

"The Nouffie messengers remain here with me, and the Queen of Boossà's 'master of the horse' has determined not to leave us till after our arrival at _Lever_, though we would much rather dispense with his company. They tell us that _Rabba_ is two days' journey by water from the town of Lever, and three from Funda, and that Funda is four days' journey from the sea. On our arrival at Rabba, says Mohammed, or after we shall have delivered a present to its chief, and the formalities of introduction are gone through, he will supply us with horses to convey us to a town wherein the magia resides, and which is about two days' journey from thence, for it will be necessary that we should pay our respects to him in person.

"The chief of Patàshie came to see me this evening by lamplight, accompanied by his sick relative, whom he pronounced to be much better, having slept soundly during the night, and experienced a mitigation of pain. I applied a little more spirits of hartshorn to his throat, and recommended temperance in eating, gentle exercise in the open air, to beware of chills, and avoid exposure to nightly damps and dews. The old chief and his nephew (for that is the relationship between them) took their leave of me with many expressions of thankfulness. Our hut has been literally crammed with visiters nearly the whole of the day. Thermometer 77, 88, 92, during the day.

"_Saturday, Sept._ 25_th._—Nothing worthy of particular notice has occurred to-day; I continue to receive the utmost hospitality and kindness from the old benevolent chiefs of Teàh and this island, the latter of whom stays with me almost all day long. He took a fancy to the only English coat which is now left me, its green colour seeming to be the principal cause of his admiration; and as it is of little consequence here how uncouthly soever a European may be dressed, I cut off part of its skirts to make him a cap. A woman belonging to the chief died to-day in a state of insanity. According to the people's account, the deceased was in good health three days ago, but this morning a malicious female demon entered into her, and began to exercise her malign propensities by tormenting her victim, throwing her upon fires, and into the water, causing her eyes to roll in a phrensied manner, and making her lie along the ground, raving and roaring most furiously. Last of all, they say, the evil spirit put an end to her torture by *eating her life*, and she died. Thermometer 74, 80, 83, during the day.

" *Sunday, Sept. 26th.*—A Mohammedan priest, furnished with pen and ink, arrived at Patàshie to pay his respects to us, and without wearying me with questions, he sat down very composedly and commenced writing an Arab charm or prayer for our health, preservation, and success. I felt no inclination to interrupt the man's benevolent intention; and when he had finished, the magia's son, who happened to be present, animated by the same laudable impulse, produced a charm, possessing, no doubt, as many virtues as the mallam's. These are nothing more than short extracts from the Koran. Both men appeared to write the Arabic character with a readiness and facility which one would scarcely expect to find in this remote country. Charms or amulets are in universal use, more especially in Yarriba, where, perhaps, the Mohammedan religion is least felt, and has made least progress. They are generally encompassed with red cloth or leather; are worn for the most part on the left arm; and from ten to twenty are sometimes observed on the person of one individual. This custom might have originally been introduced into the country by the Arabs, and disseminated by their means through all these parts of the continent. The phylacteries of the ancient Jews, which were little rolls of parchment containing written passages from the Holy Scriptures, and which used to be worn upon the forehead and the wrist of the left arm, might have given the Arabians the hint of wearing extracts from the Koran in like manner, and which, by the lapse of ages, have degenerated into the present superstitious practice of wearing charms, which is so prevalent in Africa. The same idle stories with regard to reputed wizards, necromancers, &c., which are current in Boossà, obtain as great a degree of credit here; and the people likewise believe in other absurdities equally detestable. To-day a man has been accused of eating the spirit, or living principle, of another; but in what manner he is to be punished, no one has yet informed us. Thermometer 76, 86, 91, during the day."

Monday, September 27th.—I returned in the warmest part of the day from my visit to Wowow, with no less than three men as messengers from the king, the whole of whom are to accompany us to Lever. It has ever been the policy of all the African rulers of the cities and kingdoms through which we have passed since leaving Badágry, to furnish us with a greater number of guides and messengers than we have either required or wished. In the present instance, one would have been amply sufficient for our purpose; but, as on former occasions, the Wowow men are the king's slaves, and will be obliged, on their return, to lay before their monarch whatever we may give them as a reward for their trouble; he will take from them as much as he likes, which most likely will not be less than seven-eighths of the whole, and the little left will then be divided among the mes-

II.—C

sengers, so that self-interest alone has induced the
king to send us three men, because three men will be
entitled to more wages than one.

On my arrival at Wowow on the 24th instant, I
felt too much fatigued, from the length of the journey,
and the heat of the weather, to pay my respects to
the monarch, and therefore desired to be excused
from visiting him till the morrow. Accordingly, on
the following day I had prepared myself to go to
the king's house, in pursuance of my agreement, but
was greatly surprised on learning that the eccentric
old man had excused himself from being seen on
that day, on the same plea as I had the day before,
observing that he had taken a ride to view his gar-
dens in the morning, and that the exercise had so
much tired him, that he felt no inclination whatever
to receive visiters till next day. Therefore, it was
not till the 26th that the king granted me an audi-
ence, and then he said,.with the greatest indifference,
" I have not yet been able to procure you the canoe
which I promised to get; but I have no doubt that
the ruler of Patàshie will have it in his power to
supply you with one to your satisfaction, for which
purpose I will send an express to that island without
delay, whom I will furnish with the necessary instructions to effect an immediate purchase." Thus,
with as much discussion as would fill a volume, continued with little or no intermission for seven weeks,
between the sovereigns of two countries, who during that period were sending messengers to each
other continually, the mighty business which had
employed all their thoughts, and in which they were
unceasingly engaged—the simple purchase of a canoe, is even now left unfinished ; in fact, up to the
present moment, no more has been done in the matter than when we first made known our intentions and
wishes to the King of Boossà from the city of
Yàoorie two months ago. So much for the expedition with which Africans usually transact their affairs. The king took the opportunity of informing

me that he should by-and-by set about erecting a suitable building for the reception of our country-men, whenever it should please them to come up the river to trade: for the old man cherishes the belief, in common with other rulers on the banks of the Niger, that numbers of Europeans will, some time or other, certainly visit his country for the purposes of traffic.

Before my departure, the monarch showed me, in compliance with my request, the whole of his col-lection of charms, which are written on sheets of paper, glued or pasted together. Among them I discovered a small edition of " Watts's Hymns," on one of the blank leaves of which was written, "*Alexander Anderson, Royal Military Hospital, Gos-port*, 1804." It is perhaps unnecessary to say, that Mr. Anderson was the companion, and I believe a very near relative, of the celebrated Mr. Park. From the Wowow chieftain, as well as from his good old brother, and our friend Abba, I and my attendants experienced the most liberal hospitality; and, on taking my leave of them, they wished me farewell in the most cordial and affectionate manner. Be-sides the note from Mr. and Mrs. Watson to Mr. Park, which we obtained when at Boossà, we also saw another from Lady Dalkeith, of the same date, acknowledging the receipt of some drawings from him. Thermometer 76, 89, 93, during the day.

Tuesday, Sept. 28th.—It is really tiresome to say any thing further on the provoking subject of the canoe; yet we think it necessary to remark, that not a sin-gle one is to be found here sufficiently large for our purpose, or at all answering the expectations held out to us by the prince of Wowow. Lever is there fore again fixed on as the place where our wishes are to be answered and our hopes realized; and we are given to understand that we shall leave this place for thence at an early hour to-morrow.

On walking across Patàshie to-day, in perhaps its

narrowest part, we found the island to be about a mile in width; yet, in comparison to its breadth, it is very disproportionate, being several miles in length. Patàshie is extremely populous for its size, and large clusters of huts are scattered all over the island. From a gentle eminence on the mainland opposite, its appearance bears a striking resemblance to the more beautiful parts of the seacoast.

The people have a hut here wherein all females who conduct themselves indecently, or commit any crimes or offences, are imprisoned. This building is distinguished from the others by its size, situation, and superior appearance. Outside the doorway, and on each side of it, are two clay figures, nearly as large as life, which are affixed to the wall. One of them is intended to represent a woman in an upright position, and without clothing, so that every female who sees it may be reminded of the object and origin of the institution; but the thing looks extremely odd, and the execution, as might be supposed, is rude and contemptible. The figure opposite to it is a pretty good representation of a crocodile; and is placed against the wall, I suppose, merely as an ornament. Nearly all the junior classes of the population here go entirely naked; and it is not before they attain to man's or woman's estate that they begin to clothe themselves. Red clay is in general use among females of all ranks. The magia's son intends leaving us to-morrow, on a visit to his father, whom he will inform of our movements, &c. From thence he purposes proceeding to Rabba, where he will stay till our arrival. Thermometer 76, 87, 90, during the day.

Wednesday, Sept. 29th.—After our luggage had all been packed up this morning in readiness for our departure, and every thing had been prepared for that purpose, word was brought us from the chief that we should be unable to start till to-morrow, because the Niger, he said, would receive a great influx of

water to-night, which would be considerably in our favour. As it rained heavily and incessantly nearly the whole of last night, and as we had continued heavy showers almost the whole of this forenoon. we have made no complaint or fuss at our disappointment, but quietly await the coming of to-morrow. In the evening we were urgently solicited by the hospitable chief of Patàshie for a charm to render him successful in all his shooting excursions, and in hunting the hippopotamus. This request was soon followed by a similar one from his brother. For ourselves we are obliged to follow the current of opinion, or consent to lose our credit and be regarded with detestation; and, as our charms are likely to be as effective as those of the Arabs, we sometimes oblige the natives in this respect. Thermometer 75, 85, 87, during the day.

Thursday, Sept. 30th.—Between eight and nine o'clock in the morning, horses were brought us from the chief and his nephew, to take us to the water's side, where the luggage had been previously conveyed. Here we waited a good while till canoes were brought from another part of the island, there being but one got ready at the time of our arrival. While we stood near the water's edge, hundreds of people were collected there to look at us, and among them was a native pagan priest, who was dressed more fantastically than any merry-andrew in Christendom. His clothing was manufactured almost solely of fine soft grass. His head and shoulders and part of his body were hid underneath an enormous thing in shape like the roof of a hut, with a fringe and tassels of stained grass. A tobe, made also of grass, excellently woven and of various colours, encircled his body, and reached as far as the knee; and the man wore likewise trousers of the same material, and plaited in a similar manner, but this was unstained, and of the colour of dried grass; it w s turned up at the ankles, though a deep fringe

hung to the ground.. He approached several individuals that were sitting on the turf, and stooping
over them, the priest enveloped the upper part of
their persons in his uncouth headdress; shook i
over them, which produced a strange rustling noise ;
screamed in a most frightful and unearthly tone ;
and then arose to perform the same barbarous ceremony to others.

When the canoes had arrived, and all our things
had been removed into them from the beach, we
were desired to ride to a landing-place farther down
the island, because of the rocks, which are reported
to intercept the stream at a little distance from the
place whereon we stood, and to be very dangerous
for canoes which are heavily laden. But first of all
we took a cordial farewell of the hearty old chief
of *Tedh*, who had come over to see us before our
departure. The venerable governor of Patàshie, to
whom we are under so many obligations, then preceded us on the footway, walking with a staff; and
we reached the appointed place of embarkation exactly at the same moment as the canoes. There
we found a man and woman sitting on a mat, which
was placed on the grass, refreshing themselves with
Guinea nuts and water; we partook of their fare by
invitation, and as the canoes were waiting for us to
come on board, we bade adieu, in the most expressive manner, to the good old chief of Patàshie, and
thanking all the friends that had accompanied us
thither, we jumped on board, and pushed off from
the shore, cheered by the natives that were present.

The current bore us rapidly along, but we regretted to find the river again broken up by rocks and
numerous small islands, which spoil its delightful
appearance, and render it unnavigable. A few miles
below Patàshie are three islands, abreast of each
other, and by no means destitute of beauty or verdure, which are called collectively *Ràah*. On one
of them is a large trading town, and near it the

canoemen landed to get some refreshment. We then continued our course for some time without meeting any obstacle to embarrass us; but afterward, in order to get clear of a reef of rocks, we were obliged to make our way through an exceedingly narrow channel, overhung with the branches of trees, and more than half filled with rushes and tall luxuriant grasses. This brought us into the main river again, and having passed along in front of one or two towns on the banks of the river, we came in sight of *Lever*, which was the place of our destination, and where we landed at one o'clock, after rather a short excursion from Patàshie of three hours. Lever may be distant from that island about twenty miles.

Our surprise was great indeed, when, instead of the proper person who we expected would have received us, we were welcomed on shore by a man called *Ducoo*, and who represented himself as agent and confidential friend of the prince of Rabba; but this surprise was not a little increased on learning that a party of forty or fifty armed Falátah soldiers were also in the town. Ducoo, who is a Bornouese, treated us with the courtly politeness of a Frenchman, and was equally lavish in his compliments and his offers of service; he walked with us to the chief of the town, to whom he took the liberty of introducing us, almost before he himself knew who or what we were; went himself and procured excellent lodgings for us, returned and sat down in our company to tell us some droll stories, and impart to us in confidence some very disagreeable news; then hastily rose up, went out, and came back again with a sheep and other provisions, which he had obtained by compulsion from the chief, and finally remained with us till long after the moon had risen, when he left us to our repose. A man of such excessive volubility we never recollect to have met with; but at the same time he seems to be a most useful fellow.

This *Lever*, then, after all, does not belong to the King of Wowow, though it stands on his dominions, nor has that monarch a single subject here, or a solitary canoe, so that we are as far from getting one as ever we were, and with the loss of our horses to boot. We have been cajoled and out-manœuvred very prettily by those fellows of Boossà and its adjoining state, whom we falsely conceived to be our dearest and best black friends. They have played with us as if we were great dolls; we have been driven about like shuttlecocks; we have been to them first a gazing-stock, and are now no doubt their laughing-stock, perhaps their mockery; we have been their admiration—their buffoons—their wonder and their scorn—a by-word and a jest. Else why this double-dealing, this deceit, this chicanery, these hollow professions? Why did they entrap us in this manner? Why have they led us about as though we had been blind, only to place us in the very lap of what *they* imagine to be danger? For can it be possible that the monarchs of Wowow and Boossà were ignorant of the state of things here, which is in their own immediate neighbourhood, and which have continued the same essentially for these three years? Surely they have knowingly deceived us.

As soon as we were convinced that no canoe could be had in this place, as we have all along been led to expect, we conceived it prudent, under existing circumstances, to detain the two canoes which were lent us this morning by the chief of Patàshie; one of them is tolerably large, and nearly new, but the other is of much smaller dimensions. However we are well aware that the King of Wowow has not yet paid for them, and we are afraid that he never will; and it grieves and saddens us beyond expression to do this thing; for the island ruler is a simple, kind-hearted, and good, very good old man. But what can we do! *We* have not the means of purchasing his canoes, for the King of Wowow has deprived us

of them; our resources are nearly exhausted, and
how should we be able to prosecute our journey? The Patàshie canoemen stoutly resisted our
claims, as it is natural to suppose that they would.
For our own parts we were actually ashamed to
look them in the face; but our busy, restless friend,
Ducoo, the priest, soon silenced their remarks by
threatening to cut off the head of him who should
presume from that time to set foot in either of the
canoes. To give his menace the greater weight, he
stationed two of his men to guard the forbidden
boats till the sun went down, with drawn swords, and
during the greater part of the night another of his
men paraded up and down the banks of the river
near the spot as a watch, and this man was continually playing upon a large drum.

We are furnished with four messengers besides
him from Nouffie, one of whom is from Boossà, and
the other three from Wowow. The office of these
men is to see that every thing promised us by their
respective sovereigns be executed in pursuance of
their agreement; but no one can be more intimidated
or alarmed than they. They have scarcely dared
to open their lips for the purpose of speaking since
our arrival; they look as silly as sheep, sneak about
our lodgings, and hang down their heads like prisoners under sentence of death. They are of no
service whatever to us, rather a disadvantage in fact,
but yet their wages must be paid them.

After the departure of Ducoo in the evening, the
chief of the town came to pay his respects and to wish
us good night. He related to us a pitiable account
of the evils which he and his people had undergone,
and were still enduring from the selfishness and rapacity of the Falatahs; "and they never pay us a
visit," said he, "but my spirits droop within me,
and my heart becomes heavy and sorrowful, for
these foreigners come only to plunder and lay
waste." The appearance of things at the present

time seems to confirm this assertion, for a number
of Falátahs are here for no other reason; and the
melancholy of the chief's countenance was an eloquent illustration of the imbittered state of his
heart and feelings. Thermometer 78, 89, 93, during the day.

CHAPTER XIV.

State of the Town of Lever—The Falátahs—The Travellers' Canoes
claimed—Interference of Ducoo—Detention of the Travellers—Their
Departure from Lever—The Town of Bajiebo—Chiefs—Canoes of
Bajiebo—Departure from Bajiebo—Scenery of the River—Town of
Leechee—Visit to the chief—The Passage continued down the River—
Madjie Island—Mount Kesa—Land on Belee Island—Messenger from
Rabba—Arrival of Suliken Rouah, or the King of the Dark Water—
Grand Procession of Canoes down the River—Arrival at Zagözhi*
Island—Its swampy Nature.

Friday, October 1st.—THIS morning, to our infinite
relief, the four messengers from Wowow and Boossà
spoken of yesterday were paid for having accompanied us hither, and in the forenoon they left the
town in company to go to Wowow. The Patàshie
canoemen also received their wages at the same
time, and embarked in two canoes a few minutes
afterward on their return homewards, so that there
only remains with us at present one of the Nouffie
messengers who joined us at Boossà.

This town is called indiscriminately *Lever* and
Layaba, though the latter name seems most generally applied here. Its population is great, and
though it is very extensive, it has been built and
occupied a very few years only. Its inhabitants
are all Nouffie people, and not long ago resided in a

* The first z in this word is pronounced like our z in azure.

arge village on the opposite side of the river; but on account of the civil wars which raged in their country, setting every man against his friend and against his neighbour, when property was insecure, freedom threatened, and life in danger, they were driven to seek an asylum here, where they fancied themselves out of the influence of these evils, and beyond the reach of the Falátahs, of whom they have an unconquerable dread. Here accordingly they erected their dwellings, and cleared the adjacent ground for cultivation. However, the poor people were not left a great while to enjoy unmolested the security which they had been in quest of, and which they imagined they had found at Layaba; for three years ago their relentless enemies invaded their retreat, ransacked the town, and destroyed their houses by fire. Fortunately for them, the inhabitants had timely notice of the approach of these marauders, and succeeded in recrossing the river, just before their arrival, without the loss of a single man; nor could the Falátahs follow them there, because they had no canoes. But rather than have their property destroyed a second time, and rather than be liable to continual irruptions of their enemies, who would abuse their women and enslave themselves, after their return hither the people of Layaba consented to pay a certain tribute to the prince of the Falátahs at Rabba, independent of a kind of ground-rent or acknowledgment, which is paid to the owner of the soil; so that a double duty is by this means exacted from them. Nor is this all: for parties of Falátahs, which are without employment at home, are generally prowling about the country, and levying contributions on those villages which are too feeble to resist their claims.

Such is the case here at this moment; the Falátahs entered the town on Wednesday to take from its peaceful inhabitants whatever they thought proper These men are all extremely well-dressed, and are

armed with large swords, which are carried about
their persons wherever they go. It is likely enough
that, in this town, their object, for the present at
least, will be defeated, for it is affirmed that they
are in terrible apprehension of us, understanding
that we should interfere in their unjustifiable proceedings; and appearances seem to confirm this assertion.

This afternoon their party was assembled together by beat of drum, and they crossed the river
in a hurry almost immediately after. Without asking our permission, or giving the slightest intima-
tion of their intentions to either of us, they launched
and took away the Patàshie canoe, which we call
ours, and filled it with their people; which some one
observing, he came running in haste to our hut, and
informed us that the Falátahs had stolen our largest
canoe, and were taking it away. Unacquainted then
with their true motives for this action, we were
filled with apprehension, and believing the story
which had been told us, my brother instantly repaired to the water-side, where he observed, sure
enough, our canoe filled with Falátahs, who were
waiting the signal for starting. He was agitated at
the insolence of the fellows, and ordered them to
get out of the canoe immediately, or take the consequences. They were about to obey his commands,
when our officious friend, Ducoo, the priest, stepped
forward, put his hand upon his shoulder, and with
his usual volubility, desired him to be cool, and he
would tell him all. He then informed him that he
had himself taken the liberty of launching the canoe
for the use of his friends, made an apology for not
asking permission, and said, that after the Falátahs
had crossed over on the other side, it should be
brought back to us again. This satisfied my brother,
and he left them, though he knew he had been telling a falsehood, for it was certainly his intention to
send away the canoe, so that we should never have

the use of it; but as Ducoo was to remain at Layaba a little longer, we had determined to keep him in "durance vile" till another, through his means, should be got for us.

In the mean time I had also repaired to the water-side with a pistol, which so terrified the Falátahs, that those who were on shore jumped hastily into another canoe, and all of them stole away as fast as they could, in great trepidation, for they fancied that their end was come. The priest subsequently remarked, that since our arrival, they had been greatly alarmed on account of our presence, and that he had been unable to suppress their fears. Thinking to pay us a compliment, he said we were stronger and better looking than any chief in the whole country, with the exception of the sultan of Bornou. He is himself a tall handsome fellow, and was chuckling at his own ingenuity; but we took little notice of him, and gave him not so much as a needle for his remark. This same individual has begun to show himself in his true colours; in the morning he began begging with much importunity, not only for himself, but for others, nor would he be quieted until we had satisfied his covetousness; and he then laid claim to one of our canoes, which he had the impudence to offer us for sale, and entreated that we would purchase of him! Surely the man cannot be in earnest. This is impudence with a vengeance!

Another small party of Falátahs entered Layaba this afternoon. An hour or two since, one of them attempted to take away a bow and arrows from an inhabitant of the town, who disputed his right to do so; but the Falátah enforced his demand by cutting him across the right shoulder with his sword. The wounded man saw the blood and wept, and ran away to make a complaint to his chief, who hearkened to his tale and pitied him. After a good deal of trouble, he caused the bow and arrows to be given back

to their rightful owner, but he could do no more; he
dared not punish the assailant for his crime, and he
was suffered to boast of it at large.   How different
are these people from the peaceful and happy Falátahs in Yarriba and other countries, who spend their
time solely in pastoral occupations and pursuits!
Thermometer 76°, 85°, 87°, during the day.

Saturday, October 2d.—The chief sent us another
fine sheep to-day, and a quantity of dressed provisions
swimming in palm oil.   He was induced to make us
this present from Ducoo's insinuations, who, no
doubt, has his own private ends in view.   The
priest boasts an acquaintance with the late unfortunate Major Laing, and affirms that he was near
the spot at the time of that gentleman's death.   He
can also relate the whole of the circumstances attending the melancholy fate of Mr. Park and his
associates.   But this man is an eternal talker, and
therefore we receive all his communications with
extreme suspicion.

In the afternoon a small party of men arrived here
in a canoe from the chief of the island of *Teàh*, with
a message to us, purporting that the canoes which
we had, to his infinite surprise, detained at Layaba,
did not belong, as we imagined, to his friend the
Chief of Patáshie, but were his own property ; and
as he did not acknowledge the authority of Wowow,
but had ever been subject to the King of Nouffie, he
considered that we could have no right whatever to
the canoes in question, and therefore he would entreat us to return them by the hands of his messengers.   He had lent them, because he was willing to
oblige us and please his neighbour; but he did not
conceive or think it possible that we could make so
ungrateful and unkind a return for his hospitality,
and the respect and attention which it had been his
pride and pleasure to show us.   For our own parts,
we could not forbear acknowledging the truth and
justice of the observations of the Teàh chieftain and

blaming ourselves for the step we had taken. We therefore expressed our deep and very sincere regret at the measure which we had, from a combination of circumstances, been compelled to adopt; yet we assured the chief messenger, a quiet, respectable man, that it was not altogether our own fault (for indeed it was not), as the Patáshie canoemen well knew, for the men of Wowow had forbidden them to take back the boats, promising that their sovereign would pay for them, and the Falátah agent had prevented them from doing so. We said further, that whatever might be the consequence, we had not the slightest objection for the canoes to be restored to their rightful owner; and provided the men from Teàh could obtain the consent of the priest to take them away, they were at liberty to do so whenever they might think proper. But this they were by no means disposed to do, for they both feared and hated him; and therefore they bribed the Nouffie messenger with a large sum of money to assist them in their project, and purposed taking away both canoes in the night-season by stealth. However, their intentions were frustrated by the watchful vigilance of the priest, who had mistrusted them long before they were made known to us; and when he had actually detected their plans, he ordered the canoes to be pulled up on shore, two hundred yards at least from the water's edge, and observed with vehemence, that after what he had done should they be launched again into the water and taken away, he would instantly tie a rope round the necks of the chief of the town and the Nouffie messenger that had accepted the bribe, and in that humiliating state they should be driven like beasts to their sovereign the magia.

In the evening, the inhabitants of the town assembled outside our house to amuse themselves by dancing and singing in the moonlight; for, notwithstanding all their misfortunes and oppressions, they

never refrain from indulging with all their hearts
in these sprightly and thoughtless entertainments.
Every dancer held in each hand a cow's tail; they
were all dressed grotesquely, and a great quantity of
strings of cowries encircled their legs and bodies,
which made a loud rattling noise by the violence and
celerity of their movements. They-sang as they
danced, and excited, by the oddity of their gestures,
loud clappings of applause, and bursts of laughter
from all the bystanders. The spectacle was exceedingly ludicrous; we have rarely witnessed so
much jocularity and thoughtless gayety; and we
have seldom laughed so much at any native exhibi-
tion. Though the performers panted from want of
breath with their exertions, they yet continued their
darling exercises, as is usual with them, till long
after midnight.

Like many of their countrymen, and like the natives of Yarriba, the inhabitants of Layaba appear
to bestow scarcely a moment's reflection either on
public misery or individual distress—upon their own
misfortunes or the calamities of their neighbours.
Nature has moulded their minds to enjoy the life
they lead; their grief, if they grieve at all, is but for
a moment; sorrow comes over them and vanishes
like the lightning's flash; they weep, and, in the
same breath, their spirits regain their elasticity and
cheerfulness; they may well be said to drink of the
waters of Lethe whenever they please. As long as
they have food to eat, and health to enjoy their
frivolous pastimes, they seem contented, happy, and
full of life. They think of little else.—

"Thought would destroy their paradise."

Thermometer 77°, 88°, 90°, during the day.

Sunday, Oct. 3d.—We were desired yesterday to
get our things packed up, and ourselves prepared,
for that this morning we should quit the island to
proceed on our journey. In pursuance of this ar

rangement we had got all our luggage in readiness, and only waited the coming of the chief to take our departure, when, to our great regret, one of his messengers entered our hut to apprize us that we should be unable to go away till to-morrow, his master having been dissuaded from his original purpose by the officious, bustling priest, our friend and enemy. We submitted to the disappointment as patiently and silently as we could; and in the evening we obtained a solemn promise, that whatever might be the consequence, no one should divert him from the resolution he had formed of detaining us no longer than to-day; and that early to-morrow we should certainly depart. Thermometer 76°, 89°, 88°, during the day.

Monday, Oct. 4th.—Our surprise and displeasure may be guessed, when, after our goods had been removed from our hut into the yard outside, we were informed that we should be compelled to abide in the town yet another day, notwithstanding all that the chief had told us yesterday. Our patience was now completely exhausted; and we were in great anger, for it is disheartening to be always deceived and trifled with by such scoundrels. Repairing instantly to a hut wherein we knew the chief passed most of his time, we discovered him sitting on the ground in company with the artful Ducoo and our Nouffie messenger, and engaged in a very high dispute with both of them. Our unexpected and abrupt intrusion and angry looks cut short their wrangling; and we spoke with much emphasis of the shameful manner in which we had been treated, and expressed our determination of leaving Layaba presently, in defiance of them and all their power. With the most insolent effrontery in the world the priest smiled at us, and replied, that we were entirely in his power—that we should do as *he* liked, and quit the town whenever *he* thought proper. Such language as this we thought was rather too

II.—D

bold: we pretended to be in a violent passion, and quickly undeceived him in this point, threatening, that if either he or any of his men should presume to interfere with us in our intentions or proceedings, or attempt to hinder us from getting away from the town, we should feel no more hesitation or reluctance in shooting him than if he had been a partridge or a Guinea-hen! The priest, who had never before seen any thing in us but mildness, was intimidated at the determined and resolute behaviour we had found it necessary to adopt: he was crest-fallen in a moment, and, from being one of the most boisterous and consequential fellows in the world, became quite passive; yet his presence of mind did not forsake him: he stammered out a kind of apology, attempted to sooth us by soft language and submission, in which he found little difficulty, and did all in his power to effect a reconciliation. Having settled this business, we went out, and assembling our men, attempted to draw our canoe to the riverside, but the ground was uneven, and the boat so long and heavy, that notwithstanding all our exertions we could move her only a few inches towards the river. The people were ashamed of themselves to see us labouring so hard, and to so little purpose; and the priest, likewise, observing us, was convinced that we were in earnest: therefore, whispering a few words in the ear of the chief, they both came down to the spot where we were toiling at the canoe, followed by a number of men; these, with the priest at their head, took the work out of our hands, and in less than two minutes the boat was floating on the water. Our luggage was then conveyed into the two canoes, and shortly afterward we were supplied with three men to paddle them with the assistance of our own. Here we took our farewell of the chief and the priest, the latter begging us very anxiously to speak well of him to his sovereign at Rabba.

It was not till after we were all in the canoes, and

ready to push off, that those on shore discovered
them to be overladen, and recommended us to hire
one of immense size which was lying alongside.
Without stopping to make them any reply, or listen
to any further nonsense, we desired our own men to
push the boats out into the middle of the current,
which they did very promptly, and the town of Layaba, with its chief and inhabitants, was speedily out
of sight, and soon forgotten. This was about nine
o'clock in the morning, so that, after all, we had lost
but little time in getting away.

The banks of the river near Lever are high, being,
according to our estimation, about forty feet above
the river, and steep to the water-side. The river itself appeared deep, and free from rocks of any kind;
its direction nearly south. We ran down the stream
very pleasantly for twelve or fourteen miles, the Niger, during the whole of the distance, rolling grandly
along—a noble river, neither obstructed by islands
nor deformed with rocks and stones. Its width
varied from one to three miles; the country on each
side was very flat, and a few mean, dirty-looking villages were scattered on the water's edge. We then
came to two small islands; the land appeared more
elevated, and in some few places it rose in gentle
hills. We observed three remarkable and lofty hills
on the eastern side, which rose very abruptly from
the plain, and were separated from each other only
by a few yards of ground. Both banks of the river
were overhung with large shady trees, between
which we could perceive the land behind to be open
and well-cultivated; and, if we may be allowed to
form an opinion from the number of towns and villages which were scattered over the country, we
should conceive it to be thickly inhabited also.

At one o'clock, P. M., we landed at a considerably
large and spacious town, called *Bajiebo,* which is inhabited by Nouffie people, though it is situated on
the Yarriba or western side of the river. For dirt

bustle, and nastiness of all kinds, this place, we think, can scarcely be exceeded. For two hours after our arrival we were obliged to wait in a close and diminutive hut, till a more convenient and becoming habitation could be procured for our reception, and the pleasure of the chief with regard to us should be known. Here we were visited by a number of the inhabitants, consisting both of Falátahs and *Noufanchie* (Nouffie people). Among the former was a sagacious and intelligent old man, who has travelled a long, long way on the Niger, even beyond Timbuctoo ; and he states, that that town is several miles from the banks of the river. We were sadly incommoded by these visiters, who scarcely allowed us to move or breathe ; which, joined to the heat of the weather, and the insufferable stench, rendered our situation truly comfortless and distressing.

We were at length removed from this horrible hole, and conducted to a hut in the heart of the town, in which wood fires had been burning the whole of the day, so that the wall was almost as warm as the sides of a heated oven, insomuch that it could hardly be endured. Yet, to render it more unpleasant still, a large, closely-woven mat was placed before the doorway, in order to prevent a thousand eyes from staring in upon us ; this excluded every breath of air. Our feelings, during the whole of the night, were more distressing than can be conceived: we were almost suffocated with the closeness and intense heat of the room ; and dreamed hat we were being baked alive in an oven. It appears that this town is governed by two chiefs, separate and distinct from each other, one of whom is a Nouffie man, and the other a Falátah ; for in the afternoon each of these individuals sent us a bowl of rice as a present.

Bajiebo is a flourishing and important trading town, although not walled, and one of the largest and most populous that we have yet seen. A considerable

Kaffir Canoe.

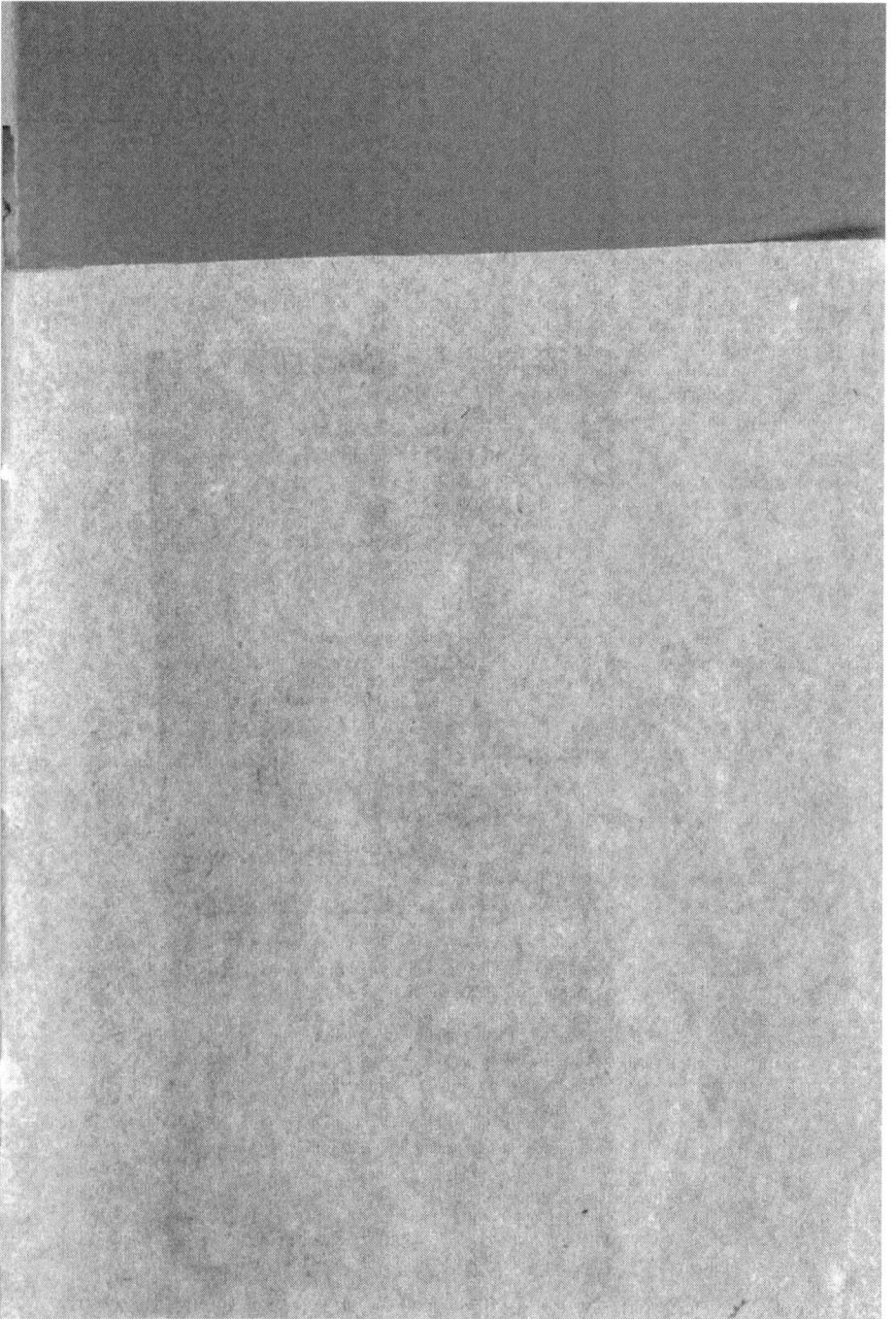

traffic is carried on by its inhabitants with their countrymen on the opposite side of the river, for which purpose they have a great number of canoes of large dimensions, which are continually employed every day in crossing from side to side. Their huts are erected so close to each other, and with so little regard to comfort and a free circulation of air, that there is scarcely a footpath in the town wide enough for more than one man to walk on at a time ; and not having the advantage of shady trees, the heat of the town is excessive and distressing. Its uncleanness, filth, and extreme nastiness have already been alluded to ; and the odour emitted from the dirty streets is offensive and almost insupportable. The people formerly inhabited a town on the opposite bank of the Niger, but as was the case with those of Layaba, they were induced, or rather compelled to settle here, on account of the commotions occasioned by the civil wars, and like them too, they have been found out by their greatest enemies.

The power of the Falátahs here is evidently very great. One of their number is styled chief, and has more authority and influence than the native ruler. We have been obliged to make a present to each of these individuals, and other high and mighty personages were likewise desirous of obtaining a similar favour at our hands, but we made light of their conversation, and would not understand their enigmas.

We have seen to-day several large canoes, the bottom of which is made of a single tree, and built up with planks to a considerable height. In many of them, sheds, or houses, as they are called, have been erected, which are thatched with straw, and in which fires are kindled, food prepared, and people sleep, and indeed live altogether. The roof is circular, and formed in much the same manner as the upper part of a covered wagon in England. These sheds are of the most essential service to the natives, as, with their assistance, merchants are en-

abled to travel with some degree of comfort, with
their wives and household, several days' journey up
and down the Niger, without being under the necessity of landing, except to purchase provisions, or
whenever they feel inclined to do so.   As the people
have nothing that equals or answers to pitch, hemp,
or tar, they use iron staples for the purpose of repairing it and keeping the planks together when a
canoe becomes leaky, or any part of it, as it frequently happens, is split by exposure to the rays of
the sun. We have seen an old canoe, which had
undergone repairs several times, with no less than
from eight to ten thousand of these staples driven
into her sides and bottom.

Our course to-day has been about S. by E.   The
thermometer has been at 70, 90, and 95.

Tuesday, October 5th.—Before sunrise this morning our luggage was removed to the beach, and between six and seven o'clock we were once more
upon the water. Just below the town of *Bajiebo*
the Niger spreads itself into two noble branches, of
nearly equal width, formed by an island.   We preferred journeying on the eastern branch, but for no
particular reason. The country beyond the banks
was very fine. The island in the middle of the river
is small, but verdant, woody, and handsome; and we
passed by the side of it in a very few minutes, with
considerable velocity. It was then that both banks
presented the most delightful appearance.   They
were embellished with mighty trees and elegant
shrubs, which were clad in thick and luxuriant foliage, some of lively green, and others of darker hues;
and little birds were singing merrily among their
branches. Magnificent festoons of creeping plants,
always green, hung from the tops of the tallest trees,
and drooping to the water's edge, formed immense
natural grottoes, pleasing and grateful to the eye,
and seemed to be fit abodes for the Naiads of the
river! Yet, with all its allurements, there is some-

thing wanting in an African scene to render it comparable in interest and beauty to an English landscape.

"By secret charms our native land attracts."

There is nothing here half so attractive or inspir ing. It is seldom, very seldom, that the morn is ushered in by the " song of earliest birds ;" which is so eminently enchanting at home, and which induces so much happiness and cheerfulness, benevolence and joy. Here there are no verdant fields, nor hedges, adorned with the jessamine, the daisy, the primrose, the bluebottle, or the violet, and the hundred other pretty flowers, which please the sight, and exhale, in springtime or summer, the most grateful and delicious fragrance. No flowers here

" Waste their sweetness in the desert air,"

for not a solitary one is anywhere to be seen. Besides, generally speaking, a loneliness, a solemnity, a death-like silence pervades the noblest and most magnificent prospects, which has a tendency to fill the mind with associations of sadness, and reflections of melancholy, very opposite to the silent cheerfulness and that internal springing joy which we feel on contemplating those goodly and charming landscapes which are the pride, the beauty, and the ornament of England. To look at the cleanliness of our cottages and the tidiness of their occupants is pleasant; but when the dirty mud huts of the natives of this part of the world, with the people themselves, do appear, in our opinion they banish every favourable impression, and destroy the effect of all.

In the course of an hour after leaving Bajiebo, we passed by two towns of considerable extent, and a hill was observed right ahead of us, covered with trees, one of which was of such singular appearance, that it might easily be mistaken at a short distance

for a tall pole, with a flag unfurled, and waving at
the top of it.

At a little before eight in the morning, we saw and
passed along at the base of a high pile of loose
granite rocks, large and dark-coloured, which are
on the Nouffie, or eastern side of the river; and almost close to them, and on the edge of the water, is
a small town. In about a half hour afterward we
arrived at an extensive town, situated on the same
side, and called *Leechee*, which is inhabited by Noufanchie, and said to be a place of considerable rank
and consequence. Here we landed by express desire, and finding an empty grass hut near the spot,
we entered and took possession of it till such time
as the chief should be made acquainted with our arrival. Here also our canoe-men left us, and returned
to Bajiebo, where we had hired them.

We were not suffered to wait long, but in a few
minutes received an invitation from the chief to
come and see him; and having walked through a
good part of the town, we at length approached his
residence, and were introduced without ceremony or
hinderance into a large and lofty hut, where we discovered the chief sitting on a platform of mud, in
great state, with about forty natives and Falátahs
in earnest conversation on each side of him. He received us with great civility and many demonstra-
tions of gladness, and desired us to draw near his
person, that he might have a better opportunity of
looking at and talking to us. However, he appeared
unwilling for us to quit *Leechee* till to-morrow, and
pressed us strongly to remain with him for the day,
which, however, not all his solicitations and importunities could induce us to accede to. A Falátah
then commenced a long and pithy harangue, in which
he endeavoured to prejudice the chief and those that
were with him against us, and to fill their minds with
alarm and apprehension, on account of our malevo-
lence and the extraordinary power which he said

we possessed; but his eloquence was unavailing, for we had the consolation to hear one of his own companions and countrymen desire him to hold his tongue, and mind his own business, and consequently his remarks were soon forgotten.

We had provided ourselves with a small present for the chief on our first setting out for his residence, but after what we had seen and heard, we fancied that it was too trifling, and feared that it would be returned as such by the chief, and that we should be exposed to abuse and ribaldry from those that were with him; therefore something was added to the gift before we presented it. We then took our leave of him and his people, and instantly made our way back to the water-side, where we waited in the grass hut, what appeared to us to be a long, long time, for the appearance of the canoemen with whom the chief had promised to supply us. In this interval, the governor sent us a pot of honey, a couple of fine lemons, and a few limes. After a considerable delay, a man for each canoe could only be procured for us, so that two of our own people were obliged to supply the place of others as well as they could.

The width of the Niger at Leechee is about three miles, and the inhabitants have plenty of canoes for the purpose of crossing the river, for fishing, and for other purposes. About half-past ten we got into our canoes, which we pushed off the shore, and proceeded at a good rate down the stream, along the side of a considerable island, which is within gunshot of the town; and after passing a large open village, of respectable appearance, which is on the western bank, we put in at a small town, a few miles below, also on the Yarriba side of the river where we were constrained to go in quest of other canoemen, because those from Leechee, though they had been with us only forty minutes, and had certainly not laboured very hard, had refused to pro-

II.—E

ceed with us any farther, nor could all our entice-
ments induce them to forego this resolution. Here
we were detained in our canoes, and exposed to the
sun for an hour and a half, in order to obtain fresh
canoemen, the inhabitants of the town being absent
in the fields.

Immediately after leaving this town we passed
another island, of goodly appearance, but we understand it is uninhabited. We then came in sight of
a double range of rocky hills, one of which is close
to the water, and both running from north-east to
nearly due south. At one P. M. we were again
obliged to put in and land at a small village, which
is situated on an island, for an exchange of canoe-
men, for, like those from Leechee, these were unwilling to go a great way from their homes. In an
hour's time a number of the islanders came down to
us, and paddled us to the opposite side of the river,
and from thence along the base of the hills already
alluded to. The appearance of these hills is wild
and gloomy, though highly romantic. Trees of
hungry growth and stunted shrubs, whose foliage
seemed for the most part dull and withering, shoot
out of the hollows and interstices, and overhang immense precipices, whose jagged summits they partly
conceal. Indeed, these hills look dismal and lone-
some in the extreme, and seem to be visited only by
wild beasts and birds of prey, or by the shadow of
a passing cloud, which serves to increase, if possible,
their dreariness and gloom. On the top of one of
them is a huge and singular block of white stone,
which, at a certain distance, greatly resembles an
ancient fortification. We arrived at the end of our
journey, and the termination of the nearer range
of hills, between four and five o'clock in the afternoon, when we landed at a fishing-town on a small
island, which is called *Madjie*, and belongs to the
Noufanchie. Here we were received with cheerfulness by the chief, who accommodated us with a

roomy hut, sent us a quantity of dressed provisions, and otherwise treated us in the most hospitable manner. The banks of the river that we have passed to-day are high, and well cultivated. The direction of the river rather to the eastward of south, and the distance from this island to Bajiebo about thirty miles. The thermometer has been at 78, 92, 94, during the day.

Wednesday, Oct. 6th.—About seven o'clock in the morning we departed from the island of Madjie, where we had slept, and pursued our journey down the river, which for a short distance takes a turn to the east, by the side of another range of hills, and afterward flows for a number of miles a little to the southward of east. Near the island of Madjie, the Niger branches into three streams, and we were recommended to follow the most easterly, because the other two were neither considered so deep nor so free from danger.

On leaving the island we journeyed very rapidly down the current for a few minutes, when, having passed another, we came suddenly in sight of an elevated rock, which is called *Mount Kesa* by the natives, and almost at the same instant we found ourselves abreast of it. It forms a small island, and is probably not less than three hundred feet in height, which renders it a conspicuous and remarkable object. It is excessively steep, and rising out of the river as it does, its appearance is irresistibly imposing and majestic beyond expression. Its base is fringed by venerable trees, and less magnificent vegetation, which also strives to spring forth from its barren and almost naked sides. The height of Mount Kesa, its solitary position, and the peculiarity of its form distinguish it from every other, and render it an object of more than common interest. It is greatly venerated by the natives of this part of the country, and, as may readily be imagined, favours the superstitious notions which are attached to it by a simple and credulous people, who, like the vulgar of Europe, are fond of the marvellous. The story attached to Mount Kesa is of a very romantic nature. The natives believe that a benevolent genius makes the mountain his favourite and continual abode, and dispenses around him a benign and heavenly influence. Here the misfortunes of the unhappy are alleviated, the wants of the needy supplied, and the lamentations of the mourner turned to joy: sin, sorrow, and suffering are unknown; solemnity gives place to merriment, and the solicitude of futurity to present enjoyment and thoughtless jocularity. But more especially, say the natives, the weary traveller here finds a refuge from the storm, and a rest from his toils; here he reposes in the delights of security, and revels in the comforts of ease. However, to obtain all this, he makes known his wants and desires to the spirit of the mountain by supplication and prayer, when they are instantly answered; he receives the most delicate and excellent food from invisible hands, and when sufficiently invigorated by refreshment, he is at liberty either to continue his journey or remain awhile to participate in the blessings of the mountain. Such is the story we received from these superstitious people of this celebrated mount. A little to the northward of it is a naked rock, which rises only a few yards above the surface of the water; but from its insignificance it is unworthy of particular description.

A canoe, in which was a Mohammedan priest, with his women and train, kept company with us down the river, and Rabba was the place of its destination. A very spirited competition was for some time maintained between his canoemen and ours, in regard to the velocity with which they could impel their respective boats; but that of the priest was three times larger and heavier than ours, and he was at length constrained to forego the contest, the

odds being so very much against him. This created
a loud laugh and a little cheering on our side, and
much merriment on both. All the canoes then proceeded abreast of each other, and the whole of the
party were on the best possible terms. The priest's
wives strove to entertain us to the best of their
ability with specimens of their music. One of them
played on a four-stringed guitar, and her companions
accompanied the instrument with their voices; and
though the noise was not very melodious, still it
was more agreeable to us than silence; indeed, we
were highly pleased with the attempt of these sooty
ladies, for how rude soever the performance may
be, music has oftentimes a pleasant and soothing
influence.

At nine in the morning we landed near a small
town to procure a fresh supply of canoemen, and
we waited for them above an hour, without visiting
the adjacent village. As soon as we had obtained
them we journeyed along the eastern side of the
river; and, at eleven A. M., perceived the smoke of
the far-famed Rabba ascending many miles before
us. In another half-hour we drew near an island
called *Belee*, which is exceedingly low, flat, and
swampy. Here we stopped at a large, but mean
and dirty-looking town, which stands close to the
water's edge.

We were shortly introduced to the chief, who is a
great, rich, and important personage, if we may believe the representations of our messenger. He informed us, that Mohamed, the magia's son, who
had left us at Patashie, had returned from his father,
in pursuance of his agreement, but, instead of remaining at Rabba, as we expected, he had come
over to Belee, and been waiting three days on the
island, in expectation of our arrival. However, having heard in the earlier part of the morning that we
were to have slept at Madjie last night, he instantly
left Belee in canoe, and proceeded up the river to

meet us. For ourselves we had neither heard nor
seen any thing either of him or his canoe. The governor further said, " You will be obliged to remain at
Belee till Mohamed's return to the island, for he has
news of importance to communicate to you; to-
morrow morning you will leave hence, and proceed
to another island, which is farther down the river,
wherein it is arranged that you shall abide till your
affairs be finally adjusted." There was some mystery
about this, which was unexpected and not very gratifying.

It was nearly evening before Mohamed returned
to Belee, and he came to us in a dripping state, with
an excuse that he had been upset in his canoe two
or three times. After the first salutations were
over, he informed us of his visit to his father, and
its result. The magia had desired him to assure us
of his "best wishes in our welfare, and his determination to protect, support, and encourage us, as
far as he was able." Mohamed then drew our attention to a young man who had entered the hut with
him, but whom we had not before observed, and introduced him as a messenger sent to us by the Falátah prince of Rabba. This man said that his master, named Mallam Dendo, had commissioned him
to acquaint us, that he heartily concurred with the
King of Nouffie in the favourable opinions and sentiments which the latter entertained for us. With
respect to our visiting Rabba, which he understood
we were very much disinclined to do, he should not
urge us; and rather imagined that we should be
more comfortable and enjoy greater tranquillity on
an island on the opposite side of the river, where he
would recommend us to stop. The chief of Belee
had previously made us acquainted with this arrangement. The Falátah messenger concluded by
observing that we should be visited on the morrow
by the " *King of the Dark Water!*" who would escort

us to the island in question, of which he is governor.

In the evening the chief of Belee made us a present of a quantity of goora-nuts, a large pot of honey, a sheep, and dressed provisions in abundance, with a huge calabash of sour beer. He boasted that he was the King of Nouffie's head slave, and a mighty man of valour; and artfully insinuated that he expected a present from us in proportion to his rank and eminence. But we have seen such numbers of kings, princes, and great men lately, that we are heartily disgusted with all who bear the epithet; they are so numerous, that they would be as difficult to count as the drops of rain in a heavy shower.

The thermometer has been at 79, 92, and 94, during the day.

The course of the river from Madjie to this island has been to the S. E., the distance about twelve miles. The eastern or Nouffie bank of the river is moderately high, and overspread with low hills, and both banks are well cultivated.

Thursday, Oct. 7th.—So early as five o'clock in the morning our canoes were loaded, and having breakfasted on a slice of yam, we were fully prepared to quit the island. But as it was not deemed either politic or proper to go away till the arrival of the great *King of the Dark Water*, who was hourly expected, and who might be inclined to construe our departure into contempt, we consented to await his coming. Though we have been exposed to a thousand nuisances, and all manner of inconveniences, and are pretty well reconciled to them all, yet rather than remain in a close black hut, full of men, whose garments are generally covered with vermin, and rarely, if ever, cleaned, and who make it a common practice to sit on the mat whereon we sleep; rather than do this, we stepped into our canoes, and having pushed off from the land, we waited the islander's

arrival under the branches of a large tree at a little
distance from the town.

Between nine and ten, A. M., we heard a number
of men singing, and keeping time to the motion of
many paddles, but we could see no one. However,
in a very few minutes, a canoe, which was paddled
by a few men only, came in sight, and we knew by
this that the Water King was approaching. It was
instantly followed by another and much larger one,
propelled by above twenty very fine young men,
whose voices we had been listening to just before,
and who were still continuing their song. Their
music was slower, but very similar to that which may
be heard on many parts of the western coast. The
King of the Dark Water was with them. As the canoe drew nearer we were not only surprised at its
extraordinary length and uncommon neatness, but
likewise at the unusual display of pomp and show
which we observed in her. In the centre a mat
awning was erected, which was variously decorated,
and on the front of it hung a large piece of scarlet
cloth, ornamented with bits of gold lace stitched on
different parts of it. In the bow of the canoe were
three or four little boys, of equal size, who were
clad with neatness and propriety; and in the stern
sat a number of comely-looking musicians, consisting of several drummers and a trumpeter, while the
young men who had the management of the boat
were not inferior to their companions either in de-
cency of apparel or respectability of appearance.
They all looked in fact extremely well.

As soon as this canoe arrived at the landing-place,
the "Water King" came out from beneath the awning, and, followed by the musicians and a suite of
attendants, walked to the hut wherein all public matters are transacted, and whither, in a few minutes,
we ourselves were desired to repair. The chief of
the island, with his elders and the more respectable
of the people, were seated, on our entrance, on

each side of their important visiter, an my brother
and I, as a mark of distinction, were invited to place
ourselves in front of him.   When the usual compliments had passed on both sides, he informed us, with
much solemnity, of his rank and title; he then alluded to the cause of his coming, which, he said,
was to do us honour, and repeated what had previously been told us by the king's son.   This being
done, he presented us with a pot of excellent honey,
and two thousand cowries in money, besides a large
quantity of goora-nuts, which are cultivated in the
country, and which are held in so great esteem, that
the opulent and powerful alone have the means of
procuring them.   Having nothing farther to say or
do, we shook hands with his sable majesty, whose
name is Suliken Rouah, expressed our acknowledgments for his handsome present, and returned to our
boats.

The "King of the Dark Water" is a fine-looking
man, well stricken in years; his skin as black as a
coal; his features are coarse but benevolent, and his
stature advantageous and commanding.   He was
dressed in a full Bornouse, or Arab cloak, of inferior
blue cloth, underneath which was a variegated tobe
made of figured satin, country cloth, and crimson silk
damask, all patched together; he likewise wore a
cap of red cloth, Hàussa trousers, and sandals of
coloured leather.   Two pretty little boys, about ten
years of age, and of equal size, and who acted in
capacity of pages, followed him into the hut.   Their
clothing was neat and becoming, and their persons
nicely clean; each of them was furnished with an
ornamented cow's tail, and they stood one on his
right hand and the other on his left, to brush away
flies and other insects from his person, and supply
him with goora-nuts and tobacco.   The king was
also accompanied by six of his wives, fine handsome
iet-black girls, dressed in neat country caps edged
with red silk.   Native cloths, made of cotton and

silk, were fastened round their waists, beneath which
they wore a sort of short frock.   The usual custom
of staining their finger and toe-nails with henna appears to be general among them; their wrists were
ornamented with neat silver bracelets, and their
necks with coral necklaces.

To such a man as the "Water King," with such
a suite and such a title, the greatest honour is expected to be paid, and we therefore showed our respect by saluting him with a discharge from two or
three muskets; and by waiting patiently his return
from the council-hut, wherein he staid two whole
hours, during which we were sitting in our canoes,
exposed to a very hot sun, for we had removed them
from under the tree by the side of his own.

It was exactly midday when Suliken Rouah re
embarked in his princely canoe, and quitted the
island of Belee.   Determined for once to make an
attempt at a more respectable appearance, for heretofore it had been extremely mean and homely, we
hastily constructed an awning of our sheets.   It was
the first time we had made use of such a thing,
though we are without umbrellas, and till then had
nothing but slight straw hats to protect our heads
from the sun.   Above the awning we elevated a
slender staff, on the top of which we fastened our
national colours, the union flag, which was kindly
given us by a gentleman on the coast, who was
commandant of Anamaboo.   When unfurled and
waving in the wind, it looked extremely pretty, and
it made our hearts glow with pride and enthusiasm,
as we looked on this solitary little banner.   We
thought it would be of service to us also if we made
as gay an appearance as the king and his followers;
and accordingly I put on an old naval uniform coat
which I had with me for state occasions, and my
brother also dressed himself in as grotesque and
gaudy a manner as our resources would afford.   Our
eight attendants also put on new white Mohamme

dan tobes, so that our canoe, with its white awning surmounted by the union flag, our canoemen in new dresses, and ourselves appearing as officers, contributed not a little to the effect of the whole scene. "The august King of the Dark Water," with his retinue in twenty canoes, condescendingly gave us the precedence, and ours was the first that moved off from land, and led the way down the river towards Rabba.

For a little while we continued to take the lead, but the chief soon went before us, for two reasons: first, that he might have an opportunity of looking at us; and secondly, that we might have a fairer chance of seeing him in all his state, for which purpose he had placed himself outside his awning on an elevated and conspicuous seat. However, he only wished to get a few yards before us, for his canoemen soon lifted their paddles out of the water, and the boat fell back to its former situation. This going before and falling behind was done repeatedly. The musicians in the large canoe performed merrily on their instruments, and about twenty persons now sung at intervals in recitative, keeping excellent time with their paddles.

A brisk wind sprung up the river full in our faces, relieving us from the extreme heat of the weather, which was remarkably fine; the scene before us was very animating, and the whole of us were in high glee and spirits. Other canoes joined us; and never did the British flag lead so extraordinary a squadron. The "King of the Dark Water" might be mistaken for a river god; and his wives, now and then showing their pretty black faces from under the awning, cast many an arch look at us with their sparkling, jetty eyes. It was not long before our revery was interrupted by a great noise from the adjacent land; and on turning we perceived the banks of an island called *Zagozhi*, which were lined with numbers of people, admiring our flag, and watching

us very earnestly, by which we guessed that this
was the place of our destination. The island is so uncommonly low that the houses and trees appeared
as if they were standing in the water, as indeed
many of them actually were. Here we arrived,
and landed between one and two P. M., having enjoyed a pleasant excursion of eight or nine miles.
Ours being the first canoe, before we landed on the
island we waited for the king to precede us, and the
moment he set his foot on the shore, we fired a
salute of four muskets and three pistols. Suliken
Rouah was rather alarmed at this, and demanded
whether we were going to make war on him. He
was soon relieved from his fear, by being told it was
an honour that we had been in the habit of paying
to all the princes we had met in our travels ; which
he no sooner understood, than he expressed himself much gratified by our attention. Suliken Rouah
went in person in quest of a dwelling-house, and led
us to one of the best which the island affords ; however, it is miserably bad ; for, as the town is built on
a marsh, every hut in it has the disadvantage, during
the whole of the rainy season, of soft damp floors
and uncomfortable roofs. Our own has positively
pools of water springing up out of the ground, and
on this we shall be obliged to sleep. The walls of
the huts are built of mud from the river, strengthened
and supported by wooden pillars, and ribs of the same
material : however, these do not prevent them from
cracking in a hundred different places ; and large
chinks, admitting wind and rain, may be observed in
the wall of every hut. They all have, indeed, invariably, a very dirty and wretched appearance, though
their inmates, generally speaking, are understood to
be opulent, clean, and respectable. Having conducted us to our hut, the chief of the island shook
hands very heartily with us, and assured us that we
should want nothing. He soon provided us with
doors of bamboo for our hut, and a number of mats

to spread on the floor, which made it tolerably comfortable. In the evening four large calabashes of
stewed rice, with fowls, and no less than ten gallons
of *pitto*, or country beer, were sent us. About seven
in the evening, messengers arrived from Rabba, to
inform us that they should come early in the morning for the presents we intended for the chief. They
said that the king would not put us to the trouble
of going to see him, as the town is full of Arabs,
whose begging propensities would be very inconvenient to us. I was much pleased with this intelligence, knowing very well the character of these
Arabs; and I sent word back that I was much
obliged to him, and should be still more so if he
would dispense with my going to the sansan or
camp at a short distance from the town to visit the
King of Nouffie.

Rabba is opposite Zagozhi, and appears from
hence, a distance of two miles, to be an immensely
large, populous, and flourishing town. It is built
on the slope of a gentle hill, and on a spot almost
entirely bare of trees. The Niger, both yesterday
and to-day, has flowed in a direction to the south
of eas

CHAPTER XV.

Friday, October 8th.—MALLAM DENDO, the cousin of Bello, we find is still living, but in a very old and feeble condition. He is besides nearly blind, and thinks he has not many more years to live. Being a cautious, peaceful old man, his chief concern is to establish his son as his successor, and fearing that there might be some dispute about it after his death, has already given up to him the reins of government. The usual form on these occasions will be observed, and is to take place on the first day of the new moon. The son is to ride through all the streets of the town on his father's white horse, preceded by all the principal people of Rabba, attended by trumpeters, &c., and thus proclaimed king.

Early in the morning, the messengers from the chiefs mentioned yesterday arrived, bringing with them two fine sheep and a great quantity of rice. They were accompanied by a messenger from the general, a Bornou man, with another sheep. We are obliged to accept of this latter much against our inclination, for it will cost us ten times its value, but it is a treat that we have not had since we left

Yàoorie. It appears that we shall be required to give presents to nine persons before we shall get away from this place.

Having prepared the presents, I collected the messengers and laid out before each of them those that were intended for their masters; they expressed themselves pleased with them, and assured us that their masters would be also. In order to make them some reward, and secure their good will, I gave something to each, and dismissed them. We also sent away Mohamed, and his countryman and associate the Nouffie guide, who had accompanied us hither all the way from Boossà. The presents we have made consist of a handsome looking-glass, with a gilt frame, a pair of silver bracelets; a snuff-box, tobacco-pipe, knife, razor, two pair of scissors, four new shillings, and a number of books on natural history, with plates. Besides these, we sent the King of Nouffie a pocket compass, and the Prince of Rabba a camera obscura, desiring each of the messengers to inform their sovereigns that the latter articles were invaluable, but that owing to the length of our journey, and the few things which were left us in consequence, we were compelled to part with them—only, however, till such time as we should return to the country again, when we hoped they would be given back to us, for a handsome present which we should bring for the purpose. Mohamed and the Falàtah messenger promised to return to Zagozhi in a couple of days; but the Nouffie guide, a surly, ill-favoured, and dissatisfied man, has no wish to see us again, and therefore he will remain at home. The old "King of the Dark Water," and after him several of his people, paid us a visit to-day, bringing with them an enormous quantity of bits of meat and pounded yam, boiled or stewed in palm oil, and abundance of less delicate provisions; and strong beer sufficient for a regiment of soldiers! A Hàussa interpreter followed in his train, so that we nad no difficulty in understanding each other; but those who subsequently visited our dwelling were not quite so fortunate, and we could not comprehend a single word which they uttered. Having brought their offering of provisions and beer in huge pots and calabashes, and laid it at our feet, they wished very much to enter into conversation with us, and were much confused and disconcerted at our ignorance of the Nouffie language, and our apparent dulness of comprehension; at first, they stared at us in vacant astonishment, then looked at each other very cunningly, and afterward looked into our faces again. Finding at length that either we could not, or would not, understand their words and gestures, they burst into a loud laugh and went away, leaving their pots and calabashes behind them. These men were extremely well dressed and respectable in their appearance.

Saturday, October 9th.—This morning we were visited by two young men, Arabs from Rabba, who had come, they said, purposely and solely to pay their respects; but in reality, the object of their coming was very different from this, as shortly afterward appeared. On their entrance into the yard of our hut, one of them, a little, short, disagreeable-looking man, uttering a sudden exclamation of joy, sprang forward, and clasped me with violence to his breast, kissing my shoulder, hands, head, cheeks, and beard with much eagerness, agreeably to the custom of his countrymen on such occasions, and also of the Israelites, as well as many other eastern nations; and having done this, he next proceeded to embrace my brother in the same rough and hasty manner, but his compliments were equally as unexpected as they were unpleasant. The Arab, as may be supposed, was very eager to claim acquaintance with me, and to bring to my memory certain scenes which had taken place on my former journey through Hàussa. Having in

some degree recovered from my surprise at his salutation, on looking at him more attentively, I recognised in him the very same individual that had
been employed by Captain Clapperton, whom he
had abused and cheated, and who was subsequently
engaged by myself as guide from Kano. He is the
person also that decamped with Captain Pearce's
sword, and a large sum of money in cowries, when
I sent him back to Kano for the tent-poles, which
he had forgotten till after he had been several miles
on his journey, and since which time I had not seen
him till to-day. His appearance is somewhat uncouth and remarkable; his figure is awkward and
uncommonly diminutive; he has a most forbidding
and intolerable squint; his mouth is turned awry;
and he has a huge and unnatural excrescence jutting
out from his chin, which adds not a little to the de-
formity of his countenance and appearance. Therefore it was not very pleasant to be embraced, and
almost hugged to death, by such a man as this. His
companion is a pale, handsome, and agreeable youth,
and is different from the other; in our presence
his behaviour was decent, and his manners rather
timorous and reserved; and when the villany of his
associate was exposed, he felt the more abashed of
the two. My brother instantly accused the fellow of
his former infidelity, and told him he was surprised
that he could have the impudence to visit and salute
him in the manner he had done, after what had
transpired between them. Instead of expressing
his sorrow and contrition, the Arab made light of
his offence, and endeavoured to laugh off the impression of it altogether; and then in the most abject
manner begged every thing he saw with so much
importunity and selfishness, that we were out of all
temper with the scoundrel, and I turned him out of
the hut in disgust. However, he could not believe
it possible that we were in earnest with him, and
waited outside the door a long time, anxiously ex-

II.—F

pecting an invitation to come in again.   " O, it must
be all in sport," said he ; but at last we threatened
to shoot him if he did not go about his business, and
being apprehensive that we should put our threats
into execution, he ran off as fast as he could.   Before
his dismissal, we gave his companion a few needles,
and he took his leave in peace.   The fellow's excuse
for leaving me in the manner he did, was, that Al
Hadjee Salah, the late Captain Clapperton's agent,
had persuaded him, saying that I was going to travel
among Caffres who knew not Allah, and who would
therefore murder him.   He was frightened, he
added; but it was easy to see that this was a mere
excuse.   His pretext for coming to us now, was,
that Sceriffe Asman, who was going to his native
country Timbuctoo, had offered to convey letters
for us, from whence they might be forwarded to
Tripoli ; and that he himself would call for them
in the morning.   This I hoped to prevent, by saying that we had neither letters to send, nor presents to give to Sceriffe, therefore we did not wish
to see him.

  A great number of Arabs are at present residing
in Rabba ; they have come from various parts, and
trade with the natives in red caps, trona, small looking-glasses of the most inferior description, red
cloth, silk, &c., which they bring chiefly from Fez-
zan.   Among these Arabs is a famous sheikh, who,
we understand, will set out in a few days on a journey to Timbuctoo and other places.

  Sunday, October 10*th.*—Mohamed and the Falàtah
messenger arrived at Zagōzhi in company this morning, in pursuance of their agreement.   The former
brought with him a fine sheep as a present from the
magïa, and Mallam Dendo sent a large pot of honey
by the hands of the latter.   Both princes, according
to the account of their representatives, were mightily
pleased with their respective presents, and expressed
their acknowledgments in the warmest and most

grateful terms; they repeated the encouraging promises which they had before held out with regard to our
journey, and have commissioned the "King of the
Dark Water," under certain circumstances, to supply us with a commodious canoe, as excellent as
our hearts can desire; strongly recommending us
to enter into arrangements with him, and deliver
our two Patàshie canoes, which are comparatively
small and of little value, into his keeping till our
departure from the country. A man is also to accompany us as far as the sea, to be our guide and
interpreter on the voyage. This intelligence has
made us quite easy in mind, and filled us with hope
and joy; for, previous to the arrival of these men,
our hearts misgave us that every thing would not
prosper well. They seem to have forgotten the
presents we had bestowed on them as well as their
master, for they have been very pressing to-day
in their solicitations for money and needles, so that
I have gone so far as to cut my coat in pieces for
them to make caps of the cloth. Mohamed, in
particular, has been incessantly annoying us in
this manner, and brought a fellow with him from
Rabba, who, he wished us to believe, was the
magia's eldest son, merely for the purpose of exacting a present from us proportionate to his rank;
but we saw through his deceit in time to prevent
our being taken in by him, and crushed it in its
infancy.

It is provoking to be continually tormented so,
and after all to receive nothing for our pains and
the sacrifices we make but discontent, black looks,
and grumbling without end. These fellows, instead
of paying their respects in the first place to the
chief of the island, had come to us directly from the
landing-place; and, because they had something of
consequence to communicate to him, in which we
ourselves were intimately concerned, after having
remained in our company long enough to ascertain

that they could extort nothing further from us, Mohamed, who had come with them, declared that they
were in a hurry to be gone, to make amends for
their delay, and therefore boldly demanded two
thousand cowries " to open," as he expressed it, or
" clean out, the mouth of the 'Water King!'" or
else, he declared, no business whatever could be
transacted with him; it was the only method, he
added gravely, with which he was acquainted, of
enticing him to speak on any subject of importance.
We knew all the time that the fellow was endeavouring to deceive us; but seeing how much our
success depended on keeping all these sort of gentlemen in good-humour, and that our interest lay in
being imposed on now and then, we complied with
his request. Considering, after what had passed,
that Mohamed and his colleagues might embezzle
this sum, which in fact they strove to do, we sent
Pascoe along with them to the chief's house. Both
he and his people continue to show us every hospitality, and to treat us with all manner of respect and
civility.

Monday, October 11th.—*Ali*, the Arab, who, it will
be recollected, introduced himself to our notice in
Yàoorie, paid us a visit to-day from Rabba, where
he has been residing some time past. We hardly
knew him again at first, on account of his altered
countenance, and the languid and emaciated appearance of his person; which, he tells us, has been
the effect of sickness and anxiety, occasioned by an
attack of the Guinea-worm, which had confined him
within doors on his mat for three weeks. Instead
of proceeding to Alórie in Yarriba, which it was
his intention of doing, he had changed his mind
suddenly, and had come to Rabba, where he was at
first courteously received and entertained. The
horses which he had in his possession belonged to
the good old Gadado of Soccatoo, by whom he was
commissioned to sell them to the highest bidder.

These animals were exceedingly large, handsome,
and spirited, so much so indeed, that the prince of
the Falàtahs took a great fancy to them, and purchased them, at an extravagant price, very shortly
after they had been first exhibited in public by Ali.
But not having money sufficient at his disposal at
the time, Mallam Dendo promised to give the value
of the animals partly in cowries and partly in handsome tobes of native manufacture, which the seller
agreed to receive as willingly. He has, however,
been detained here ever since, and to the present
time has been put off day after day with empty
promises. Ali does not think that this procrastination proceeds from any dishonest feeling on the part
of the prince of the Falàtahs, but that it is really from
want of the means of paying him, owing to the expenses attending several warlike expeditions in which
he has been recently engaged.

Such, generally speaking, is the manner of trading
in this country, a few years' credit being thought
very little of; and it is not unusual to meet with individuals who have been unable to obtain payment of
debts for ten or a dozen years at least.

We had a long chat with Ali, and gave him a few
old things which were useless to us; but we soon
found it necessary to send him away, as he began
complaining very grievously of poverty and wretchedness.

The Arab, in course of conversation, remarked,
that it would be a good speculation to send some
needles for sale at the Rabba market, which is extremely large and well attended; therefore, we took
the hint, and sent Jowdie and Ibrahim, two of our
men, with a certain quantity to dispose of, and they
both returned in the evening with the fruits of their
success, having obtained the sum of eight thousand
cowries for them. This has given us fresh spirits
again, for we had not a single cowrie to give to our
men. The inhabitants of Rabba purchased them

very eagerly, at from fifteen to thirty cowries each needle, and they were anxious to get more, when they found that our men had disposed of the whole.

It has been the policy of Mallam Dendo, who, by all accounts, is an able and crafty chief, and a courageous man, to advance foreigners of all nations to certain lucrative and important posts, either about his person, in the army, or as governors of conquered towns; and by this means he conciliates, in a great measure, the black or original population of the country, confirms his reputation, and establishes his sovereignty with little trouble over lands and districts which he may have subjugated and added to his dominions. It appears that the prince of Rabba is wholly independent of Bello, the Sultan of Soccatoo, or at most that he pays only a nominal allegiance to that monarch, though an amicable intercourse is constantly kept up between them.

Mallam Dendo lately planned an expedition against the kingdom of Funda, which was instantly carried into execution, though former enterprises of the kind had uniformly terminated in confusion and defeat. This also was a complete failure; for as his soldiers were drawing near the city of Funda, as the story goes, and had attained an eminence for the purpose of reconnoitring the surrounding country, they saw, or thought they saw, to their infinite amazement, a large army coming out to meet them, and all the soldiers armed with muskets, clothed after the manner of foreigners in blue and white dresses. This put them all in a consternation; and without stopping to look behind them, they fled with the utmost speed, and returned to their own homes without accomplishing any thing. Here they attempted to vindicate their cowardice by telling their countrymen a very marvellous story of their having encountered an army of white men, whose formidable equipments and warlike appearance had made their hearts droop within them, and they had fled. In allusion to this story, Mallam Dendo asked Pascoe, in confidence yesterday, whether he did not think that many of our countrymen were assisting their adversaries?

Mallam Dendo, it is said, can send one thousand horse soldiers, well equipped and mounted on noble animals, to the field; and the number of foot soldiers he has at his command is so great, that it is not known. All runaway slaves are encouraged to join the ranks on condition of receiving their freedom; and they are joined by a vast number from the surrounding country. The natives are commanded by captains from among their own countrymen, and the Falàtahs also by theirs; the greatest good-will prevails among them, and we have nowhere observed quarrelling of any kind.

The Falátahs are now in possession of the whole of Nouffie, Ederesa having relinquished his claim, as he had been deserted by the greater part of his troops, who joined the army of Mallam Dendo. Both the magia and Ederesa have little or no authority. The Falátah prince has sent his messengers, both by land and water, to collect the taxes and tributes throughout the country of Nouffie, which were last year paid to Ederesa. Yarriba will soon follow the condition of Nouffie, and the Falátahs, in the course of a few years, will reach the sea. An idea of their character may be formed from their usual boast, that they could conquer the whole world if the salt water did not prevent them.

Friday, Oct. 12th.—As we have already said, Rabba market is very celebrated, and considered by traders as one of the largest and best in the whole country, of which it may be styled the emporium; a variety of articles, both of native and foreign manufacture, are there offered for sale; and it is generally well supplied with slaves of both sexes. Yesterday, one of our men counted between one and two hundred men, women, and children, who were all exposed for sale in ranks or lines. These poor creatures have, for the most part, been captured in war ; and it is said, that the Falátahs rarely treat them with unkindness, and never with brutality. The price of a strong healthy lad is about forty thousand cowries (8*l.* sterling) ; a girl fetches as much as fifty thousand, and perhaps more if she be at all interesting ; and the value of men and women varies according to their age and abilities. Slaves are sometimes purchased at Rabba by people inhabiting a country situated a good way down the Niger, and from thence they are delivered from hand to hand till they at length reach the sea. Ivory is likewise sold, most likely to the same individuals, and large tusks may be purchased at a thousand cowries each, and occasionally at a much cheaper rate. We have eleven elephants' tusks of our own, which were presented to us by the Kings of Wowow and Boossà, but we have been unable to dispose of them at Rabba because no strangers are at present in the city.

All the principal inhabitants of Rabba are complaining bitterly of the want of money, and the peculiar hardness of the times. Formerly, they say, it was not so ; and they ascribe their present poverty and embarrassments to their late reverses in war and misfortunes at home. Their recent unsuccessful attack on the *Cumbrie* people, who reside in the province of Engaskie, near Yàoorie, and which we have alluded to in our visit to that country, has quite humiliated and disheartened them. To be outwitted and overthrown by the unwarlike Cumbrie, who are considered as a despicable race by all people, and to have lost so many men and horses in that expedition, have been a source of great mortification to their vanity, and derogation of their high name. In order to redeem their national character from the stain which it has thus received, and to re store the reputation for bravery and resolution which had before so eminently distinguished them from their neighbours, but which is now so deeply tarnished, the Falátahs at Rabba are actively employed in hastening preparations for the invasion of Yarriba ; and are resolved, it is reported, to set out in a very few days for Katunga, the capital, which is to be their first object of attack. They anticipate success, without the dread of opposition; and they already boast of acquisitions which they have not yet gained, and exult in the thoughts of the splendour and opulence they shall enjoy in cities which they have not yet seen. Our old friend, the monarch of Yarriba, on his part, has been put on his guard, and is, we hear, determined to resist any hostile attempt which may be made against his country.

Mallam Dendo sent for Pascoe this morning in a great hurry, with a message, that he was waiting impatiently his arrival at Rabba, having something of the utmost consequence to communicate. As may easily be conjectured, we were rather surprised at this unexpected summons, and waited Pascoe's return with much anxiety, for we had no doubt whatever that we were principally concerned in it. When, however, he *did* come back, and enter our hut, he looked very wistfully, and informed us, with considerable agitation both of voice and manner, that Mallam Dendo had expressed to him the greatest dissatisfaction at the things which he had received from us as a present, declaring them to be perfectly worthless, and, with the exception of the looking-glass, "fit only for a child !" that he well knew we could have sent him something more useful and of greater value, if we had thought proper ; but that if we persisted in our refusal to do so, he should demand of us our guns, pistols, and powder, before he would consent or permit us to leave Zagózhi. This news made us very uneasy and unhappy, and we sat down in gloom and thoughtfulness, without uttering

a word, for we believed this to be a death-blow to all
our hopes. To part with the only defensive weapons
in our possession we felt determined not to do; it
brought to our recollection the fable of the lion deprived of his teeth and claws. We knew that if we
were to be deprived of these, we should be entirely
in the power of a set of fellows who are remarkable
neither for generosity nor nobleness of principle,
without the means of helping ourselves; and we re
solved never to part with our guns unless compelled
to do so by force, or from the most urgent necessity.
Having reflected deliberately on our situation, we felt
convinced that something on our part must be done,
by way of conciliation, if we had any intention of
quitting the country, and of prosecuting our enterprise. The chief also wanted to know why we had
not gone to Sansam to see the magia, having been
only five days' journey from him when at Yàoorie,
and added, that one of us must go immediately. We
were much hurt, and pointed out to the messenger
our only box of presents, and told him it was all we
possessed to last us to the sea, adding, that if we
were to give his master more we should have nothing left to obtain us even food on our voyage. At
this moment we thought of Mr. Park's tobe, which
was given to us by the King of Boossà; and thought,
that as it was the only thing which we had to offer,
it *might*, in consequence of the splendour of its appearance, and its intrinsic value, prove an acceptable present to the covetous prince, and we fondly
hoped that it might be the means of a perfect reconciliation on both sides: therefore, under these considerations, we immediately despatched Ibrahim with
it to Rabba, though our hearts misgave us at the
time, that it would after all be thought lightly of, as
an excuse for further extortions. Of course, we
deeply lamented the necessity to which we were reduced on parting with this curiosity, but it was inevi-
table. We sent word by Ibrahim also, that having

no good presents to give him was the reason I had
not visited Bello when we were at Yàoorie, and
that I declined doing so for the same reasons now.
Our plan was to make friends with the Rabba chief,
and this, we have some hopes, the tobe we have just
sent to him will effect.

In less than two hours after his departure, Ibrahim
returned from his errand with a quick step and cheerful looks, and informed us that the tobe was accepted
by the prince with rapturous admiration.   By this
present we had made him our friend for ever; he regretted that the Falátahs had no canoes, but were
they possessed of any, he would make us a present
of as many as we might want, and accelerate our
departure from Zagozhi with all his influence. "Ask
the white men," said he, "what they would desire,
and if Rabba can supply them with it, tell them they
shall always have it.   Well!" he continued, "I must
purchase this tobe; I will not accept it as a gift,—
that would be against my principles, and besides it
would be wrong for me to be guilty of such injustice.   Now I shall be something like a king," he
added, turning the tobe inside and out; "let no man
know of it; my neighbours will behold me with
envy; and as for my own people, I will surprise them
some morning by putting it on when they are going
to war; it will dazzle their eyes.   How great will
be their astonishment!"   In this manner the prince
of the Falátahs talked to Ibrahim. We hardly know
what conclusion to draw from it, but rather imagine
that this present of the tobe will in the end be advantageous to our interests, though we very much
regret its loss.   Our man has been desired to visit
Rabba again to-morrow, when a present of some
kind will be sent us as an acknowledgment, for such
is the custom of the country.

Wednesday, October 13*th.*—In pursuance of the
chief's arrangement, we sent Ibrahim and Pascoe to
him this morning.   He received them with civility,

said he was highly pleased at their coming, and
wished to know in what manner he could best express his acknowledgments to us for the present we
had made him, which he termed a "princely gift,"
promising to make us all the return for it in his
power, by forwarding our departure, and assisting
us in the object of our visit as much as he was able.
Pascoe, who had previously been tutored by us, and
who is not deficient in sagacity, made answer, and
said, that our first wish, and the one which he believed we were most anxious about, was to obtain a
large canoe, and pursue our journey on the Niger as
fast as possible; that as we had little money, and
but few presents, and as the "King of the Dark
Water" had refused to exchange a canoe of the
above description for those which we had obtained
at Patàshie, unless we would consent to pay him
ten thousand cowries, we should be obliged to him
to settle that little affair to our satisfaction, otherwise he said we should be embarrassed with insuperable difficulties. And that, if the prince of
Rabba approved of it, a few mats, tobes, or sandals
would be highly acceptable; and would be considered
by us as a sufficient remuneration for the presents we
had made him. This answer pleased the prince,
and he cheerfully agreed to the whole of Pascoe's
propositions. He then went out and procured a
bundle of the handsomest-coloured mats, for the
manufacture of which Rabba is famous, and came
back, and delivered them into the hands of Pascoe
as an offering to us, with two large bags of rice, and
a bunch of plantains. He gave Ibrahim also a handsome tobe and cap for himself; and promised to send
a messenger to the *King of the Dark Water* to settle
the business of the canoe, by whom he would likewise send valuable tobes, to be worn by my brother
and myself. He then presented Pascoe with a
thousand cowries; and he returned with Ibrahim to
Zagòzhi, quite overjoyed with success.

A foot messenger from the King of Nouffie arrived at Rabba in the morning. His sovereign had despatched him privately to Mallam Dendo, with an insinuation to him, "that if it met with his approbation, he (the magia) would order us to be detained at Zagozhi until we should consent to make him a present of a certain number of dollars, or something equivalent to them in value; that he disbelieved the story of our poverty altogether, and would therefore search our luggage, in order to discover whether our assertion was true or false, that we had no greater presents to make." So much dissimulation, meanness, and rapacity which this trait in his character exhibits, we had little reason to expect from the King of Nouffie after expressing for us, so warmly and repeatedly as he has done, protestations of the most cordial, candid, and lasting friendship. We could not forbear feeling very indignant at this foul breach of the laws of hospitality and good faith, which we had experienced in every part of the country previous to this. Perhaps it was well that we had presented the prince of Rabba with Mr. Park's tobe, for he treated the message and its bearer with contempt, and answered energetically: "Tell the magia, your sovereign, that I would rebuke him for this expression of his sentiments; that I detest his base insinuations; that I will never consent to his wishes; and that I reject his proposal with disdain. What! shall the white men, who have come from such distant lands to visit our country, who have spent their substance among us, and made us presents, before we had leisure to do any good for them, shall they be treated so inhumanly? Never! They have worn their shoes from their feet, and their clothes from their persons, by the length and tediousness of their journeys; they have thrown themselves into our hands, to claim our protection and partake of our hospitality; shall we treat them then as robbers, and cast them from us like dogs? Surely

not. What would our neighbours,—what would our
friends—our foes, say to this? What could be a
greater reproach than the infamy which would attach itself to our characters and to our name, should
we treat these poor, unprotected, wandering strangers, and white men too, in the manner your monarch, the King of Nouffie, proposes? After they
have been received and entertained with so much
hospitality and honour in Yarriba, at Wowow, and
at Boossà, shall it be said that Rabba treated them
badly; that she shut her doors upon them and plundered them? No, never! I have already given my
word to protect them, and I will not forfeit that
sacred pledge for all the guns and swords in the
world." Such was the answer which the King
of Nouffie's messenger received from the Falátah
chieftain. Surely it was worthy of a prince.

Our men saw and conversed with this Nouffie
messenger, who had made no secret of his errand,
and the above answer was related to Pascoe by the
prince of the Falátahs himself.

The imbecility of the magìa, and his want of
power, are strikingly apparent; he exercises a nominal authority only over his people, Mallam Dendo
being evidently the ruling monarch of the whole
kingdom of Nouffie. The former never enters into
any public undertaking without consulting the Falátah ruler, and first obtaining his consent to the measure, be it urgent or otherwise.

Several Hàussa merchants arrived at Rabba this
morning, with a number of fine horses for sale. As
soon as they entered the town, they went to pay
their respects to the prince, when Pascoe happened
to be in his company, and they conversed together
in the Falátah language, not thinking for a moment
that it could be understood by him. In allusion to
us, for we are generally brought on the *tapis* on such
occasions, they spoke very much in our praise,
mentioned Captain Clapperton, "the unfortunate

Abdallah," in terms of the highest admiration, and had seen with wonder the splendid and curious presents which he had made to Sultan Bello at Soccatoo. "I know the white men too," said the prince, "they are good men; in fact I have reason to speak well of them, for I also am a white man, and therefore I am of opinion that they are of the same blood as ourselves." It is in this manner that Falátahs endeavour to claim relationship with Europeans, though these people are either of a swarthy complexion, or black as soot; and this passion to be considered fair is often carried to a most ridiculous height. White men, how sorry soever their outward appearance may be, are certainly considered, not only by Falátahs, but by the native blacks, as a superior order of beings, in all respects more excellent than themselves. At Yàoorie we recollect having overheard a conversation between two men, who were quarrelling in the very height of passion. "What!" exclaimed one of them to his fellow, "thou pitiful son of a black ant! dost thou presume to say that a horse was my father? Look at these Christians! for as they are, I am; and such were my ancestors; answer me not, I say, for I am a white man!" The speaker was a negro, and his skin was the colour of charcoal.

Thursday, October 14*th.*—It is time that our journey should be completed, for our goods are very nearly exhausted; and so far from being in a condition to make further presents, our means will scarcely be adequate to procure the bare necessaries of life. Our stock of cloth, looking-glasses, snuff-boxes, knives, scissors, razors, and tobacco-pipes has already been given away, and we have only needles and a few silver bracelets left to present to the chiefs whom we may reasonably expect to fall in with on our voyage down the Niger. Henceforward we must endeavour to shun as many large towns on the banks of the river as we may venture to do with safety. In order to obtain a little money, in addition to what we have already been enabled to procure from the sale of a quantity of needles, both for present use and future convenience, I sent my watch this afternoon to the Falátah general, who is the Bornouese that made us a present a day or two ago, and he agreed to purchase it for the sum of sixty thousand cowries; but having the misfortune to let it fall shortly afterward, as he was in the act of mounting his horse, the glass was broken by the accident, and it was so much damaged outwardly, that its beauty of appearance is entirely destroyed. It was returned to us towards evening, with a present of a bunch of plantains and a beautiful leopard's skin, as a remuneration for the injury which it had sustained, but without sending any apology, or the most distant allusion to the accident! The watch, however, still *ticked*, and the brightness of its inner case was untarnished, therefore we sent it over instantly to Mallam Dendo, who received it with eagerness, and purchased it on the spot for a large sum of money, which he has promised to pay us to-morrow, and Pascoe has accordingly left it in his hands.

The story which we had heard when at Yàoorie, relative to the decease of old Mallam Lendo, father of the present prince of the Falátahs, was not true, as that individual is still alive. But the rumour we suppose to have originated from the old chief's abdication in favour of his son, which took place at the time, and his relinquishment of all public business in consequence of that resolution, though it is said that he still influences his son's conduct in all private as well as public concerns. He now sits, as the Arabs tell us, in one position every day from morning till night, with three large calabashes around him, one of which is kept constantly filled with *tuah*, another with cowries, and a third with goora-nuts; and he revels in the delights which these calabashes afford him all day long. He has the reputation also, now that he is become old, of being both a miser and a glutton. He receives but few visiters, and those are of a particular description, with whom acquaintance has made him familiar, and whose company, equality of age, and a similarity in tastes and inclinations have rendered desirable. These friends are at liberty to eat a handful of *tuah*, or chew a goora-nut in his company, whenever they please. Old Mallam Dendo is considered a very eccentric character by all those who have either seen or heard of him, and his singular manner of living is the common theme of conversation among all ranks. His son is said to inherit none of his father's foibles or propensities; he is revered as a leader, and beloved as a man, though the Arabs do not speak well of his consistency. For some reason, the report of the old man's death is industriously propagated.

Friday, October 15*th.*—We are generally awakened every morning at daybreak, and on particular occasions long before the sun rises, with the noise of the grinding of corn and the loud cheerful singing which accompanies it from the females engaged in that laborious occupation, for females only are employed in it. The same custom prevails in Yarriba, in Borgoo, and at Yàoorie, and in fact throughout the whole of western, central, and northern Africa, as far as we can learn. Instead of the mill formerly used in Judea, and in all eastern countries, with its handle of wood or iron in the rim, the people here simply employ two large stones, flat and smooth, with the uppermost of which they rub the grain till it becomes sufficiently fine. Perhaps this is a more ancient, as it is a more simple contrivance, than the corn-mills used by the females of the east, to which it is greatly inferior. However, Dr. Clarke, the traveller, is of opinion, that the former "are the primeval mills of the world," and he also says, that "they are still found in all corn countries where

II.—G

rude and ancient customs nave not been liable to
those changes introduced by refinement."

Rabba which has before been alluded to, appears
from Zagōzhi to be a considerably large, neat, clean,
and well-built town, though it is unwalled, and is not
otherwise fenced. It is irregularly built on the
slope of a gently-rising hill, at the foot of which
runs the Niger; and in point of rank, population,
and wealth, it is the second city in the Falátah
dominions, Soccatoo alone being considered as its
superior. It is inhabited by a mixed population of
Falátahs, Noufanchie, and emigrants and slaves
from various countries, and is governed by a ruler
who exercises sovereign authority over Rabba and
its dependencies, and is styled sultan or king. The
regal power is despotic, though exercised with
mildness, and the succession hereditary. The Arabs
and all strangers have an enclosure of dwellings to
themselves, which is in the suburbs of the town.
Rabba is famous for milk, oil, and honey. The
market, when our messengers were there, appeared
to be well supplied with bullocks, horses, mules,
asses, sheep, goats, and abundance of poultry.
Rice and various sorts of corn, cotton, cloth, indigo,
saddles and bridles made of red and yellow leather,
besides shoes, boots, and sandals, were offered for
sale in great plenty. Although they observed about
two hundred slaves for sale, none had been disposed
of when they left the market in the evening. The
inhabitants grow abundance of corn and rice, and
other productions common to the neighbouring
countries, and they cultivate the plantain shrub
with success. They possess large flocks and herds
of the finest description, and their horned cattle are
remarkable for their size and beauty. They have
also a prodigious number of excellent horses, of
which they take the greatest care, and they are
universally admired for their strength and elegant
proportions. These animals are used only for war,

recreation, and in travelling. It is the pride and
pleasure of the higher classes to dress well, and
display their persons and their horsemanship to
advantage, and it is gratifying to witness the grace
and dexterity with which they preserve their command over these beautiful creatures. In the management of their horses they are perhaps not inferior to the Arabs, from whom they have, in all
probability, derived most of their lessons in the art.
Rabba is not very famous for the number or variety
of its artificers, and yet in the manufacture of mats
and sandals they are unrivalled. However in all
other handicrafts Rabba yields to Zagozhi.

Zagozhi, situated as it is, directly opposite Rabba,
participates in many of its advantages, though still
it has various inconveniences peculiar to itself.
The town is built on a bog, for such it appears to
us, and it lies so close to the water, that in fact
hundreds of huts are literally standing in it. So
little regard do the people appear to have for what
is termed comfort, that they suffer the walls of their
dwellings either to fall to pieces, or permit large
chinks and holes to remain in them, which freely
admit the wind and rain; while the floors, which
are made of earth or clay, are so soft and damp,
that a slender stick may easily be thrust into them
by the hand to any depth. Our own is of this description. In so moist a situation as this, it may
readily be supposed the air in the night season is
illuminated with fireflies. The huts of the natives
are infested with mosquitoes and other more disgusting insects, which abound indeed in millions.
When the Niger subsides, and leaves Zagozhi exposed with all its dirt to the influence of the sun,
the noxious vapours and exhalations with which the
air must of necessity be impregnated will render it
no doubt very insalubrious; but at present the inhabitants make few or no complaints.

In their huts the people exhibit no very favour-

able specimens of taste or cleanliness; and in this
respect, certainly, they are greatly inferior to their
neighbours on the other side of the river. However, in their persons they are by no means so neg-
ligent, for they always appear extremely well
dressed; and we have rarely met with so large a
number of tall, handsome, well-formed men and
comely women as in this place.

The care which the Falátah bestows, and the
pride which he takes in his horse, are employed
and indulged by the inhabitants of Zagózhi in an
equal proportion in their canoes; the Niger is covered with these little vessels, and to be skilful in
the management of them is their greatest boast.
The chief of the island has about six hundred
canoes, all of which will be employed, when the
young Mallam Dendo is proclaimed king, in conveying the Falátah troops across the river on their
expedition into Yarriba. They are fond of aquatic
occupations, even to a passion, and carry them to
excess. All the trade by water in these parts is in
their hands, and they are proprietors of the ferry to
and from Rabba, which is a source of considerable
emolument to those engaged in this speculation.
They are also excellent fishermen, and, in fact, the
population of Zagózhi are almost amphibious, so
prone are they to be perpetually sporting in bogs or
dabbling in water. But they do not confine themselves all the year round entirely to the river, for
they cultivate the soil as well, and, like their countrymen of Nouffie, in the manufacture of various
articles they evince considerable ingenuity and expertness. The cloth which they manufacture in
common with their countrymen, and the tobes and
trousers which they make, are most excellent, and
would not disgrace a European manufactory; they
are worn and valued by kings, chiefs, and great men,
and are the admiration of the neighbouring nations,
which vainly attempt to imitate them. We have

also seen a variety of caps, which are worn solely
by females, and made of cotton interwoven with
silk, of the most exquisite workmanship. The
people here are uncommonly industrious, be they
males or females, and always busy either in culi-
nary or other domestic occupations.

In our walks we see groups of people employed
in spinning cotton and silk; others in making wooden
bowls and dishes, mats of various patterns, shoes,
sandals, cotton dresses and caps, and the like;
others busily occupied in fashioning brass and iron
stirrups, bits for bridles, hoes, chains, fetters, &c.;
and others again employed in making saddles and
horse accoutrements. These various articles, which
are intended for the Rabba market, evince considerable taste and ingenuity in their execution.

We have not seen a single public amusement since
we have been among them. In this respect they
are an example to their neighbours. They seem
quite independent of all authority and above all restraint, except that of the legitimate *King of the
Dark Water*, and their own interests induce them to
obey him alone. They care as little for the Falátahs
as the Falátahs for them; the peculiarity of their
situation renders them secure from foreign invasion,
and insensible to the calamities and distresses which
overwhelm the natives of many parts of the continent. They have liberty stamped on their features,
and lightness and activity, so rarely to be seen in
this country of sluggards, are observable in all their
actions. The generality of the people are well-
behaved; they are hospitable and obliging to strangers; they dwell in amity with their neighbours, and
live in unity, peace, and social intercourse with themselves; they are made bold by freedom, affluent by
industry and frugality, healthy by exercise and
labour, and happy from a combination of all these
blessings.

The population of Zagozhi cannot well be estimated, on account of its lowness and the prevailing flatness of the country round, on which neither a hillock nor eminence of any kind can be discerned. However, it must be immense; and we consider it to be one of the most extensive and thickly inhabited towns, as well as one of the most important trading places in the whole kingdom of Nouffie, not excepting even Coulfo. According to our estimation, the island may be about fifteen miles long and three in breadth, but the greater part of it is now nearly over-flowed. Notwithstanding this, the natives appear to enjoy good health.

Novelties, however trifling, attract the notice of the people of Rabba, as glittering baubles excite the attention of a child; and as children, too, become tired of their plaything a few moments only after it is put into their hands, so do they throw aside in disgust, when it ceases to be a novelty, that which they would have given half their substance to obtain a few seconds before it actually became their own. They are

Pleased with a feather, tickled with a straw.

The prince of the Falàtahs is already tired of my watch, which he purchased yesterday, and he returned it this afternoon, with all its machinery broken; and, like the Bornouese soldier, without making any acknowledgment for his carelessness. However, we *have received permission to quit Zagozhi to-morrow morning, to pursue our journey down the Niger;* and though all the promises of the magia have terminated in nothing—though a Nouffie guide has been denied us—and though it is likely that we shall be perplexed with a thousand difficulties, yet we are in high spirits and great good-humour at the thoughts of our release, for we know that we shall go our way with alacrity and confidence.

We have been busily employed in packing up and

making preparations for our departure from Zagozhi
to-morrow morning. We are in hopes of having no
difficulties about the canoe, and are desirous of obtaining one that will hold all of our party, as it will
be a much more satisfactory arrangement for us,
and more convenient than two small ones. The
chief of the island visited us in the morning, and
promised to send a messenger with us as far as *Egga*,
on the banks of the river. This is the last town,
we are told, down the river belonging to the Nouffie
territory, and its distance from hence is said to be
four days' journey. He tells us also, that the river
is quite safe, according to the reports of the Nouffie
people who trade between this place and Egga.

This afternoon, the chief was unwilling to part
with a canoe under any consideration, yet, as a token
of his friendship and regard, he has offered to spare
us one for twenty thousand cowries! in addition to
our own which we brought from Patáshie island.
A messenger from the prince of Rabba arrived here
just after this proposition was made us, with full
powers to treat with the Water King for our canoe.
" I will see," said the man, " whether I can make him
comply with your wishes or not ; he will not show
me any of his airs, I am sure." This messenger
brought with him a large bag of rice as a present
from Mallam Dendo, who desired him to inform us,
that " he wished us well, and should be most happy
to hear of our return to the country by way of the
Niger." As soon as he had delivered his message to
us, he repaired to the dwelling of the Zagozhi chief,
and returned to us from his errand shortly afterward, with the intelligence of his having succeeded
in obtaining the long-talked-of canoe, which would
be in readiness to receive us on board at an early
hour to-morrow. This has removed a great weight
from our minds.

Last night my brother was troubled and terrified
in his sleep by a frightful dream of scorpions, and,

to his astonishment, when he awoke this morning, he discovered one of those reptiles on his mat, which he had crushed to death in his sleep.

The "Dark Water King" has been informed of our poverty, we believe, and his goodness is declining very perceptibly in consequence. Nor do his people, we are sorry to say, regard us with the same respect and partiality as formerly, nor treat us with as much beer as they did. Doubtless they have imbibed a similar notion, that the white men are poor, and *their* kindness and good-nature are also fast dwindling away. Perhaps all this is natural: even from our friends and relations, hospitality and tenderness do not, under such circumstances, last for ever. It is true the natives have pitied us; but pity is composed of sorrow and contempt; and here, as in more polished countries, we have found it to be unsubstantial and fleeting. After the first gush of feeling, the tear of compassion gives place to the frigid indifference of contempt. To be pitied is to be despised. Such is the case here, and such is the way of the world.

CHAPTER XVI.

The canoe exchanged—Wooden Shoes of Zagózhi—Departure from Zagózhi—Difficulty of obtaining Paddles—The Niger below Rabba—A Night on the River—Hippopotami—Dácannie Island—Progress of Mohammedanism—Scenery of the River—Gungo Island—Native Canoes—Want of an Interpreter—Natives of Gungo—Danger of the Canoe—Height of the River—Fofo Island—Falátah Mode of obtaining Tribute—Arrive at Egga—The Chief of Egga—Curiosity of the People—An important Visiter—Fears of the Canoe-people, and their Refusal to proceed.

Friday, October 16th.—WE were up and stirring at a very early hour in the morning, packing up our clothes and getting our luggage ready for embarkation. But when this was all done we met with a sudden and unforeseen embarrassment,—the sable "King of the Dark Water" laughed at the idea of giving us a canoe on the faith of receiving payment from the prince of the Falátahs, and refused at first to deliver up to us our own, which we had obtained from Patàshie, and which we had kept with so much anxiety and trouble. At length, after much importunity, we induced the chief to restore them into our hands; and our things and the clothes of our people, with a quantity of rice, corn, calavances, and honey, were removed into them from our late residence.

When all this was done, and we were quite ready to start, the old chief came down to the water-side to bid us farewell, according to his avowed purpose, but in reality to offer us a commodious canoe in exchange for our own, if we would consent to give him ten thousand cowries in addition to them. This was agreed to on our parts after a little delay, for we considered that it would be infinitely more comfortable to have our people and all our things with us in the same canoe; and that it would be less laborious, rather than be liable to casualties and accidents by separation. We had fortunately realized a sufficient number of cowries from the sale of needles at Rabba, and while I was shifting our things from our canoe into another, my brother walked back with the old chief to his residence, where he found all the people of the house gathered round the trunk of a large tree which was burning in the hut. Here he paid the chief ten thousand cowries for the canoe, which having done, he rejoined me at the water-side. I had forgotten to mention that the principal inhabitants, owing to the softness of the soil during the rainy season, wear large wooden shoes when they go abroad in bad weather; but the lower class of people and ourselves generally went barefoot. It is merely a flat piece of a very hard species of wood

II.—H

as long as the foot, supported at each end by thick
pieces, as shown in the sketch. A small piece of
leather passing through holes in it, and leaving a
noose on the upper part, serves to confine the great
toe to it, and the heel is also secured by another
piece passing over the instep. The annexed sketch
is a representation of it.

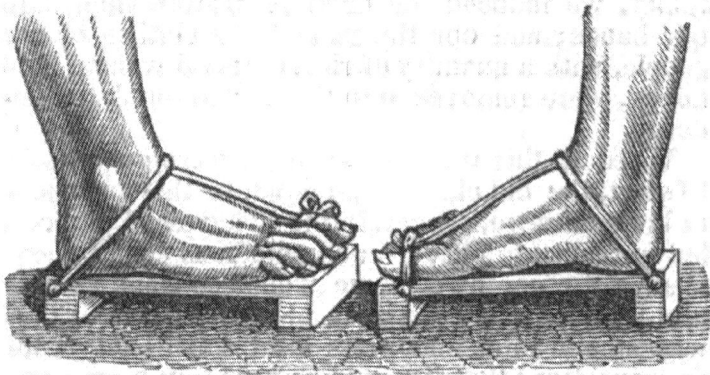

The canoes made here are of a particular descrip
tion, very much resembling what are called punts in
England, but are perfectly straight and flat-bottomed.
They are generally formed out of one log of wood,
and are of an immense size. That which we purchased is about fifteen feet in length and four in
breadth, but they make them nearly as large again.
As soon as our goods were all transferred into the
purchased canoe, which, after all, was not near large
enough for our purpose, we found it to be extremely
leaky, and patched up in a thousand places. We
saw that we had been cheated by the artful "King
of the Dark Water," but rather than enter into an
interminable dispute on the subject, which might involve us in further difficulties, we held our peace,
and put up with the imposition without a murmur.
We had been prevented from perceiving the canoe's

defects before by the excitement of preparation and
the hurry of departure. And yet after we had all
got into her, we waited till we were weary for the
arrival of a messenger that was to have accompanied
us a little way on our journey; but he did not come,
and we resolved to leave without him. Therefore
at nine o'clock in the morning we bade farewell to
the King of the Dark Water and the hundreds of
spectators who were gazing at us, fired two muskets,
accompanied with three cheers, and launching out
into the river, we were soon out of their sight.

Leaving Zagözhi.

Notwithstanding his recent artful proceedings,
this old man had behaved to us with the most attentive hospitality, in which he was imitated by his
principal people, who were as friendly to us as we
could desire. We could not expect that the first
flow of feeling and generosity should continue.
"Whatever is violent," it has been often remarked,
"is seldom lasting;" and when this remark is applied
to the passions of unlettered and uncivilized man,
surely we ought not to be surprised at their advances
of friendship becoming less frequent and their hospitality decreasing with their admiration.

It is inconceivable what difficulties we have experienced in obtaining paddles for our canoe; nowhere have we found people willing to sell us any,
and until we reached Zagözhi we could induce no

one to spare us a paddle; they would not do it for
the world. However at Madjie, and other places,
we returned the hospitality which we received from
the chiefs, by suffering our men to go out at night
when it was dark, and when the villagers were
asleep, and steal what we found an invincible difficulty in procuring by fairer means. The paddles
thus obtained were concealed from their owners,
and from our ill-natured Nouffie guide, in the bottom
of a canoe under a quantity of mats; and though our
men were suspected of the offence, yet we were
permitted to pass on unmolested. It was by such
mean and unworthy shifts as these that we found
ourselves in a condition this morning of proceeding
down the Niger for the first time, without any
foreign assistance whatever. We were overjoyed
at this, for nothing can be more irksome and unpleasant than to be at the beck and under the control of an interested guide or messenger, to stop the
canoe whenever he may think fit, and to land at
every town which might suit his own convenience.
It is pleasant, very pleasant, to *feel* that one is his
own master.

As we have already said, Zagozhi was soon out
of sight; but though we journeyed with tolerable
rapidity, the city of Rabba remained long in view.
We fancied at first that we were pursued from
thence by several canoes which were filled with
people, but we learned soon after that they were engaged in trade, and only pursuing their customary
avocations. The breadth of the channel between
Zagozhi and Rabba is not more than two miles in
our estimation, and the direction of it about south-
east. Our course from the landing-place was along
the shore of the island on the Rabba side for about
twenty minutes, when we arrived at its extremity.
The river then ran east, and its breadth appeared to
be about four miles.

A little before nine A. M., we passed a ferry where

we observed a great many canoes crossing and recrossing with passengers and horses to the Yarriba
side. On inquiry we found that they were going to
the market of Alorie. This is the same place mentioned as lying to the south-west of Katunga. A
range of low hills appeared on each side of the river
as far as the eye could discern, but at some little
distance from the bank, sometimes about five miles;
and we passed along the side of a large cone-shaped
hill, completely detached from the range, and rising
with abruptness at a few paces only from the water's
edge. The borders of the river were exceedingly
flat, low, and swampy, and appeared as though they
were partially overflowed, for trees and shrubs were
shooting up in many places out of the body of the
water.

We observed several large and small towns as we
paddled along, all of them in situations extremely
low, which gave them a truly uncomfortable and
wretched appearance. Besides fish, the principal
food of the inhabitants is rice, of which they cultivate vast quantities. The rice grounds are now almost all inundated; some of them are as much as
three or four miles from any perceptible human hab
itation.

We made no stop whatever on the river, not even
at meal-times, our men suffering the canoe to glide
down with the stream while they were eating their
food. At five in the afternoon they all complained
of fatigue, and we looked around us for a landing-
place, where we might rest awhile, but we could
find none, for every village which we saw after that
hour was unfortunately situated behind large thick
morasses and sloughy bogs, through which, after
various tedious and provoking trials, we found it
impossible to penetrate. We were employed three
hours in the afternoon in endeavouring to find a
landing at some village, and though we saw them
distinctly enough from the water, we could not find

a passage through the morasses, behind which they lay. Therefore we were compelled to relinquish the attempt, and continue our course on the Niger. We passed several beautiful islands in the course of the day, all cultivated and inhabited, but low and flat. The width of the river appeared to vary considerably; sometimes it seemed to be two or three miles across, and at others double that width. The current drifted us along very rapidly, and we guessed it to be running at the rate of three or four miles an hour. The direction of the stream continued nearly east.

The day had been excessively warm, and the sun set in beauty and grandeur, shooting forth rays tinged with the most radiant hues, which extended to the zenith. Nevertheless the appearance of the firmament, all glorious as it was, betokened a coming storm; the wind whistled wildly through the tall rushes, and darkness soon covered the earth like a veil. This rendered us more anxious than ever to land somewhere, we cared not where, and to endeavour to procure shelter for the night, if not in a village, at least under a tree. Accordingly, rallying the drooping spirits of our men, we encouraged them to renew their exertions by setting them the example, and our canoe darted silently and swiftly down the current. We were enabled to steer her rightly by the vividness of the lightning, which flashed across the water continually, and by this means also we could distinguish any danger before us, and avoid the numerous small islands with which the river is interspersed, and which otherwise might have embarrassed us very seriously. But though we could perceive almost close to us several lamps burning in comfortable-looking huts, and could plainly distinguish the voices of their occupants, and though we exerted all our strength to get at them, we were foiled in every attempt, by reason of the sloughs and fens, and we were at last obliged to abandon

them in despair. Some of these lights, after leading
us a long way, eluded our search, and vanished from
our sight like an *ignis fatuus*, and others danced
about we knew not how nor where. But what was
more vexatious than all, after we had got into an
inlet, and toiled and tugged for a full half hour against
the current, which in this little channel was uncommonly rapid, to approach a village from which
we thought it flowed, both village and lights seemed
to sink into the earth, the sound of the people's
voices ceased of a sudden, and when we fancied we
were actually close to the spot, we strained our eyes
in vain to see a single hut,—all was gloomy, dismal,
cheerless, and solitary. It seemed the work of enchantment; every thing was as visionary as " scep-
tres grasped in sleep."

We had paddled along the banks a distance of not
less than thirty miles, every inch of which we
had attentively examined, but not a bit of dry land
could anywhere be discovered which was firm enough
to bear our weight. Therefore we resigned ourselves
to circumstances, and all of us having been refreshed
with a little cold rice and honey, and water from
the stream, we permitted the canoe to drift down
with the current, for our men were too much fatigued with the labours of the day to work any
longer. But here a fresh evil arose, which we were
unprepared to meet. An incredible number of hippopotami arose very near us, and came plashing,
snorting, and plunging all round the canoe, and
placed us in imminent danger. Thinking to frighten
them off, we fired a shot or two at them, but the
noise only called up from the water, and out of the
fens, about as many more of their unwieldy companions, and we were more closely beset than before. Our people, who had never in all their lives
been exposed in a canoe to such huge and formida
ble beasts, trembled with fear and apprehension, and
absolutely wept aloud; and their terror was not a

little increased by the dreadful peals of thunder
which rattled over their heads, and by the awful
darkness which prevailed, broken at intervals by
flashes of lightning, whose powerful glare was truly
awful. Our people tell us, that these formidable
animals frequently upset canoes in the river, when
every one in them is sure to perish. These came so
close to us, that we could reach them with the butt
end of a gun. When I fired at the first, which I
must have hit, every one of them came to the surface of the water, and pursued us so fast over to the
north bank, that it was with the greatest difficulty
imaginable we could keep before them. Having
fired a second time, the report of my gun was
followed by a loud roaring noise, and we seemed to
increase our distance from them. There were two
Bornou men among our crew, who were not so
frightened as the rest, having seen some of these
creatures before on Lake Tchad, where, they say,
plenty of them abound.

However, the terrible hippopotami did us no kind
of mischief whatever; no doubt, at first, when we
interrupted them, they were only sporting and wallowing in the river for their own amusement; but
had they upset our canoe, we should have paid dearly
for it.

We observed a bank on the north side of the river
shortly after this, and I proposed halting on it for
the night, for I wished much to put my foot on firm
land again. This, however, not one of the crew
would consent to, saying that if the *gewow roua,*
or *water elephant*, did not kill them, the crocodiles
certainly would do so before the morning, and I
thought afterward, that we might have been carried
off, like the Cumbrie people on the island near
Yàoorie, if we had tried the experiment. Our canoe is only large enough to hold us all when sitting,
so that we have no chance of lying down. Had we
been able to muster up thirty thousand cowries at

Rabba. we might have purchased one which would
have carried us all very comfortably. A canoe of
this sort would have served us for living in entirely,
we should have had no occasion to land excepting
to obtain our provisions; and having performed our
day's journey, might have anchored fearlessly at
night.

Finding we could not induce our people to land,
we agreed to continue on; all night. The eastern
horizon became very dark, and the lightning more
and more vivid; indeed, we never recollect having
seen such strong forked lightning before in our lives.
All this denoted the approach of a storm. At eleven
P. M. it blew somewhat stronger than a gale, and
at midnight the storm was at its height. The wind
was so furious, that it swept the water over the sides
of the canoe several times, so that she was in danger of filling. Driven about by the wind, our frail
little bark became unmanageable; but at length we
got near a bank, which in some measure protected
us, and we were fortunate enough to lay hold of a
thorny tree, against which we were driven, and which
was growing nearly in the centre of the stream.
Presently we fastened the canoe to its branches, and
wrapping our cloaks round our persons, for we felt
overpowered with fatigue, and with our legs dan-
gling half over the sides of the little vessel into the
water, which for want of room we were compelled
to do, we lay down to sleep. There is something,
I believe, in the nature of a tempest, which is favourable to slumber, at least so thought my brother; for
though the thunder continued to roar, and the wind
to rage—though the rain beat in our faces, and our
canoe lay rocking like a cradle, still he slept soundly.
The wind kept blowing hard from the eastward till
after midnight, when it became calm. The rain then
descended in torrents, accompanied with thunder
and lightning of the most awful description. We
lay in our canoe drenched with rain, and our little

vessel was filling so fast, that two people were obliged to be constantly baling out the water to keep her afloat. The water elephants, as the natives term the hippopotami, frequently came snorting near us, but fortunately did not touch our canoe.

The rain continued until three in the morning of the 17th, when it became clear, and we saw the stars sparkling like gems over our heads. Therefore, we again proceeded on our journey down the river, there being sufficient light for us to see our way, and two hours after, we put into a small, insignificant fishing-village, called Dùcannie, where we landed very gladly. Before we arrived at this island, we had passed a great many native towns and villages, but in consequence of the early hour at which we were travelling, we considered it would be imprudent to stop at any of them, as none of the natives were out of their huts. Had we landed earlier even near one of these towns, we might have alarmed the inhabitants, and been taken for a party of robbers, or, as they are called in the country, *Jacallees*. They would have taken up arms against us, and we might have lost our lives; so that for our own safety we continued down the river, although we had a great desire to go on shore.

In the course of the day and night, we travelled, according to our own estimation, a distance little short of a hundred miles. Our course was nearly east. The Niger in many places, and for a considerable way, presented a very magnificent appearance, and we believe it to have been nearly eight miles in width.

Sunday, Oct. 17th.—After drying our persons and wet clothes before large fires which we had kindled for the purpose, we sat down at the root of a tree, and partook of a meagre refreshment of rice and honey. While we were at breakfast, the promised messenger from Zagōzhi arrived at the village, in a canoe of his own, and came up to us, and introduced

himself. He said that he had followed our track
during the night, and had heard the report of our
guns, but though he strove to come up with us, yet
he had been not able. The hippopotami had annoyed
him in the same manner as they had us, and had given
him much apprehension and uneasiness, but had done
his canoe no manner of injury. We found several
Falátah mallams on the island, who have been sent
by the Chief of Rabba for the purpose of instruct-
ing the natives in the Mohammedan faith. The
island is inhabited by Nouffie fishermen, a harmless,
inoffensive race of men, who only a few weeks ago
were obliged to adjure their pagan deities for the
Koran, whether against their inclination or otherwise. This is another of the effects of the Falátahs' spreading their conquests over the country.
Wherever they become masters, the Mohammedan
religion follows. In consequence of Ederesa having relinquished his authority in favour of Mallam
Dendo, his subjects have become Mohammedans,
and this faith will no doubt shortly spread through
Yarriba.

The mallams were attentive and civil to us as
strangers, and directed the natives to find firewood
for us, and bring it to our encampment, for which, in
return, we made them a present of a few needles.

It was between nine and ten in the morning, when
the guide desired us to proceed onward, and promised to follow us in a few minutes. With this arrangement we cheerfully complied, and instantly
pushed off the shore, for of all persons a messenger is the most unpleasant companion; he is fond
of procrastination, sullen when rebuked, and stops at
every paltry village wherein he fancies that he can
levy his contributions without the fear of interruption.

At ten A. M. we observed several mountains of
singular and picturesque appearance, which are situated a few miles beyond the extreme borders of the

river, bearing north-east of us. They appeared like
three complete sugar-loaves, with little hills about
them. And shortly afterward we came in sight of
other mountains, yet more interesting and romantic;
but these were very elevated, and so far before us, that
they could hardly be distinguished from faint blue
clouds. Among them were table hills, and others
which formed perfect cones, while others again
were of the most grotesque and unshapely description. By what we could see, we were of opinion
that they formed a regular chain of mountains.

The messenger whom we left behind at *Dùcannie*
soon overtook us, in pursuance of his agreement,
and kept us company till we drew near to two cities
of prodigious extent, one on each side of the river,
and directly opposite each other. The beach was
lined with the canoes of their inhabitants. To that
lying on our right, the guide expressed his intention
of going, and endeavoured to entice us with many
promises to accompany him there, but this we refused, for we had previously formed a resolution to
husband our resources to the utmost of our ability;
and well knowing, likewise, the number and rapacity of the "great men," who expect presents in all
large towns, and the detention to which we should
be subjected in them, we had made up our minds to
land at little hamlets only (unless compelled to alter
this arrangement from circumstances), where we
might do just as we pleased, without being amenable
for our actions to those powerful beings who are
styled the "*mighty*" of the earth.

Accordingly, we parted company, and took our
leave of the Zagōzhi messenger, who agreed to follow us as before, and in an hour afterward, which
was about the middle of the day, we put in at a
small village, situated on an island called *Gungo*.
The banks now became high and beautifully cultivated. On our right we passed many villages and
towns, and on our left, the mountains before men-

tioned. Palm-trees grew in profusion, and the
towns and villages were not more than two or three
miles from each other. We observed some hundreds
of large canoes, with a hut in their middle, passing
along the river, some crossing and recrossing to the
opposite banks, while others were pursuing their
course along them. They mostly seemed to contain families of people, for while the men were pad-
dling, the women and girls were singing to a guitar
with their little delicate voices, and produced a very
pretty effect. When we passed close to any of their
canoes, they would suddenly stop their music and
exclaim *Ki, ki, ma nenee acca chiken zhilagee!* repeatedly, expressing the utmost astonishment, both
in their features and gestures. We got this translated for us by Pascoe, and it signifies *Oh, dear! Oh,
dear! what do I see in that canoe!* The *ki ki* is evidently an exclamation of surprise, and might be
rendered Oh! only; but our interpreter gave us his
own translation, and we have accordingly preserved
it. We contented ourselves with a look at the innocent black faces of these damsels, and passed on.
We find that all the Yarriba side of the river is deserted by the natives, who have fled into the country, and left the Falátahs in quiet possession of all
their towns and villages.

The river near this island takes a slight bend to
the southward of east, the current continues to run
very rapidly, and the breadth of the river is from
three to five miles, according to our estimation.
This island is about a mile and a half in circumfer-
ence, lying nearly in the middle of the river. Here,
for the first time since leaving the coast, we could
not make ourselves understood. We could muster
up five different languages spoken by the Africans,
but the Hàussa language was not even understood
here, nor any other that we could speak; so we had
recourse to signs and motions, and soon made the
natives comprehend that we wanted something to

eat, and a hut to sleep in for the night. The choice
of several empty ones was quickly offered us, which
were all equally comfortless and miserable, on account of the lowness of the village, part of which
was overflowed by the river. However, we took
possession of one which is made of wicker-work,
rather for the benefit of cool and fresh air than for
any other advantage peculiar to itself, for it is built
in a splashy situation, and a stream of water from
the Niger rushes over half its floor. The other part
of it was cleaned out for us, and we endeavoured
to make ourselves comfortable. Shortly after, a
large bowl of boiled corn, and another of fish, were
sent to us, together with about ten pounds of the
flesh of hippopotami. The former we were quite
contented with, but as for the latter, being nearly
all fat, we could not fancy it, and accordingly gave
it to our people. They were not a little amused at
this delicacy on our part, for they assured us it was
the finest meat they had ever tasted, and it forms a
principal part of the food of the natives.

The natives of Gungo seem to be a mild, inoffensive, quiet, and good-natured people. They procure
a livelihood almost solely by fishing, and the fruits
of their labour are exchanged with their neighbours
for corn and yams. About sunset, the inhabitants
of the whole island, amounting to about a hundred
men, women, and children, dressed in very decent apparel, and headed by their chief, a venerable old man,
paid us a visit. The chief was dressed in the Mohammedan costume, and he arranged his people, and
made them sit down round our hut in the most orderly manner. They remained in this situation
about an hour, satisfying their curiosity in looking
at us, and making their remarks to each other, expressive of amazement and delight; during which
time, signs only could be understood between
us. The men evinced no alarm, but the women

and pretty little plump-faced children* were much
frightened by our white faces, and seemed not a
little glad to get away. Before they retired, we distributed about two hundred needles among them, and
they went away highly pleased with their present.

Monday, October 18*th* —Weather dull and cloudy.
At a little after six, every thing was in readiness for
our departure. As we were about to launch out into
the stream, the chief came down to the water-side,
and presented us with a piece of hippopotamus flesh,
in a clean white calabash, expressive of his gratitude for our visit. This meat was pronounced by
our people to be rich and delicious. We presented
him with a hundred needles, and the young girls who
had brought us the provisions with a few beads.
They were much pleased with our presents, and I
have no doubt our visit has made an impression on
their minds that will not be easily effaced. Having
read prayers to our people, a custom which we have
never neglected either morning or evening, we bade
adieu to the Chief of Gungo and his people. They
were assembled at the river-side to see us go, and as
our canoe left the shore they all lifted their hands,
wishing us a prosperous journey.

We had not been on the water more than half an
hour after leaving Gungo, before the wind rose to a
gale, causing the river to be agitated like a sea, and
our canoe to be tossed about like a cocoanut shell.
It also rained heavily, insomuch that in a moment
we were wetted to the skin, and our canoe soon became half filled with water. We were then in the
middle of the river, and in danger of sinking every
instant. Our men struggled hard to pull the canoe
among the rushes on the right bank, for the purpose
of holding on by them till the wind and rain should
abate, and the water become smooth. It was not
without great exertion that this was effected, for the

* Negro children when very young, are generally interesting, even to
a European.

wind was against us, the water was in commotion, and our fragile little vessel, as a sailor would express it, "shipped several seas." No sooner had we got into the morass, and were congratulating ourselves on our deliverance, than a frightful crocodile, of prodigious size, sprang forth from his retreat, close to the canoe, and plunged underneath it with extraordinary violence, to the amazement and terror of us all: we had evidently disturbed him from his sleep. He was the largest I ever saw; and had he touched our canoe, would have upset it. The rain, in addition to the water that washed in from the river over the bows of our canoe, employed three persons constantly baling to keep her afloat.

The wind and rain having subsided, we left our retreat about half-past eight, and kept on down the river.

About ten in the morning, we arrived opposite a large village, which is situated on a low, flat island; and the current at this place rushing with the impetuosity of a torrent over a broad sandbank, notwithstanding we exerted all our powers to avoid it, we were completely foiled: the canoe became unmanageable; we were carried along with irresistible velocity; and in less than two minutes, she struck against the roof of a hut which was covered with water. By the sudden and forcible shock which the canoe hereby sustained, one of our men was thrown with violence overboard, but the others, more fortunate, clung to the boughs of a tree. Though the current was so exceedingly rapid, the water was very shallow, and the man was enabled to join his companions shortly afterward: he appeared more frightened than hurt. The village is nearly washed away, with the exception of about a dozen houses; so high are the waters of the river. We observed a number of large canoes receiving the inhabitants in them, for the purpose of conveying them to the mainland.

At Zagozhi we had been strongly recommended

to put into a large and important trading town, called
Egga, which was reported to be three days' journey
down the river from thence, and we had been promised a guide or messenger to accompany us thither,
but we have neither heard nor seen any thing of him
since yesterday. Beyond Egga, it is said the Falátah
interest does not extend, and by all accounts, after
leaving that place, the banks of the Niger are in
habited by different races of people, who are less
gentle and humane, and not so civilized as the Noufanchie. We had so far proceeded without the guide,
because he did not choose to keep up with us, and
because we would not consent to wait for him. But
here, from motives of prudence, we thought proper
to make inquiries concerning the Egga we had been
told of, lest by any means we should pass it without
seeing it; and we were persuaded, should this be
the case, that the difficulty of pulling back against
the current would be insuperable. Therefore, we
approached as near the village as we could, and hal-
looed and bawled to the inhabitants, some of whom
we could observe kneedeep in water, walking about
the streets; but they were at so great a distance
from our canoe, or so busily employed in their own
concerns, that it is probable they did not perfectly
understand the nature of our inquiries, and their
answers were too indistinct for us to comprehend
their meaning. However, instead of answering our
questions, two or three mallam priests gave us to
understand that the Niger has been more than usually
full this season; that it had overflowed its natural
boundaries, and washed away a considerable portion
of their village, which was apparent from the great
number of frames of huts which we had seen stuck
in the sand outside, more especially the circular tops
of them, which had a very odd appearance in the
river. The remains of the village are even now
half under water, and the unfortunate inhabitants
must therefore be in very great distress.

II.—I

Seeing that we could gather no further informa
tion from these villagers, we left the place, and
shortly afterward came abreast of those remarkable
mountains which we saw before us yesterday. They
appeared now in the shape of three flat table-moun-
tains, and seemed to be very close to the river. One
or two of them exhibit a perfect picture of barren-
ness and sterility; others are covered with stunted
vegetation; but others again appear more fertile,
being cultivated with corn almost to their summits,
and have a very agreeable appearance. At their
bases are several pleasant-looking villages, most
charmingly situated, and embellished with tall and
goodly trees.

Journeying along by the side of them, we observed
a mountain a long way to the eastward of us, whose
summit resembled an immense dome. At midday,
we stopped awhile at a small island to obtain the
necessary information respecting Egga; but could
only learn that that town was still a great way off.
A large Falátah canoe, with musicians on board, followed us here, and for some distance after we had
left it, but we do not think with any hostile intention.

At four in the afternoon, our men were tired with
their exertions, and complained sadly of fatigue and
exhaustion, so that we were induced to put in at a
small island called *Fofo*, where we resolved to sleep.
The river to-day has been very serpentine; its general course south-east, and east-south-east; and its
breadth from two to six miles.

After we had landed, a man who asserted that he
had just arrived from Funda introduced himself to
our notice: he states that it is three days' journey
from hence down the Niger to the frontiers of that
kingdom; and that its metropolis, which is of the
same name, is situated at an equal distance inland
from the water-side; so that, if this information be
true, it will be utterly impossible for us to visit the
city of Funda, as it was our intention to do, for we

are without horses, and the means of procuring them; and the attempt to penetrate so great a distance through the bush in our present languid and debilitated state would be impracticable, and highly improper. Besides, what presents have we to offer to the king?

For the first time since leaving Yarriba, we saw a cocoanut this evening, which gave us infinite pleasure. On inquiring where it grew, we were told that it had been brought from a place near the sea, seven days' journey from Fofo. The evening was far advanced, before a hut could anywhere be found for our reception, owing, it was said, to the absence of the chief; nor did we experience, on his return to the village, the slightest degree of kindness or hospitality. In the course of the day, we observed a great number of hippopotami as we came down the river, and many canoes of a large size. The consternation of the people at seeing us was very great; they gazed at us with vacant countenances, and never once thought of asking us if we wanted a hut or any thing to eat. We had been an hour with them, undergoing their scrutiny, and affording them subject for their remarks, when two Rabba messengers came to us, saying, that as none of the people of Fofo had offered us a hut, we were welcome to theirs. We accordingly accepted their offer, and were glad to get under their protection. We had not been here long, before three large calabashes of cakes, made of Indian corn, fried in palm oil, were ent to us by the women, who it seems take much more interest in us than the men, and we were quite ready for our meal.

The chief has kept aloof from us, being in trouble at present, from not having a sufficient number of cowries to pay his annual taxes to Rabba, for which purpose it seems the messengers are here. It is customary to allow them a certain number of days to do this, at the expiration of which time, if the tribute be not paid, the messengers watch their opportunity, and carry off one or two of the inhabitants. These are then sold in market at Rabba as slaves, and their produce pays the tax. The same custom we had seen practised at Lever, even after the tax had been paid.

We have passed many islands to-day. The Nouffié bank is high and hilly, but well cultivated. There seem to be many villages, and much cultivation on both sides.

Tuesday, October 19th.—Having taken a slight breakfast, we were not unmindful of the attentions of our female friends yesterday, and returned their kindness with a paper of needles, and it was gratifying to see them so thankful. We were informed by the Falátah messengers, that we shall pass the Coodoonia river this morning, the same that I crossed on the former mission near Cuttup. We gave them a few buttons and parted very good friends. The morning was dull and cloudy, and showers fell occasionally, but as the weather cleared up a little before eight o'clock A. M., we embraced the opportunity of quitting the island of Fofo. Some of the people hereabouts display as little curiosity at seeing us as if we were as black as themselves. In half an hour we observed and passed a river of tolerable size, which entered the Niger from the northward. This is no doubt the Coodoonia which the Falátahs mentioned. The banks this morning have exhibited a more beautiful appearance than we had observed for several days before; nevertheless, they wanted the charm of novelty to recommend them. Very elevated land appeared on each side of the river, as far as could be seen; which appeared to be formed of a range of hills, extending from north-north-east to south-south-west. At eleven o'clock, we touched at a large village to inquire whereabouts Egga lay, and were informed that we had not a long way to go. We journeyed onwards for about half an hour, when we perceived a large, handsome town behind a deep morass. Several little inlets led through it to the town, distant about three miles from the bank of the river, which, as we drew near we learned was the place of which we were in quest. It was the long-sought Egga, and we instantly proceeded up a creek to the landing-place. The town is upwards of two miles in length, and we were struck with the immense number of large, bulky canoes which lay off it, and which were filled with trading commodities, and all kinds of merchandise which are common to the country. They also had huts in them, like the canoes we had seen before. All of them had blood smeared on their sterns, and feathers stuck in it as a charm or preservative against robbers and the evil-disposed.

We halted a few minutes before landing, no one having conveyed intelligence of our arrival to the chief. A young Falátah was the first who invited us on shore, and we despatched Pascoe to the chief, to tell him who we were, and what we wanted. He quickly returned, saying that the old chief was ready to receive us, and we immediately proceeded to his residence.

In a few minutes we arrived at the *Zollahe*, or *Entrance Hut*, in which we found the old man ready to receive us. We discovered him squatting on a cow's hide spread on the ground, smoking from a pipe of about three yards long, and surrounded by a number of Falátahs and several old mallams. We were welcomed in the most friendly and cordial manner, and, as a mark of peculiar distinction, we were invited to seat ourselves near the person of the chief. He looked at us with surprise from head to foot, and told us that we were strange-looking people, and well worth seeing. Having satisfied his curiosity, he sent for his old wives that they might do the same, but as we did not altogether relish so much quizzing we requested to be shown to a hut.

The chief is a very aged and venerable-looking man, with a long white beard, and of more patriarchal appearance, perhaps, than any one we have ever seen; yet he laughed, played, and trifled like a child. A house "fit for a king," to use his own expression, was speedily got ready for our reception, and as soon as he had learned, with surprise, that we subsisted on the same kind of food as himself, we were led to our dwelling, and, before evening, received a bowl of *tuah* and gravy from his wives. We were soon pestered with the visits of the mallams and the chief's wives, which latter brought us presents of goora-nuts as a sort of introduction to see us. As soon as the news of our arrival spread through the town, the people flocked by hundreds to our hut, for the purpose of satisfying their curiosity with a sight of the white people. The mallams and the kings had given us trouble enough, but the whole population of Egga was too much for us, so we were literally obliged to blockade the doorways, and station three of our people at each to keep them away. At sunset, finding they could get no nearer to us, they departed, and we retired to rest in peace; for we were in much want of it.

The course of the river to-day has been, for the most part, east-south-east; the width varying from two to five or six miles.

Wednesday, October 20th.—Benin and Portuguese cloths are worn at Egga by many of its inhabitants, so that it would appear that some kind of communication is kept up between the seacoast and this place. The people are very speculative and enter prising, and numbers of them employ all their time solely in trading up and down the Niger. They live entirely in their canoes, over which they have a shed, that answers completely every purpose for which it is intended, so that, in their constant peregrinations, they have no need of any other dwelling or shelter than tha. which their canoes afford them. Cocoanuts are sold about the streets in great quantities, and various little parcels of them have been sent us from several individuals, but we understand that they are imported from a neighbouring country, and are here considered as very valuable.

The chief visited us about eight in the morning, and begged that we would allow his wives and principal people to come and see us. We could not but comply with his request, and accordingly all the old and young ladies visited us, each bringing gooranuts, or some little present. They were very inquisitive, and remained with us much longer than we wished; our hints had no effect on them, and we were obliged to bear with their disagreeable society. The heat of the weather is excessive our doors and windows are often blocked up by the people, and our room filled with these visiters is scarcely tolerable. The ladies no sooner departed than they were followed by a party of men, accompanied by one of the chief's people, as a sort of introduction; and in this manner was the greater part of the day passed.

Their belief that we possessed the power of doing any thing was at first amusing enough, but their importunities went so far, that they became annoying. They applied to us for charms to avert wars and other national calamities, to make them rich, to prevent the crocodiles from carrying off the people, and for the chief of the fishermen to catch a canoe-load of fish every day, each request being accompanied with some sort of present, such as country beer, goora-nuts, cocoanuts, lemons, yams, rice, &c., in quantity proportionate to the value of their request.

The curiosity of the people to see us is so intense, that we dare not stir out of doors, and therefore we are compelled to keep our door open all day long for the benefit of the air; and the only exercise

which we can take is by walking round and round
our hut like wild beasts in a cage. The people
stand gazing at us with visible emotions of amazement and terror; we are regarded, in fact, in just
the same light as the fiercest tigers in England. If
we venture to approach too near the doorway, they
rush backwards in a state of the greatest alarm and
trepidation; but when we are at the opposite side
of the hut, they draw as near as their fears will permit them, in silence and caution. But, from an
insolent Falátah, and one or two troublesome head-
men, whom it would be impolitic to offend, we have
experienced infinitely more inconvenience,—they
have haunted us like evil spirits. These individuals
enter our hut in the morning, and, whatever we
may have to do, they squat themselves down on our
mats with the most provoking effrontery, and are
unwilling to leave us, except for a few moments at
a time, till long after we lie down to rest.

A "great man," a stranger, visited us to-day, with
an extraordinary display of native pomp, and he
brought along with him a pot of honey, which he
presented as a recommendation. He was dressed
in a damask tobe of crimson silk, and the rest of his
apparel corresponded with this piece of finery. He
informed us without solicitation that he was an
agent, sent by the Prince of Rabba to collect the
tribute that was owing at the different villages along
the banks of the Niger; and insinuated that in point
of rank he was superior to the old chief of Egga,
spelling hard for a present proportionable to his
boasted dignity. This man, who is nothing more
or less than the Chief of Rabba's tax-gatherer, was
accompanied by two shrewd-looking Falátahs, whose
part it appeared was to impress us with a proper
dea of the great importance of their friend. They
spoke of him in the highest terms to us, telling us
he had come from a great distance for the purpose
of visiting us, and concluding their praises with a

request that we should make him a present. Be
sides his damask tobe, he wore large silk trousers,
a turban and red cap, and red morocco slippers.
However, we wanted the few things we had left to
give to those who could be of service to us, and we
determined on giving him nothing. I therefore told
him that we were very poor, and could not afford to
give him any thing worth his acceptance, but by
way of remembrance presented him with a comb
for his beard. At this he looked at his companions,
and they at him; when, after a little time, they
asked, "Is this all you intend to give this great man,
who is even greater than the chief of Egga himself?" To which I replied in the affirmative. He
then thought perhaps that he could do for himself
what his friends could not, by saying to us, "If any
one should ask me what you gave me, what shall I
say?" To which I replied very quietly, "Say I
gave you a comb, or nothing; whichever you please."
This was quite enough; he was convinced at length
that we could give him nothing, although it was
long before he would believe it. We thought at
first that we should have spared his dignity, by telling him, with as much delicacy as we could, that we
had nothing to part with; but he took leave of us
much less annoyed than we had expected by our
refusal, and we saw him no more. The Falátah
influence is scarcely felt here, though the town was
pillaged and burnt as recently as two years ago, and
many of the ruins may still be seen.

Egga is of prodigious extent, and has an immense
population. Like many other towns on the banks
of the river, it is not unfrequently inundated, and a
large portion of it, as at the present moment, actually overflowed. No doubt the people have their
reasons for building their habitations in places which
appear to us so very inconvenient and uncomfortable. The soil in the vicinity of the town consists
of a dark heavy mould, uncommonly fruitful, and

produces in abundance and with trifling labour all
the necessaries of life, so that provisions are plentiful and cheap. The inhabitants eat little animal
food besides fish, which are likewise sold at a very
reasonable rate. Hyenas are said to abound in the
woods in incredible numbers, and they are so bold
and rapacious as to have carried away nearly the
whole of the sheep which were once in the town
Perhaps Egga can boast of having a greater number
of canoes, both large and small, than any single
town to the northward.

Thursday, October 21*st.*—Though the venerable
chief of Egga has to all outward appearances lived
at least a hundred years, he is still active; and, instead of the peevishness and discontent too often
the accompaniment of lengthened days, possesses all
the ease and gayety of youth. He professes the
Mohammedan religion; and it is his custom to rise
every morning long before daybreak, and, having
assembled all his priests round him, performs his
devotions, such as they are, repeating his prayers
in a loud, shrill tone, so that we can hear him
in his pious employment; and as our hut is directly
opposite to his, and but a few paces from it, he is
determined to give us no rest as long as we remain
with closed doors. As soon as these devotional
exercises have been gone through, several of his
companions, with a disposition as thoughtless as
childish, and as happy as his own, get together in
his hut, and, squatting on the ground with the old
chief, they form a circle, and beguile the time by
smoking and conversing till long after sunset, and
separate only for a few minutes at a time in the
course of the day for the purpose of taking their
meals. This company of gray-beards, for they are
all old, laugh so heartily at the sprightliness of their
own wit, that it is an invariable practice, when any
one passes by, to stop and listen outside; and they
join their noisy merriment with so much good-will.

that we hear nothing from the hut in which the aged group are revelling during the day but loud peals of laughter and shouts of applause. Much of this gayety, however, must be affected, in order to gratify the ruling passion of the old chief for joke and frolic. Examples of this nature are uncommonly rare. Professors of Mohammedanism affect, generally speaking, the solemnity of the owl; and though they understand no more of their faith than of the doctrines of Christianity, they regard all natives of a different persuasion with haughtiness and disdain.

The old chief longed to-day to give us a specimen of his activity and the vigour which he yet possessed; and for this purpose, when the sun was going down, his singers, dancers, and musicians assembled round our hut with a great concourse of people, who could not boast a proficiency in those refined attainments, but who came to witness the accomplishments of their aged leader. The old man advanced proudly into the ring, with a firm step and a smiling countenance, and casting upon us a glance full of meaning, as if he would have said, " Now, white men, look at me, and you will be filled with admiration and wonder"—

" He frisked beneath the burden of *five*-score ;"

and shaking his hoary locks, capered over the ground to the manifest delight of the bystanders, whose applauses, though confined, as they always are, to laughter, yet tickled the old man's fancy to that degree, that he was unable to keep up his dance any longer without the aid of a crutch. With its assistance he hobbled on a little while, but his strength failed him, and he was constrained for the time to give over, and he sat himself down at our side on the threshold of the hut. He would not acknowledge his weakness to us for the world, but endeavoured to pant silently, and suppress loud

breathings that we might not hear him. How
ridiculous yet how natural is this vanity! He made
other unavailing attempts to dance, and also made
an attempt to sing, but nature would not second his
efforts, and his weak piping voice was scarcely
audible. The singers, dancers, and musicians continued their noisy mirth till we were weary of
looking at and listening to them, and as bedtime
was drawing near, we desired them to depart, to the
infinite regret of the frivolous but merry old chief.

It is our intention to continue our journey to-
morrow, though the elders of the town have been
remonstrating with us that it will be highly dan
gerous to go by ourselves, and endeavouring to per-.
suade us with many words to alter this arrangement
for our own sakes. They have promised to procure
us a convoy of traders, if we would consent to wait
three days longer, which would leave Egga at the
end of that time to attend a famous market, called
Bocquá. But the attentions of our venerable friend
already begin to slacken, being too intently engaged in his favourite pursuits to think much of
us or of our wants, more especially since he has
received his present; and we cannot easily maintain a quiet, equable temper, or keep up a flow of
spirits for any length of time together, when we
can get little or nothing to eat. We are therefore
determined to go to-morrow at all risks, though we
shall have no guide to accompany us; we have
confidence in ourselves, and the mountains of the
natives generally prove to be no bigger than mole-
hills. The chief has been soliciting a charm of us,
to prevent the Falátahs from ever again invading
his territory. The old man's allegiance to the King
of Nouffie appears to us to be merely nominal.
When we sent word to the chief that we intended
going to-morrow morning, he begged us to remain
at Egga a few days longer, and declared the banks
of the river to be inhabited by people who were

little better than savages, and plundered every one that came near them. He assured us that they were governed by no king and obeyed no laws, and that each town was at war with the others. I asked him if he would send a messenger with us, but he refused, saying, that the Falátah power and his own extended no farther down the river: that Egga is the last town of Nouffie, and that none of his people traded below it. "If that is the case," I said, "it will be as safe for us to go to-morrow as any other day;" and with this determination I left him.

I then proceeded to give directions for our people to prepare themselves for starting, when, to my astonishment, Pascoe and the mulatto so often alluded to were the only two who agreed to go; the rest of them refused to a man. I then found out that the people of the town had been telling them stories about the danger of the river, and that they would all certainly either be murdered or taken and sold as slaves. Nor could all I said to them change their determination. I talked to them half an hour, telling them they were cowards, and that my brother's life and mine were as good as theirs; till at length, tired of them, and seeing that I made no impression on them, I told them to go away from our sight, and that we could do without them. But now they demanded their wages, or a *book* to enable them to receive them at Cape Coast Castle, to which they said they would return by the way they had come here. This I refused instantly to comply with, and added, that if they chose to leave us here, they should not receive a farthing; but if they would go on with us down the river, they should be paid. They were indignant at this, and went directly to the chief to lay their case before him, and to induce him to detain us. The old man, however, would not listen to them, but sent them about their business; and it is not unlikely, rather than lose all their wages, that they will proceed with us.

My brother and I determined to satisfy the curi
osity of the people to-day, and we accordingly walked
about outside our hut for two hours. The natives
were much pleased at this, and much order and regularity were preserved by two old mallams, to
whom the duty had been assigned of removing those
away who had seen us when any fresh ones arrived.
It was the old chief's particular wish that all his
people should see us, and they all conducted themselves in a very becoming manner. We had presented the chief with a pair of silver bracelets on
our arrival, on which the arms of our gracious
sovereign were engraved, and he wore them to-day
with evident satisfaction. These were no less objects of curiosity to the people than they had been
to the king, and hundreds of them came to look at
them on his wrists, overjoyed at seeing their chief
so smart. They even came and thanked us for our
kindness to the old man.

The people of this town appear all very neatly
dressed; the population is one-half of the Mohammedan religion, and the other the original pagan.
The town is about four miles in length and two in
breadth: the morass which surrounds it is full of crocodiles. The streets are very narrow, and, like most
places where there are large markets, are exceedingly filthy. The reason for building their houses
so close together is, that the Falátahs may not be
able to ride through them so easily and destroy the
people; it is said that they have been expecting an
attack from these people a long time. The Portuguese cloth which we observed here on our arrival
is brought up the river from a place called Cuttumcurrafee, which has a celebrated market for Nouffie
cloths, trona, slaves, Nouffie knives, bridles, stirrups,
brass ornaments, stained leather, and other things.
The cloth is of a very indifferent manufacture. The
large canoes lying here bring all the above articles
from the Rabba market.

CHAPTER XVII.

Friday, October 22d.—At half-past six this morning our people set about loading the canoe according to my expectations, but with a bad grace, and nothing but sulky looks, grumbling, and fearful apprehensions passed among them. They were, however, unwilling to lose their wages, which would certainly have been the case had they persisted in their refusal to proceed, and they seemed to have no wish to remain at Egga. Having no one to look to for protection, it is not improbable but that they would have been made slaves immediately after our departure, so that they had made up their minds to accompany us, although, when they took their paddles and we were fairly starting, they seemed to feel their situation more keenly than ever, and said that we were going to take them to a country where they all would be murdered. We endeavoured as much as possible to pacify their fears, but were obliged to have recourse to threats, and therefore said that we would throw them overboard if they were not quiet and worked the canoe properly. This and other threats to the same effect silenced them, and we were not sorry to see it, for we should have had a difficult matter to get others to fill their places had they persisted in leaving us.

At seven o'clock, all being ready, we bade farewell to the old chief, whose good humour had

afforded us so much amusement, although his
wives had nearly suffocated us, and on leaving the
landing-place of Egga we fired off three muskets as a
parting salute. Several of the principal inhabitants
came hurrying down to the water-side to take their
leave, to give us their blessing, and wish us a successful voyage. Our men at first paddled sluggishly,
and the canoe went slowly through the water. It
was nine before we reached the middle of the river.
A little below Egga we passed two very beautiful
small islands, which were covered with cultivation,
and well inhabited; we did not stop, but kept our
course down the river. A few miles from the town
we saw, with emotions of pleasure, a sea-gull,
which flew over our heads; this was a most gratifying sight to us. It reminded us forcibly of the object we had in view, and we fondly allowed it to
confirm our hopes that we were drawing very near
to our journey's end. We likewise beheld, for the
first time, about half a dozen large white pelicans,
which were sailing gracefully on the water.

It was a fine cheerful morning; our spirits were
buoyant, and our hearts light, as we passed smoothly,
swiftly, and pleasantly along. We had been informed
at Egga that we should soon meet with canoes
of very different construction from any which we
had before seen, and have to communicate with
various tribes and nations different in all respects
from the people with whom we have heretofore
maintained any intercourse. We were likewise
cautioned to be guarded in our conduct and demeanour, because those tribes are pronounced by the
Noufanchie to be bloody, savage, and ferocious in
their habits and manners. We had also been advised
to part with our strange-looking canoe, which might
attract their curiosity and excite suspicion, and in
consequence endanger our personal safety. After
making every allowance for exaggeration, still we
fancy there is sufficient truth in these reports to make
us watchful and cautious, and to put us on our guard

The borders of the river during the morning were generally low and swampy: high land appeared beyond them, but at some distance from the water; and the intermediate spaces are occupied by extensive morasses. The current swept us into one with great force, because we happened to keep too near, nor were we able to extricate ourselves from this unpleasant situation without infinite labour and difficulty, and much loss of time. The hills seen on the 19th now appear to take the same direction as the river, which is here about south-east. The west side of the river is low, while a double range of hills border the eastern bank. These appear very fertile, and covered with verdure nearly to their summits. In the afternoon, both the banks of the Niger became more fertile, more pleasing, and more elevated. We saw, in the earlier part of the day, several small and wretched-looking villages, which lay nearly under water, and also very extensive plantations of rice, at an immense distance from any human habitation; but the tops of these plants only were visible, and no cultivated land anywhere appeared. Afterward, however, the soil was more rich and grateful, and the country more varied in its appearance. At eleven A. M. we passed a very large market-town on our left, situated at the foot of a high hill and very near the water's edge. The hill was immediately over it, and seemed ready to fall upon it every instant. We inquired the name of it among our people, but they knew nothing of it, and our time was too precious to stop, although several canoes from it passed near us. We observed an immense number of canoes lying off it, built in the same manner as those of the Bonny and Calabar rivers. This is another symptom of communication with those people, and confirms our opinion that we are drawing near the sea. A great many of them were moving to and fro on the river; some passed close to us,

II.—K

and their crews gazed at us with astonishment, but
did not offer to interfere with us. It is a source of
annoyance that we have no means of conversing
with these people, and it may prove of serious inconvenience hereafter.

For many miles we could see nothing but large,
open, well-built villages on both banks of the river,
but more especially on the eastern, and tracts of
land covered with verdure, or prepared for cultivation, between them. Here Nature seems to have
scattered her favours with an unsparing hand. Yet
we touched at none of these goodly places, but continued our journey till the sun began to decline, and
the men to be fatigued, when we stopped at a small
hamlet on an island, intending to sleep there. At
first, the inhabitants mistrusted our intentions, and
were alarmed at our appearance. They no sooner
saw us than they raised the warcry, and every man
and woman armed themselves with swords and dirks,
bows and arrows, assuming a threatening and alarming position. We called out lustily to them in the
Hàussa language, but they were unable to understand either our words or gestures. Fortunately, in
a few minutes a woman, who could converse a little
in the Hàussa tongue, came down to us at the water-
side, and we informed her that we were friends and
Christians, travelling down the river to our native
country, and that it was not our wish to make war
with them. All this she repeated to those around
her, and succeeded, but partially, however, in removing their prejudices and suspicions. Had it not been
for the timely arrival of this woman, we should certainly have had a volley of arrows among us, for we
were taken for Falátahs at first, and we observed the
woman persuading them to the contrary. Still the
people could not, or rather would not, accommodate
us with a lodging for the night, which was contrary
to our expectations, though we solicited them with
much importunity to grant us this favour, and though

we assured them that the most homely, the most
shattered hut would answer our purpose, for we
cared not for matters of such trifling consequence.
They were all deaf to our entreaties; but fearing
that we could enforce our request, they did all they
could to induce us to proceed onwards a little farther,
when we should arrive at a city of considerable importance, called *Kacunda*, at which place we recollected that the people of Egga had strongly advised
us to stay. They also told us, that at Kacunda we
should get plenty of provisions, and receive much
attention from the inhabitants; and also, that we
should meet with people from Funda who understood the Hàussa language.

We therefore left the village, but were almost immediately afterward hailed by them to come back
again, and remain there for the night. Our men
were glad of this, for they were tired, and they
struggled hard to stem the current, but it was so impetuous, that, instead of nearing the village, we
found that we were fast receding from it; therefore,
we had no other resource, when the attempt was discovered to be impracticable, than to follow the advice which had previously been given us by the villagers, and we continued down the stream.

Kacunda is situated on the western bank of the
river; and, at a little distance, it has an advantageous
and uncommonly fine appearance. The only access
to the town is by winding channels that intersperse
an unwholesome swamp, which is nearly two miles
in breadth. It was evening when we arrived there.
The people at first were alarmed at our appearance,
but we were soon welcomed on shore by an old Mohammedan priest, who speedily introduced us into
an excellent and commodious hut, once the residence of a prince, but now the domicile of a schoolmaster. This old man had come from Cuttumcurrafee He told us that he heard of two Christians
being in Borgoo, and supposed that we were them.

The room to which he took us is the largest we have
ever seen, and is used by him for the purpose of in-
structing the children of Kacunda in the Mohammedan prayers. This old man seemed to take a great
deal of interest in us, for seeing the people alarmed
at our first appearance, he exerted himself in quiet-
ing them, saying, that we were quite harmless, and
took us immediately under his protection. He told
us that a hut was preparing for us at a short distance
in the town, but the weather being excessively hot
and fatiguing, we preferred remaining where we were,
thinking also, that any other we might be taken to
would not be so large and airy as this. Therefore
we requested his permission to be allowed to stay
with him, to which the old man readily assented.

We are informed that the Chief of Kacunda resides a distance of four miles from where we are
now, and near the market-place. The old mallam
would not allow us to go and visit him, but promised
to send a messenger for the chief's brother to come
and see us to-morrow morning, an arrangement with
which we were perfectly satisfied. About ten gallons of country beer were sent to us, with some good
pounded corn and stewed fowls, for our supper, and
having made a hearty meal, we retired thankfully to
rest.

The river runs in a serpentine direction between
this place and Egga, varying between south and
south-east; there are several islands in it, all of
which are cultivated and inhabited. The current is
very rapid, and certainly runs at the rate of four or
five miles an hour, if we may judge from the difficulty with which we even paddled against it without
making any progress towards the island after we had
left it. Near this island, which lies nearer the north
than the south bank of the river, the former is rather
low, but still well cultivated; and below this, it continues low as far as opposite to Kacunda. The south
bank is rather higher. We are informed, that at the

town we observed on the left bank in the morning, a little below Egga, the dominion of the chiefs of territories is no longer acknowledged, but that at every other on the banks of the river below it, each town has its own chief. The Nouffie territory terminates at Egga.

Saturday, Oct. 23*d.*—Kacunda, properly speaking, consists of three or four villages, all of them considerably large, but unconnected, though situated within a very short distance of each other. It is the capital of a state or kingdom of the same name, which is quite independent of Nouffie, or any other foreign power. Its government is despotic, and all power is invested with the chief, or king, who exercises it with lenity : in all cases of emergency, he never depends upon his own judgment entirely, but consults the opinion of the elders of the people. Kacunda maintains little intercourse with Nouffie, or any other considerable nation, but confines its trade almost exclusively to divers people inhabiting the banks of the Niger to the southward ; and slaves purchased here are said to find their way to the sea. In their persons, the natives are chiefly tall, well-formed, and muscular. Their ornaments are few; strings of red cornelian stone (which is plentiful in Nouffie), cut into something like the shape of a heart, and which are smooth, flat, and highly polished, are what they are most fond of wearing, and, in many cases, these are their only decoration. The only dress that the natives wear is a piece of cotton cloth round the loins. This is made by themselves, and is died of various colours, according to the taste of the owner. The women wear small earrings of silver, but use no paint, nor bedaub their persons with any sort of pigment. In the productions of the country there is nothing peculiar; and in the manufacture of cloth, &c., these people are greatly inferior to their neighbours. The Nouffie language is not understood in Kacunda, notwithstanding its proximity to that kingdom; but, as in almost every place which we have visited, the Hàussa tongue is spoken fluently by several individuals.

The chief excused himself from visiting us this morning, but sent his brother in his stead, to assure us of the pleasure he felt in our arrival, and that he welcomed us with the utmost gratification.

At 11 A. M. a large double-bank canoe, paddled by fourteen men, arrived at Kacunda, and we shortly found that the king's brother had come in her to see us. He was saluted, on landing, with a discharge from five old rusty muskets. A messenger was immediately despatched to us, announcing that he was ready to see us, and I sent word that I begged he would come. The brother came, attended by a long train of followers, and in the name of the chief he presented us with a few goora-nuts, a goat, some yams, and an immense quantity of country beer. They were all dressed in the Mohammedan costume, although pagans, and appeared very clean in their persons. Several gallons of ale were likewise sent us in huge calabashes from the more wealthy part of the population of the town. Our meeting was very cordial, and we shook hands heartily with, and immediately explained to him our business. On seeing the goat he had brought with him, I told him we were sorry he had brought so valuable a present, as we had nothing to give him in return which would be worth presenting to his brother; that we had been so long in the country, all our presents were expended before we arrived at Kacunda. I then took out a pair of silver bracelets, and begged he would present them to his brother, and tell him the reason we could give him nothing better. He took them from me, but did not seem to be much interested about them, or to care at all for them. But looking round our room, he perceived several little things to which he took a fancy, and which, being of no value whatever to us, were readily presented to him ; and it was satisfactory to see him much pleased with them.

We had now become great friends, and he commenced giving us a dreadful account of the natives down the river, and would have us not think of going among them, but return by the way we had come. He said to us, with much emphasis, " If you go down the river you will surely fall into their hands and be murdered."—" Go we must," I said, " if we live or die by it, and that also to-morrow." I then asked him if he would send a messenger with us, for that he might ensure our safety, coming from so powerful a person as the Chief of Kacunda. But he replied directly, " No, if I were to do such a thing, the people at the next town would assuredly cut off his head; but," he added, " if you will not be persuaded by me to turn back, and save your lives, at least you must not leave this by daylight, but stop until the sun goes down, and you may then go on your journey—you will then pass the most dangerous town in the middle of the night, and perhaps save yourselves." We asked him whether the people he spoke of had muskets or large canoes? To which he replied, " Yes ; in great numbers—they are very large and powerful, and no canoe can pass down the river in the daytime without being taken by them and plundered ; and even at night, the canoes from here are obliged to go in large numbers, and keep close company with each other, to make a formidable appearance in case of their being seen by them."

We had no reason whatever to doubt this information, and being well aware how little we could do if we should be attacked by these formidable fellows, we determined on going at night, according to the custom of the rest, and propose starting at half-past four to-morrow evening. I told the chief's brother of our intentions, at which he seemed quite astonished ; and we have no doubt that this determined conduct, which we have everywhere shown, and apparent defiance of all danger, in making light of the dreadful stories we have heard, has had much influence on the minds of the people, and no doubt inspired them with a belief that we were supernatural beings, gifted with more than ordinary qualifications. Having communicated our intentions to our friend and given him all the little trifling things he wished for, he departed with the present for his brother the chief.

The few things which we sent back to the chief, trifling as they were, gave him complete satisfaction: they were received by him in a much more gracious manner than we had anticipated. He besought us earnestly to write him a few charms—one of which is to ensure a continuance of peace and prosperity to the kingdom; another to prevent quarrels, abuses, and disturbances in the market-place; to obviate the shedding of human blood therein, which has recently been of frequent occurrence; and to bring to the market a greater number of buyers and sellers, which would proportionably augment the amount of duty exacted from them. Another charm he wants of us is to possess the virtues of a panoply, for preserving all persons, while bathing, from the fangs of the crocodiles, which infest the adjoining slough in great numbers, and which, it is said, have lately carried off and destroyed several children. Another charm he requires is, to have still more powerful properties, and cause a neighbouring rivulet, which has heretofore been dried up in the summer season, to be filled with water, and flow all the year round.

All ranks of people are firmly persuaded that we are necromancers, or at least that we are capable of performing any miracle, and therefore they believe that the making of these charms is but a trifling effort compared with what we *might* do, were we to exert the whole of our power. An attempt to undeceive the ignorant, credulous, and deluded people we know would be unavailing and useless, and fear that it would be dangerous; therefore we dare not meddle with their superstitions or prejudices, but conform to their wishes, and let them enjoy their own opinions in peace.

Several of the inhabitants have brought us little presents of goora-nuts, Chili and Cayenne pepper, a bit of fish, or any such trifle, in the expectation of receiving a hundred times their value in the shape of charms. We have been pestered all day by a young native, to get a charm from us to enable him to catch plenty of fish. The poor fellow followed us about like a child begging for a toy, and offered us a variety of little trifling things which he could afford, such as country beer, goora-nuts, &c.; and we believe there was nothing he had that he would not have willingly given us, so great was his faith in the power we had of bestowing on him the means of enriching himself by catching fish. There was no getting rid of him without complying with his request, so we gave him a small piece of paper on which something had been written, of no consequence whatever. The poor fellow no sooner got it, than he looked at it with much earnestness, and proceeded with great solemnity to fasten it to the end of his fishing-line. Having done this, he set off with great glee to go and fish, congratulating himself, no doubt, on the multitude of fishes his charm would obtain him.

It is painful to contemplate the melancholy ignorance and superstition in which the minds of the natives are involved; nor is this confined to Kacunda alone; at Egga, and other places up the river, they are equally as bad. Ready for the first impression, and easily imposed on, the minds of these poor creatures naturally receive as truth whatever is told them. Their faith in charms, and their credulity in the power of white men, is not to be wondered at. The former they are taught by the Mohammedan mallams, and these again are equally as credulous

II.—L

as the natives of the efficacy of any thing coming from us.

The natives are successful in their fishing expeditions, and generally use a line with a piece of iron fastened to the end of it, bent in the shape of a hook. They use a large worm as bait, and more frequently part of a fish. The line is made of a tough grass neatly twisted. In these excursions they sometimes carelessly expose themselves to the attacks of the alligators, of which there are great numbers in the river, and the natives are frequently sufferers by them. In fetching water for use from the river at night, they often become a prey to them. They destroy the crocodile and eat its flesh, as well as that of the hippopotami, which are equally as numerous. The eggs of the former also they are very fond of.

We have been visited by the chief of a neighbouring province, and an impostor, who represents himself as son to Ederesa, the ex-king of Nouffie, both of whom, like their less presumptuous brethren, are disappointed in their hopes of receiving valuable presents, for we are daily diminishing the few things which are left, and must not be prodigal in giving away.

As at Egga, we are here earnestly solicited by the mallams to stop two or three days, to give the market-people an opportunity of accompanying us to Bocquâ, every one warning us that we shall be in jeopardy of our lives, unless we take this precaution. The manners of the people all along the banks of the Niger from hence they also represent to us as being in the highest degree dangerous. They are said to be public robbers, without laws or regulations of any kind; that they live under no king, and acknowledge no human authority—in a word, that they are a community of ferocious outlaws. We hear nothing but stories about the inhabitants of Egga, who, when they attend the Bocquâ market for the purposes of trade, are obliged to sail in companies of

ten or twelve canoes, for mutual encouragement and
protection; and that even then the merchants dare
not travel in the daytime, but pass those places
which are considered as dangerous in the darkness
of night, when there is least fear of molestation :
such stories, similar to that of the king's brother, are
told us to prevent our proceeding.

Well might the King of Yarriba hesitate on sending either Captain Clapperton or ourselves to the
banks of the Niger, when he knew that he had
neither a single town so far to the eastward nor a
single subject from Yàoorie to the sea. Above
Egga, as far as Wowow, the western bank of the
river, which he boasts as being in his dominions, is
thickly inhabited solely by Noufanchie; and below
that town they are peopled by strange and distinct
tribes, who have never heard his name, nor an echo
of his glory and power ! We observe here, for the
first time, that the natives have a custom of marking
themselves, so that their tribe may be known from
the rest. The distinguishing mark of the people of
Kacunda is three cuts down the face from the temple to the chin, which gives them an odd appearance.
They are a mild, harmless, and inoffensive race of
people, and very industrious. Their huts are the
largest and cleanest we have seen in the whole
country. Our old friend the schoolmaster informs
us that we shall very soon pass the *Tshadda* river, as
it is only a day's journey distant from here down the
river. He was a very communicative old man, and
informed me that the city of Funda is not on the
banks of the Quorra, but situated a distance of three
days' journey up the Tshadda. According to his
report, the Tshadda is a large river, nearly as much
so as the Quorra. Canoes, he said, frequently go
up the Tshadda to Bornou, and that it was only fifteen days' journey from hence to that place by the
Tshadda. The countries of Jacoba and Adamowa,
he said, are at peace with Bornou, and the commu-

nication open from both those places by water as
well as land. The pagan countries, it appears, are
all greatly alarmed by the expectation of an attack
from the Falátahs when the dry season arrives.
The Tshadda, he said, was very safe, and much frequented by canoes. A town called Cuttumcurrafee,
which has been before alluded to, he informed us
was seated at the junction of the Tshadda with the
Quorra.

Sunday, Oct. 24th.—The children of the more
respectable inhabitants of Egga are placed at a very
early age under the tuition of our friendly host the
schoolmaster, who teaches them a few Mohammedan
prayers; all, indeed, with which he himself may be
acquainted in the Arabic tongue. In this consists
the whole of their education. The boys are dili-
gent in their exercises, and arise every morning between midnight and sunrise, and are studiously employed by lamplight in copying their prayers, after
which they read them to the master one after another, beginning with the eldest. This is repeated
in a shrill, bawling tone, so loud as to be heard at
the distance of half a mile at least, which is believed to be a criterion of excellence by the parents;
and he who has the strongest lungs and clearest
voice is of course considered as the best scholar,
and caressed accordingly. The Mohammedans,
though excessively vain of their attainments, and
proud of their learning and intellectual superiority
over their companions, are nevertheless conscious
of the vast pre-eminence of white men over themselves, for they have heard many marvellous stories
of Europeans, and their fame has been proclaimed
with a trumpet-voice among all people and nations
of the interior, insomuch that they are placed on an
equality with supernatural beings. As an illustration of this, a priest, himself a writer of charms,
made a pressing application to-day for an amulet
from us, which he begged might possess properties

so extraordinary and amazing as to be the wonder
of the whole country; and so firmly persuaded was
he that it was in our power, and ours only, to grant
this request, that we could not induce him by any
means to forego his application. He gave us a large
pot of beer, and would not leave our hut until he had
exacted a promise that we would give him the paper
which he had craved so piteously. We have likewise been perplexed with other demands of a similar
nature, and the tearful importunities of the poor ap-
plicants has troubled us exceedingly. In all obsti-
nate cases of this nature, we have found it expedient to follow the example of Mr. Park, which is,
to give the superstitious people a copy of the *Lord's
Prayer*, which, at least, can produce no mischievous
effects.

The chief's brother paid us a visit again this morning, and urged us by every argument which he could
think of to defer our departure, for our own sakes,
for two or three days, that canoes might be got
ready to accompany us on our voyage; and he endeavoured again to impress on our minds the danger
which we should inevitably incur if we were determined to go alone. Yet, it was apparent to us,
after all that he had said, that covetousness was his
predominant feeling, and therefore we paid little attention to his remarks, further than that we consented to wait till the afternoon for a man to accompany us in capacity of messenger to the so-
much-talked-of Bocquâ market, where, it is asserted,
we shall be perfectly safe; and beyond which place
the people are represented as being less rapacious,
so that we shall have little to fear from them.

The description which the chief's brother has
given us of the people residing a day's journey from
hence is too shocking to describe. To use a very
common and familiar expression, " What every one
says must be true," and we begin to give credence
to the rumours so often repeated of the fierceness

and cruelty of this race of human beings which occupy both sides of the Niger; between Kacunda and
Bocquâ, though we make every allowance for exaggeration, because the natives are fond of the marvellous, and are apt to magnify the most trifling circumstances into incidents of the last importance.

As the afternoon came on, we inquired in vain for
the promised guide; and when we found that the
chief, or rather his brother, felt no disposition whatever to redeem his pledge, we made immediate preparations to leave the town, to the manifest disappointment of the latter, who made a very dolorous
lament, and did all in his power, except employing
actual force, to induce us to change our resolution.

At three in the afternoon, we offered up a prayer
to the Almighty Disposer of all human events for
protection on our future voyage, that he would deign
to extend to us his all-saving power among the lawless barbarians it was our lot to be obliged to pass.
Having done this, we next ordered Pascoe and our
people to commence loading the canoe. I shall
never forget them, poor fellows; they were all in
tears, and trembled with fear. One of them, named
Antonio, a native of Bonny, and son to the late
chief of that river, who had joined us from his majesty's brig the Clinker, with the consent of Lieutenant Matson, her commander, was as much affected as the rest, but on a different account. For
himself, he said that he did not care; his own life
was of no consequence. All he feared was, that
my orother and I should be murdered; he loved us
dearly: he had been with us ever since we had left
the sea, and it would be as bad as dying himself to
see us killed.

At half-past four in the afternoon, in pursuance
of our plan, we bade adieu to the kind inhabitants
of Kacunda, and every thing having been conveyed
to the canoe, and our men in their places, we embarked and pushed off the shore in sight of multi-

tudes of people. We worked our way with incredible difficulty through the morass, before we were
enabled to get into the body of the stream. The
poor natives gazed at us with astonishment, and followed us with their eyes as long as they could, no
doubt expecting that we should never be seen or
heard of more.

We were now fairly off, and prepared ourselves
for the worst. "Now," said I, "my boys," as our
canoe glided down with the stream, "let us all stick
together. I hope that we have none among us who
will flinch, come what may." Antonio and Sam
said they were determined to stick to us to the last.
The former I have before alluded to; the latter is a
native of Sierra Leone, and I believe them both to
be firm fellows when required. 'Old Pascoe and
Jowdie, two of my former people, I knew could be
depended on; but the new ones, although they
boasted much when they found that there was no
avoiding it, I had not much dependence on, as I had
not had an opportunity of trying them. We directed the four muskets and two pistols to be loaded
with ball and slugs, determined that our opponents,
whoever they might be, should meet with a warm
reception; and having made every preparation for
our defence which we thought would be availing,
and encouraging our little band to behave themselves
gallantly, we gave three hearty cheers, and com-
mended ourselves to Providence.

Our little vessel moved on in grand style under
the vigorous and animated exertions of our men.
There were no tears now, and I thought, as they
propelled her along with more than their usual
strength, that they felt they were a match for any
canoe that would dare to attack us. Shortly after
leaving Kacunda, the river took a turn due south, between tolerably high hills; the strength of the current continued much about the same. A few miles
farther on, we observed a branch of the Niger,

rather diminutive, running off in a westerly direction; but are not certain whether this was only a creek, or a branch of the river: the banks of it were covered with palm-trees, and little hills were scattered over them. We found ourselves opposite a large, spreading town, from which issued a great and confused noise, as of a multitude quarrelling, or as the waves of the sea rolling upon a rocky beach; we saw also other towns on the western bank of the river, but we cautiously avoided them all. The evening was calm and serene, the heat of the day was over, the moon and stars now afforded us an agreeable light, every thing was still and pleasant; we glided smoothly and silently down the stream, and for a long while we saw little to excite our fears, and heard nothing but a gentle rustling of the leaves, occasioned by the wind, the noise of our paddles, or now and then the plashing of fishes, as they leaped out of the water.

About midnight we observed lights from a village, to which we were very close, and heard people dancing, singing, and laughing in the moonshine outside their huts. We made haste over to the opposite side to get away, for fear of a lurking danger, and we fancied that a light was following us, but it was only a " will o' the wisp," or some such thing, and trees soon hid it from our sight. After the moon had gone down, it became rather cloudy, so that we could not discern the way as plainly as we could have wished, and the consequence was, that we were suddenly drifted by the current into an eddy, and, in spite of all our exertions to get out of it, we swept over into a small, shallow channel which had been formed by the overflowing of the river, and it cost two hours' hard labour to get into the main stream again. The course of the river was turned to the south-east by a range of very high hills. We also passed a great number of islands.

Monday, Oct. 25th.—At one A. M. the direction

of the river changed to south-south-west, running
between immensely high hills. At five o'clock this
morning, we found ourselves nearly opposite a very
considerable river, entering the Niger from the eastward; it appeared to be three or four miles wide at
its mouth, and on the bank we saw a large town,
one part of which faced the river, and the other the
Quorra. We at first supposed it to be an arm of
that river, and running from us; and therefore directed our course for it. We proceeded up it a short
distance, but finding the current against us, and that
it increased as we got within its entrance, and our
people being tired, we were compelled to give up
the attempt, and were easily swept back into the
Niger. Consequently we passed on, but determined
on making inquiries concerning it the first convenient opportunity. But we conclude this to be the
Tshadda, and the large town we have alluded to to
be Cuttumcurrafee, the same which had been mentioned to us by the old mallam. At all events, we
had satisfied ourselves it was not a branch of the
Niger. The banks on both sides, as far as we could
see up it, were very high, and appeared verdant and
fertile.

The morning was dull and cloudy; yet, as soon
as the sun had partially dispersed the mists which
hung over the valleys and upon the little hills, we
could distinguish irregular mountains jutting up almost close to the water's edge, whose height we
were prevented even from guessing at; because
their summits were involved in clouds, or inwrapped
in vapours, which yet lingered about their sides. A
double range of elevated hills appeared beyond them
on the south-east side; and on the north-west side
a chain of lesser hills extended as far as the eye
could discern. They appeared very steril. Those
on the north-west were formed of clumps, very
much resembling the shape of those we had seen in

Yarriba, which are here called the Kong mountains.

At seven o'clock the Niger seemed free of islands
and clear of morasses on both sides, and its banks
were well wooded and much higher than we had
observed them for a long time previously; nevertheless, it ran over a rocky bottom, which caused its
surface to ripple exceedingly. Just about the same
hour, one of the canoes, which we were told of as
of different make to our own, passed us. In shape,
it much resembled a common butcher's tray, and it
was furnished with seats like those used on various
parts of the seacoast. It was paddled by eight or
ten little boys, who sung as they worked; and they
were superintended by an elderly person who sat in
the middle of the canoe. The motion of their paddles was regulated by a peculiar hissing noise which
they made at intervals with their mouth; and it was
pleasing to observe the celerity with which this little
vessel was impelled against the stream. In the
early part of the morning, after daylight, we passed a
great many villages. The banks of the river were
ornamented with palm-trees, and much cultivated
ground, which extended to the foot of the mountains, and among the avenues formed between them.

At 10 A. M. we passed a huge and naked white
rock, in the form of a perfect dome, arising from
the centre of the river. It was about twenty feet
high, and covered with an immense quantity of
white birds, in consequence of which we named it
the Bird Rock : it is about three or four miles
distant from Bocquâ, on the same side of the river.
It is safest to pass it on the south-east side, on
which side is also the proper channel of the river,
about three miles in width. We passed it on the
western side, and were very nearly lost in a whirl-
pool. It was with the utmost difficulty we preserved the canoe from being carried away, and
dashed against the rocks. Fortunately, I saw the

danger at first, and, finding we could not get clear
of it, my brother and I took a paddle, and animating
our men, we exerted all our strength, and succeeded
in preventing her from turning round. The distance of this rock from the nearest bank is about a
quarter of a mile, and the current was running with
the velocity of six miles an hour, according to our
estimation. Had our canoe become unmanageable,
we should inevitably have perished. Shortly after,
seeing a convenient place for landing, the men being
languid and weary with hunger and exertion, we
halted on the right bank of the river, which we imagined was most convenient for our purpose. The
course of the river this morning was south-south-
west, and its width varied as usual from two to five
or six miles. The angry and scowling appearance
of the firmament forewarned us of a heavy shower,
or something worse, which induced us hastily to
erect an awning of mats under a palm-tree's shade.
As soon as we had leisure to look around us, though
no habitation could anywhere be seen, yet it was
evident the spot had been visited, and that very
recently, by numbers of people. We discovered
the remains of several extinct fires, with broken
calabashes and pieces of earthen vessels, which
were scattered around ; and our men likewise picked
up a quantity of cocoanut-shells, and three or four
staves of a powder-barrel. These discoveries, trifling as they were, filled us with pleasant and hope-
ful sensations; and we felt assured, from the circumstance of a barrel of powder having found its
way hither, that the natives in the neighbourhood
maintained some kind of intercourse with Europeans from the sea.

The spot, for a hundred yards, was cleared of
grass, underwood, and vegetation of all kinds ; and,
on a further observation, we came to the conclusion
that a market or fair was periodically held thereon.
Very shortly afterward, as three of our men were

straggling about in the bush, searching for firewoo 1
a village suddenly opened before them: this did not
excite their astonishment, and they entered one of
the huts which was nearest them to procure a little
fire. However, it happened to contain only women;
but these were terrified beyond measure at the sudden and abrupt entrance of strange-looking men,
whose language they did not know, and whose
business they could not understand, and they all ran
out in a fright into the woods, to warn their male
relatives of them, who were labouring at their usual
occupation of husbandry. Meanwhile, our men had
very composedly taken some burning embers from
the fire, and returned to us in a few minutes, with
the brief allusion to the circumstance of having discovered a village. They told us also that they had
seen cultivated land, and that these women had run
away from them as soon as they saw them. This
we thought lightly of; but rejoiced that they had
seen the village, and immediately sent Pascoe,
Abraham, and Jowdie, in company, to obtain some
fire, and to purchase a few yams for us. In about
ten minutes after, they returned in haste, telling us
that they had been to the village, and had asked for
some fire, but that the people did not understand
them, and instead of attending to their wishes, they
looked terrified, and had suddenly disappeared. In
consequence of their threatening attitudes, our people had left the village, and rejoined us with all the
haste they could. We did not, however, think that
they would attack us, and we proceeded to make
our fires, and then laid ourselves down.

Totally unconscious of danger, we were reclining
on our mats,—for we too, like our people, were
wearied with toil, and overcome with drowsiness,
—when in about twenty minutes after our men had
returned, one of them shouted, with a loud voice,
"War is coming! O, war is coming!" and ran
towards us with a scream of terror, telling us that

the natives were hastening to attack us. We started up at this unusual exclamation, and, looking about us, we beheld a large party of men, almost naked, running in a very irregular manner, and with uncouth gestures, towards our little encampment. They were all variously armed with muskets, bows and arrows, knives, cutlasses, barbs, long spears, and other instruments of destruction; and, as we gazed upon this band of wild men, with their ferocious looks and hostile appearance, which was not a little heightened on observing the weapons in their hands, we felt a very uneasy kind of sensation, and wished ourselves safe out of their hands. To persons peaceably inclined, like ourselves, and who had done them no harm, we could look on their preparations with calmness; but as it is impossible to foresee to what extremities such encounters might lead, we waited the result with the most painful anxiety.

Our party was much scattered, but fortunately we could see them coming to us at some distance, and we had time to collect our men. We resolved, however, to prevent bloodshed if possible,—our numbers were too few to leave us a chance of escaping by any other way. The natives were approaching us fast, and had by this time arrived almost close to our palm-tree. Not a moment was to be lost. We desired Pascoe and all our people to follow behind us at a short distance, with the loaded muskets and pistols; and we enjoined them strictly not to fire, unless they first fired at us. One of the natives, who proved to be the chief, we perceived a little in advance of his companions; and, throwing down our pistols, which we had snatched up in the first moment of surprise, my brother and I walked very composedly and unarmed towards him. As we approached him, we made all the signs and motions we could with our arms, to deter him and his people from firing on us. His quiver was dan-

gling at his side, his bow was bent, and an arrow,
which was pointed at our breasts, already trembled
on the string, when we were within a few yards of
his person. This was a highly critical moment—
the next might be our last. But the hand of Providence averted the blow; for just as the chief was
about to pull the fatal cord, a man that was nearest
him rushed forward, and staid his arm. At that
instant we stood before him, and immediately held
forth our hands; all of them trembled like aspen
leaves; the chief looked up full in our faces, kneel
ing on the ground—light seemed to flash from his
dark, rolling eyes—his body was convulsed all over,
as though he were enduring the utmost torture, and
with a timorous, yet undefinable expression of countenance, in which all the passions of our nature were
strangely blended, he drooped his head, eagerly
grasped our proffered hands, and burst into tears.
This was a sign of friendship—harmony followed,
and war and bloodshed were thought of no more.
Peace and friendship now reigned among us; and
the first thing that we did was to lift the old chief
from the ground, and to convey him to our encampment. The behaviour of our men afforded us no
little amusement, now that the danger was past.
We had now had a fair trial of their courage, and
should know who to trust on a future occasion.
Pascoe was firm to his post, and stood still with his
musket pointed at the chief's breast during the
whole time. He is a brave fellow, and said to us,
as we passed him to our encampment with the old
man, "If the *black* rascals had fired at either of you,
I should have brought the old chief down like a
Guinea-fowl." It was impossible to avoid smiling
at the fellow's honesty, although we were on the
best of terms with the old chief,—and we have little
doubt that he would have been as good as his word.
As for our two brave fellows, Sam and Antonio,
they took to their heels, and scampered off as fast

as they could directly they saw the natives approaching us over the long grass, nor did they make their appearance again until the chief and all his people were sitting round us; and even when they did return, they were so frightened, they could not speak for some time.

All the armed villagers had now gathered round their leader, and anxiously watched his looks and gestures. The result of the meeting delighted them —every eye sparkled with pleasure—they uttered a shout of joy—they thrust their bloodless arrows into their quivers—they ran about as though they were possessed of evil spirits—they twanged their bowstrings, fired off their muskets, shook their spears, clattered their quivers, danced, put their bodies into all manner of ridiculous positions, laughed, cried, and sung in rapid succession—they were like a troop of maniacs. Never was spectacle more wild and terrific. When this sally of passion to which they had worked themselves had subsided into calmer and more reasonable behaviour, we presented each of the war-men with a quantity of needles, as a further token of our friendly intentions. The chief sat himself down on the turf, with one of us on each side of him, while the men were leaning on their weapons on his right and left. At first no one could understand us; but an old man made his appearance shortly after, who understood the Hàussa language. Him the chief employed as an interpreter, and every one listened with anxiety to the following explanation which he gave us :—

"A few minutes after you first landed, one of my people came to me, and said that a number of strange people had arrived at the market-place. I sent him back again to get as near to you as he could, to hear what you intended doing. He soon after returned to me, and said that you spoke in a language which he could not understand. Not doubting that it was your intention to attack my village at night, and carry off my people, I desired them to get ready to fight. We were all prepared and eager to kill you, and came down breathing vengeance and slaughter, supposing that you were my enemies, and had landed from the opposite side of the river. But when you came to meet us unarmed, and we saw your white faces, we were all so frightened that we could not pull our bows, nor move hand or foot; and when you drew near me, and extended your hands towards me, I felt my heart faint within me, and believed that you were ‘ *Children of Heaven,*’ and had dropped from the skies." Such was the effect we had produced on him; and under this impression he knew not what he did. " And now," said he, " white men, all I want is your forgiveness."—" That you shall have most heartily," we said, as we shook hands with the old chief; and having taken care to assure him we had not come from so good a place as he had imagined, we congratulated ourselves, as well as him, that this affair had ended so happily. For our own parts, we had reason to feel the most unspeakable pleasure at its favourable termination; and we offered up internally to our merciful Creator a prayer of thanksgiving and praise, for his providential interference in our behalf; for the Almighty has indeed, to use the words of the Psalmist of Israel, " delivered our soul from death, and our feet from falling; and preserved us from any terror by night, and from the arrow that flieth by day; from the pestilence that walketh in darkness, and from the sickness that destroyeth at noonday." We were grateful to find that our blood had not been shed, and that we had been prevented from spilling the blood of others, which we imagined we should have been constrained to do from irremediable necessity. Our guns were all double-loaded with balls and slugs, our men were ready to present them,

and a single arrow from a bow would have been the
signal for immediate destruction. It was a narrow
escape ; and God grant we may never be so near a
a cruel death again. It was happy for us that our
white faces and calm behaviour produced the effect
it did on these people. In another minute our
bodies would have been as full of arrows as a por-
cupine's is full of quills.

The old chief returned to the village, followed by
his people, whom he addressed by the way from an
ant-hill, on which he mounted himself. He put himself into a great variety of attitudes, and delivered
them a speech which lasted more than half an hour.
Whether this was relating to ourselves or not we
could not ascertain; but it seemed more than probable. They came back to us again in the afternoon,
bringing with them a large quantity of yams and
goora-nuts as a present, and invited us with urgent
importunity to sleep in their huts for the night,
promising to treat us as well as their circumstances
would permit. We thanked them for their kindness, but for many reasons we did not embrace their
offer. However, it seemed as though this refusal
on our parts caused them to be mistrustful of our
intentions; for the villagers were discharging their
muskets from sunset till nearly eleven o'clock at
night, when the chief paid us a third visit, and
brought with him eight thousand cowries, and a
large heap of yams, which he laid at our feet. Poor
fellow! his countenance beamed with joy on discovering that we were *really* his friends. At length
he was induced to place confidence in us; and as he
wished us good-night he seemed well pleased with
the tranquil appearance of things, and went away.

In the course of our conversation with the chief,
when all his villagers were assembled around us,
we pointed to their guns, and the bits of red cloth
they had with them, and made them understand that
they all came from our country, at which their ad-

II.—M

miration and wonder was much increased. The old man who had performed the part of our interpreter so admirably is an old Funda mallam. He understood the Háussa language perfectly, and told us he had come here from Funda to attend the market which was held here every nine days. He informed us that many people came from the seacoast with goods from the white men to purchase slaves, a great number of whom, he said, came from his country. He told us that this place is the famous Bocquá market-place, of which we had heard so great talk, and that the opposite bank of the river belonged to the Funda country. We now asked the old mallam the distance from this place to the sea, and he told us about ten days' journey. We then pointed out the hills on the opposite side of the river, and asked him where they led to? "The sea," was his answer. "And where do they lead to?" we inquired, pointing to those on the same bank of the river as ourselves. He answered, they run a long way into a country we do not know. We then asked him if he had ever heard of a country called Eyeo or Yarriba? To which he replied, he had never heard of any country of either of those names. Our next concern was about the safety of the river navigation; and we anxiously inquired his opinion of it lower down, and whether there were any rocks or dangerous places? As to the river navigation, he satisfied us by saying he knew of no dangers, nor had he ever heard of any; but the people on the banks, he said, were very bad. We asked him if he thought the chief would send a messenger with us if we were to request him, even one day's journey from this place? Without the least hesitation he answered us—" No; the people of this country can go no further down the river; if they do, and are caught, they will lose their heads. Every town that I know of on the banks of the river is at war with its neighbour, and all the rest likewise."

We asked him then, how far Bornou was from Funda? To which he replied, " Fifteen days' journey." We were also anxious to know the character of the people on the borders of the Tshadda; and he informed us they were all good people, nearly all Mussulmans. There was one bad place to pass, he said, which was Yamyam. Here our conversation was interrupted by the old chief, who wished to return to the village, and the mallam was obliged to accompany him. He was a fine, respectable old man, and answered all our questions with a readiness which evinced the superiority of his class.

We offered up a prayer to the Almighty for his signal protection during this eventful day, and retired to rest.

Tuesday, October 26*th.*—When I awoke in the morning, the first person I saw was our trusty old man, Pascoe, very busy roasting yams for our breakfast. This man has been a most valuable servant to us, and is the only stanch fellow among all our people. In spite of a good deal of rain that had fallen in the night, we got up much refreshed this morning; for our mat awning, although rather a frail covering, had excluded the rain and kept us tolerably dry. Early in the morning the chief of the village, the old man that acted as interpreter, and a number of men and women visited our encampment, and behaved themselves in the most becoming and friendly manner. Not satisfied with what they had given us yesterday, the villagers offered us another large heap of yams, which, however, we refused to accept without making a suitable recompense. We accordingly gave them some beads in exchange for them, although I believe they would have been contented had we possessed nothing to offer them in return.

We now learned from the interpreter that buyers and sellers attend this market, not only from places adjacent, but also from remote towns and villages,

both above and below, and on each bank of the
Niger. A small tribute is exacted by the chief from
every one that offers articles for sale at the market,
and in this consists the whole of his revenues. All
the villagers that came out against us yesterday are
his slaves. We were likewise informed that directly
opposite, on the eastern bank, is the common path
to the city of Funda, which is indeed, as we had been
told at *Fofo*, situated three days' journey up the
Tshadda from the Niger ; that the large river which
we observed yesterday falling into the Niger from
the eastward is the celebrated *Shar, Shary*, or *Sharry*,
of travellers, or, which is more proper than either,
the *Tshadda*, as it is universally called throughout
the country. The interpreter said further that the
smaller stream which we passed on the 19th, flowing from the same direction, is the "*Coodoonia*."

The chief assured us that we had nothing to fear,
having passed all those places from which we might
have expected danger and molestation, during the
night. However, he cautioned us to avoid, if possible, a very considerable town lying on the eastern
bank, which we should pass in the afternoon, the
governor of which, he affirmed, would detain us a
considerable time in his territories, though he might
treat us well. A little way below Bocquâ, he said,
on the left border of the river, resides a powerful
king, sovereign of a fine country called *Attà*, who
would force us to visit him, if by any means he
were to be forewarned of our approach. He said
that he did not think he would do us any injury, but
that the chief was a very extraordinary man, and if
he had us in his power would detain us longer than
we wished. Perhaps he might keep us in his town
two or three months, but he would at least detain
us till all his people had satisfied their curiosity, and
then he might allow us to depart. As the chief of
Bocquâ was decidedly of opinion that it would be
in the power of this prince to render us the most

essential service if he were our friend, we requested
of him a guide and messenger to accompany us to
Attà, and introduce us to the king; but he answered
without hesitation, that a man from him would be
captured and slain the moment he should make his
appearance there, but for what reason we are left to
conjecture. This did not argue, however, very favourably as to the clemency or merciful disposition
of the monarch of Attà, and therefore we resolved
to keep out of his reach by running along close to
the shore on the opposite side of the water. The
chief concluded by observing that in seven days we
should reach the sea, a piece of intelligence with
which we were not a little pleased. The old interpreter had told us that we should get there in ten
days; therefore we cannot be far from it.

The females of Bocquâ are good-looking and very
neat in their persons. The men have not the custom, as at Kacunda, of cutting marks on the face or
on any part of the body. Having finished our usual
scanty breakfast of a roasted yam and some water
from the river, we commenced loading our canoe
and preparing for our day's journey. We had now
passed the worst place on the river, which is between
this and Kacunda, and there was no further necessity for travelling by night. This we by no means
regret; for although we are exposed to the heat of
the sun by day, yet there are dangers in the river in
consequence of the water being so high, which are
more easily avoided by daylight than in the dark.
It is not easy to keep clear of eddies, and when influenced by them our canoe is swept out of the main
stream of the river, and it is with difficulty we regain our course. The canoe being all ready, we
shook hands cordially with our friend the chief, and
the principal male and female villagers, and a few
minutes after seven fired a salute of two or three
muskets, gave three cheers, and departed from Bocquâ. We soon passed their little town, which had

a neat appearance, and was fortified by a strong wooden fence.

Both banks of the river still continued hilly and were fringed with primeval woods, which were bending over the water. At eleven, A. M., we were opposite a town, which, from the description that had been given of it, we supposed to be Attà. It is situated close to the water's edge on the south-east bank of the river, in an elevated situation, and on a fine green sward: its appearance was unspeakably beautiful. The town is clean, of prodigious extent, and ornamented with verdant shrubs and tall goodly trees. A few canoes were lying at the foot of the town, but we escaped observation, and passed on near the opposite shore. Afterward the margin of the river became more thickly wooded, and more umbrageous than before; and for upwards of thirty miles not a town or a village, or even a single hut, could anywhere be seen. The whole of this distance our canoe passed smoothly along the Niger, and every thing was silent and solitary; no sound could be distinguished save our own voices and the plashing of the paddles with their echoes; the song of birds was not heard, nor could any animal whatever be seen; the banks seemed to be entirely deserted, and the magnificent Niger to be slumbering in its own grandeur.

From Bocquâ the river runs in a valley between mountains of a considerable height. Between Attà and Bocquâ market the course of the river is about south-west, with several turnings in it. The hills on the north-west side seemed to decrease in height about the middle of the day, and those on the eastern side are changing their course to the southeast, while the river still flows to the south-west. About two in the afternoon the nature of the banks was entirely changed; from being high they became low and swampy, particularly the left bank, and were covered with thick jungle, which mostly over-

hung the water. At half-past two we passed two
charming little islands, which appeared to be uninhabited, and at four we saw a branch of the river
running off in a southerly direction, inclining a little
to the east. It appeared to be a quarter of a mile
wide. At about five in the evening, our people being tired, we descried a canoe, and pulled towards
it; but those that were in it were frightened on seeing us, and jumped out and hid themselves in the
forest. In two or three minutes we perceived on
the left bank a few dilapidated huts, and we pulled
the canoe ashore, intending to remain there for the
night. A number of women first observed us; they
were also alarmed, and hurried away to an adjacent
village, where we saw them providing themselves
with muskets and other uncivil weapons, and very
formidable Amazons they appeared to be. However we did not seem to regard them, but jumped on
shore with our mats, and sat down on the ground
very comfortably under the branches of a cocoanut-tree, the first that we have seen since leaving
Yarriba. We had not been long seated before a
number of people made their appearance, running
hastily towards us with swords and muskets in their
hands. Seeing that we were sitting down quietly,
without making any hostile display, they hesitated
and stopped at a short distance from us, and wished
to know what we wanted at their town. We had
recourse to our usual method of expressing ourselves by signs, and the natives, finding that we were
really harmless beings, ventured to draw nearer, and
very soon became reconciled to us. Shortly after
they were joined by some more of their companions,
and among them was a young man who imperfectly
understood the *Bonny* language; so that Antonio,
one of our men, who is son to " *King Pepper*," chief
of that country, was enabled to enter into conversation with him, and presently made him comprehend
every thing relative to us, which he repeated to the
villagers. We had been thus employed a short time,

and had become great friends with these people, the
women chatting with a familiarity we had not been
accustomed to up the country, and began to find
ourselves very comfortable, when the chief, a tall,
Herculean, awkward figure, with a sullen and most
forbidding countenance, made his appearance. He
introduced himself without the smallest ceremony,
and very briefly desired us to accompany him to his
hut in the principal village, which is called *Abbazacca*. The road to this place is by a narrow footway, overhung by rank grass three times our own
height. This formed a complete arch over our
heads, and the path was exceedingly intricate. On
arriving there, a clean shed was prepared for us,
which, though small, was one of the largest in the
village. Through the interpretation of Antonio we
informed the chief who we were, and where we
wished to go. He immediately said he would accompany us to a large town lower down the river,
of which his brother was governor, and where we
should meet with people from Bonny, Calebar, Brass,
and Bini, which latter place we conclude is meant
for Benin. The natives of all these places, he informed us, come up to his brother's town for the purpose of buying slaves, and we shall then be at liberty
to accompany whichever party we please. It was
important to ascertain which was the largest branch,
as soon as we found that these different rivers communicated with the Niger, and we asked him the
question, through Antonio, which was considered
the largest river. This he was unable to say, but
we were told by Antonio afterward, that he thought
the Bonny was the largest. He informed us that if
we intended going to the town of which his brother
was governor to-morrow, that we must get up very
early, otherwise we should not arrive there before
sunset. After thanking the chief for his communications and attention to us, we took our leave of
him for the night.

Before we had retired to rest, a few stale eggs

which we could not eat, and a calabash of very inferior tuah, were sent us by the chief, with a hint
that a present would be acceptable in the morning.
This was very inhospitable treatment of us, and we
could not help thinking the chief was a mean old
fellow, for we saw plenty of poultry and goats in his
yard, which he knew would be more acceptable to
us than his stale eggs. At eight in the evening we
lay down to sleep, but could find no rest, on account
of an army of gigantic mosquitoes, which desperately
attacked us from all quarters, and serenaded us till
morning with their unwelcome song. The course
of the river to-day has been nearly south-west, and
its width varying from two to three miles.

Wednesday, October 27th.—At daybreak we arose
from our mats after no very comfortable night's rest
in consequence of the attacks of the mosquitoes.
We took a little refreshment, and commenced our
preparations for starting. At six o'clock the chief,
who as well as his villagers had long been on the
alert, came to us for his present, and, as we suspected last evening, we found considerable difficulty
in satisfying the surly old man. I accordingly gave
him a pair of silver bracelets, a pair of scissors, five
hundred needles, and a handsome country cloth
which the queen of Boossà had given us. The fellow was discontented with this, which was more
than we had given away a long time. He began to
grumble, and told us plainly that he would not let
us leave his village till something better was given
to him. To enforce his threats, fourteen of his
slaves stood around him armed with muskets, whose
appearance alone, I suppose, he thought would be
sufficient to intimidate us into compliance. We by
no means wished to have any disturbance, and therefore endeavoured as much as we could to persuade
him that we had nothing more to give him. I directed all our travelling things to be taken out of our
boxes before him, and had them put back again and

locked up. This would not satisfy him, and he desired them to be searched again, and that he himself
might be allowed to examine them. Our patience
was now quite exhausted: " Tell the chief," said I
to Antonio, "the boxes shall be opened no more,
and let him stop my people from loading the canoe
if he dare." My brother and I had armed ourselves
with the loaded pistols and swords, as well as all
our people, and on telling the chief what we had
done, we ordered them to proceed loading the canoe, which they obeyed directly. The chief stood
amazed, and did not offer to interfere with us. This
old rascal had muttered and grumbled at every thing
which was offered him ; *this* was of no use, and *that*
of no value, and he would desire all that we had,
such was his covetousness. After having gone the
length he did, and having shown his insolent airs,
without producing the expected impression, he feared
that he should get nothing at all, and therefore accepted the present we had offered him at first. The
country cloth alone which had been given us by the
queen of Boossà was ten times more than he deserved.

At *Abbazacca* we saw an English iron bar, and
feasted our eyes on the graceful cocoanut-tree,
which we had not seen so long. We were delighted
also with the mellow whistling of gray parrots.
Trifling as these circumstances may appear, yet they
made our hearts beat with delight, and awakened
in us a train of very pleasing associations. We indulged in a delusive, yet fanciful revery, and we
fondly hoped,—but what good would it be to tell of
what we hoped so fondly ?

It was the avowed intention of the chief to send
a man with us as messenger to a large town, which
he described to be a day's journey from Abbazacca,
and of which he said that his brother was governor ;
but imagining, no doubt, that he would not be paid
to his satisfaction, and that, should he accompany

us himself, the reward would be greater, he changed
his mind, and resolved on the latter expedient.
Therefore he got into one of his own canoes, and
between seven and eight in the morning, our canoe
having been loaded without any interference from
the chief or his people, and without taking any
further notice of him, we led the way from the village through a large and unwholesome swamp which
is before it, and were soon followed by him. We
succeeded in getting into the open river with incredible difficulty.

In consequence of the lightness of his canoe, and
its superiority to our old one, which we had got at
Zagozhi, the chief passed us with the utmost facility,
and touched at various towns and villages, to inform
their inhabitants of the fact of our journeying down
the river, and that Christians were coming from a
country they had never heard of. We were solicited
to stop at one or two of these, in order to please the
curiosity of the people, hundreds of whom ran out
into the water to obtain a better view of our persons,
but we did not get out of our canoe. These brought
us presents of eggs, which we accepted very gladly
and passed on.

During the first part of the day the course of the
river was about west-south-west, the breadth varying from two to four miles, according to our estimation. At noon we saw a small branch running off to
the south-east. The Chief of Abbazacca, who had
kept company with us, seemed to get impatient as
his canoe was so much swifter than our own, and
coming close to it, told us to pull as strong as we
could, or that we should not reach his brother's
town by daylight. However, we did not pay much
attention to his remarks, but quietly kept on our
usual rate. The north-west side of the river was
now low, and covered with thick jungle, and the
bank in many places was overflowed, so that the
jungle appeared to be growing out of the water.

The south-east bank was rather higher, and cultivated pieces of ground were seen now and then about
three or four miles apart, with villages about them.

At two in the afternoon we came abreast of a village of pretty considerable extent, intending to pass
it by on the other side. We had no sooner made
our appearance than we were lustily hailed by a little
squinting fellow, dressed in an English soldier's
jacket, who kept crying out as loud as his lungs
would permit him, "Holloa, you Englishmen! you
come here." However we were not inclined to obey
his summons, being rather anxious to get to the
town mentioned to us by the chief of Abbazacca,
and as the current swept us along past the village,
we took no notice of the little man; and we had
already sailed beyond the landing-place, when we
were overtaken by about a dozen canoes, and the
people in them, stopping us, desired us to turn back,
for that we had forgotten to pay our respects to the
king. The name of this village, we now find, is
Damuggoo. Ever willing to please and oblige all
parties, as far as we are able, and being in no condition to force ourselves from the men that had interrupted us with so little ceremony, we pulled with
all our strength against the current, and, after an
hour's exertion, landed amid the cheers and huzzas
of a multitude of people. The first person we observed at the landing-place was our little friend in
the red jacket, who we found out afterward was a
messenger from the chief of Bonny. His business
here was to buy slaves for his master.

My brother and I were instantly conducted over a
bog to a large fetish-tree, at the root of which we
were made to sit down, and were shaded by its
branches from an intolerably hot sun. Here we
waited till the arrival of the chief, who made his appearance in a few minutes, bringing with him a goat,
with a quantity of yams and other provisions, as a
present. We arose to salute him, and he shook

hands with us, welcoming us to his town with a reserved and sorrowful, yet friendly air. In his dress
and person we saw nothing remarkable, save that
his countenance displayed mildness and benevolence,
mingled with a great deal of seriousness and native
dignity. His stature is above the middle size, and
he is rather advanced in years. He requested us to
stop a few days at his town, which we promised him
we would do, having told him that we were going to
the sea. The Chief of Bonny's messenger, he said,
was going there in a few days, and he would recommend us to remain with him till he went, that we
might accompany him. We had no objection to
this, and thought that the little squinting fellow, who
was a very important personage in his own estimation, might be useful to us, and be some sort of protection to our party where he was known. He was
at all events a man of some consequence even from
his red jacket alone, which rendered him a conspicuous object among the dark natives by whom
he was surrounded; so we congratulated ourselves
with the thoughts of being quite safe.

The chief put a great many questions to us respecting ourselves and our country, the places we
had come from, their distance up the river, and also
concerning the river itself, and was astonished at
our answers. He told us that he had never heard
of any countries higher up the river than Funda and
Tacwà, by which latter we found he meant the
Nouffie country. He said that he had never heard
of Yarriba, Borgoo, or Yàoorie. A mallam now
joined our company, who appeared to be a respectable man. We found afterward that he was one of
Ederesa's people, and had been sent for by the chief
of Damuggoo for the purpose of writing charms to
protect him from all evil which might threaten him
and his village. This man seemed happy at seeing
people who had come from his own country, which
he told us, he had heard nothing of during the last

year. He was pleased in being able to talk with
those who could give him information concerning
it, and he offered us his services in all manner of
ways, and told us he would do every thing in his
power to make us comfortable.

A messenger now arrived to inform us that our
hut was ready. The chief, on our taking leave of
him, told us we were only eight days' journey from
the sea, and that we should soon get there. We
were then conducted through filthy streets of mud
to a very diminutive hut, which we find excessively
warm, owing to the small quantity of light and air,
which are admitted into it only through a narrow
aperture, opening into a gloomy and dismal passage.
The appearance of the inside is better than that of
the outside, being plastered rudely with clay, and
surrounded with indifferently carved fetish figures,
either painted or chalked a red colour.

The news of our arrival having spread through
the village, the people flocked in hundreds to see us.
They so completely blocked up every place through
which we might receive air, that we were nearly
suffocated; nor could we succeed in driving them
away. We made our people arm themselves with
swords and sticks to keep them off, but to no purpose; their curiosity overcame their fears, and they
pressed on us as thickly as ever. This was no
longer to be borne, and we were obliged to send to
the chief, requesting his interference. His reply
was, that if the people would not go away when they
were desired, we were to fire at, and kill as many of
them as we pleased. This we could not think of
doing, and therefore desired he would command
some of his own people to come and drive them
away. They soon arrived, armed with large, heavy
sticks, which they laid about the natives in so merciless a manner, that, to our great relief, our hut was
soon cleared, and we again enjoyed the fresh air.

At six in the evening the chief sent us some fofo

and a quantity of stewed goat, sufficient for thirty
persons. We were not a little surprised by the addition of a small case-bottle of rum—a luxury which
we have not had since we were at Kiama. It is
long since we have tasted tea or coffee; but the
rum was a treat that we did not expect, although it
was the worst kind of trade-rum I ever recollect to
have tasted.

Here, to our infinite surprise, we saw on landing,
besides the little man dressed in a soldier's jacket,
several others partially clothed in European apparel,
all of whom have picked up a smattering of the
English language from Liverpool vessels which frequent the Bonny river for palm-oil. The messenger
from the chief of that country, who has come hither
to purchase slaves and ivory, asserts, that the ship
Bamboo and four other Liverpool vessels are now at
anchor in the river. Bonny is said to be four or five
days' journey from hence.

After making a hearty meal· off the stewed goat
and fofo we laid ourselves down to rest, but the
mosquitoes were so troublesome, that they prevented
us from getting any till nearly morning. We have
generally found that the mosquitoes are more troublesome and vigorous in their attacks shortly before
rain than at any other time. The course of the
river has been much in the same direction as yesterday; the current very rapid.

CHAPTER XVIII.

The Chief of Damuggoo—Fetish Deity—Visit to the Chief—Unfavour-
able Termination of a Fetish Ceremony—Another Canoe promised—
Superstitious Credulity of the People—Story of the King of Atta—
Impatience of the Travellers to proceed—The Town of Damuggoo—
Its Resources—Punishments—Unfavourable Opinions respecting the
Success of the Travellers—Farewell Ceremonies—Departure from
Damuggoo—Travelling Companions—The Disaster of Kirree—John
Lander's Narrative of it—The Palaver or Council at Kirree—Decision
of the Council—The Eboe People.

Thursday, October 28th.—At daybreak we had a
heavy tornado, accompanied with much thunder and
lightning.   At ten A. M. the chief visited us, accompanied by the Nouffie mallam.   His dress consisted
of a red cloth cap, a very handsome red twilled silk
tobe, made in Nouffie, with trousers of the same
material, and sandals.   He brought with him some
palm wine, eggs, bananas, yams, &c., and desired us
to ask for any thing we might want, telling us that
we should have every thing we wished that the town
could afford.   He told us that neither he nor his
father had seen a white man, although they had
much wished it, and that our presence made him
quite happy.   He then gave us a pressing invitation
to come to see him, which we readily accepted.   He
seemed to be one of the worthiest fellows whom we
have yet met.

We shortly after proceeded to his residence, and
passed through a variety of low huts which led to
the one in which he was sitting.   In addition to his
former dress, he had a very handsome leopard's skin
thrown over him.   In his hand he held a staff
covered with the skin of a wild beast; and two
pages, one on each side, were cooling him with cir
cular fans, made of bullock's hide.   He accosted us

with cheerfulness, and placed mats for us to sit on; and rum was produced to make us comfortable withal. He wished to know in what manner we had got through the country, for he had learned we had come a long journey—from a great city called Yàoorie, of which he had never before heard the name. We again briefly related to him from whence we had come, where we had been, and whither we were going, taking care to make frequent allusions to the civility and kindness which we had experienced even from the greatest monarchs. He appeared astonished at our narrative, and promised, as far as he was able, to imitate those good men in his treatment of us as his guests. He then expressed the infinite pleasure the sight of white men afforded him, and how happy his father would have been in his lifetime, had he been honoured by the presence of such wonderful strangers. When Antonio, our interpreter, explained to him that we were ambassadors from the "great king of white men," he seemed to feel peculiar delight. "Something must be done for you to-morrow," said he, and left us to conjecture for a short time what that something would be; but we soon learned that he intended to make rejoicings with all his people; that they would fire off their muskets, and pass a night in dancing and revelry. He told us that when we left him to go down the river, he intended to send one of his canoes with nine people in her, to accompany us all the way to the sea. He requested us to wait eight days longer, when he expected his people back from the Bocquâ market. " I think," he added, "that the Chief of Bocquà's messenger and our own people will be sufficient protection for you." We readily assented to his proposal, and told him that as our presents were all expended, we would send him some from the seacoast, if he would allow a person to accompany us thither on whom he could depend to bring them back to him. He expressed himself

II.—N

much gratified by our promises, and said that his
own son should accompany us; and that although
his people had never been lower down the river than
to a place called Kirree, about a day's journey from
hence, he had no doubt that we should reach the sea
in safety. After expressing mutual good-will, friendship, and satisfaction with each other; and as soon
as the king had promised with solemnity that he
would consent to our departure in the time he had
specified, we shook hands and parted.

In taking leave of us, the old chief told us that no
one should be allowed to visit us excepting those to
whom we gave permission; and we accordingly had
all the principal people of the town, both males and
females, to see us. These persons were very well
dressed, and conducted themselves in an orderly
manner.

In the course of the afternoon, however, we were
perplexed with the visits of thousands of people besides, whose curiosity was irresistible, and who
scarcely allowed us room to breathe. Above Egga
the people are by no means inquisitive; but in and
below that town nothing can be compared with the
surprise and amazement with which the natives beheld us, and pressed round to satisfy their curiosity.

Friday, October 29th.—The promise of " something," which was made us yesterday, has been fulfilled to-day with great *éclàt*. In the morning a bullock, wild in the bush, was offered us, with a proviso
that one of our party could shoot him. Pascoe,
therefore, went out with his gun, and discovered the
animal ruminating among the trees; and levelling
his piece, he shot him dead the first fire. Part of
the carcass was given to the king, as is the custom;
and we were not unmindful of our old friend the
mallam; so, having sent him some, the remainder
of it was brought home for our own consumption.
It is usual here for the cattle to run wild in the bush,
being never admitted into the town; and when one

is wanted for food, the natives go into the woods
and shoot it. They are not so expert in killing
them as our man Pascoe, whom we had desired to
load his gun with two balls, and to endeavour to hit
the bullock under the ear. He was so successful,
that the poor animal died in an instant without a
struggle, much to the astonishment of the chief and
his people, who were witnesses of the transaction.

At the back of our hut stands a fetish god, in a
small thatched hut, supported by four wooden pillars, which is watched continually by two boys and
a woman. We were desired to roast our bullock
under him, that he might enjoy the savoury smell
of the smoking meat, some of which he might also
be **able** to eat if he desired. We were particularly

Fetish Deity of Damuggoo.

enjoined to roast no yams under him, as they were considered by the natives too poor a diet to offer to their deity. The natives are all pagans, and worship the same kind of figures as those of Yarriba.

A feast and great rejoicings are to take place to-day, in consequence of our arrival, and the preparation of the bullock only seems to be the first step towards it. The natives are getting their muskets ready, and all the swivels in the town are brought and placed under the fetish tree we have mentioned.

At six in the evening the ceremonies were commenced by a volley of musketry being fired off by command of the chief, and we were afterward saluted with a discharge from the swivels. This was a signal for the inhabitants to come forward and follow the example of their monarch, which they did with so much spirit and effect, that continual firing was kept up till between eleven and twelve o'clock, at which time the people paraded the town for the remainder of the night, dancing, singing, and making merry. Pascoe tells us that every man had a musket. They must be very numerous, for the fire is as incessant as if it were in a field of battle, so that it is quite impossible for us to get any sleep while it is going forward.

Saturday, October 30th.—Notwithstanding all the firing last night, and though the natives loaded their guns with three times their proper charge, we have not heard of any accident happening. All this had been done very much against our inclination, but it was the highest token of respect which could be shown us, and which had never before been granted to any individual: we therefore considered it our duty to visit the chief and thank him for the honour. So accordingly, a little before noon, we went to see him, accompanied by four of our people. On our arrival, we found him surrounded by his priests, who were employed in making a fetish, to ascertain whether we should reach the sea in safety. The

Nouffie mallam was also seated by the chief's side, engaged in writing Mohammedan prayers on a plain white cotton cap, which the chief was to wear on all occasions, to render him secure from danger of every description.

He received us very kindly, and desired us to sit down with him and remain a short time, offering us a glass of rum, which we were obliged to accept. It was with much difficulty we were able to drink it, for we felt little inclined to do so; in addition to which the heat of the place was so excessive, that we could hardly breathe, although two of our people kept fanning us all the time we were with him. Having expressed our thanks to the chief, for the honour he had done us by the rejoicings of the night before, we complimented him on his resources, and expressed our admiration of that greatness of mind which he had displayed in applying them to the gratification and delight of strangers, whom he had made his warmest friends. "The great white king will be pleased to learn that I have treated his subjects so well," said the chief; "and you may inform him of my dignity, my riches, my strength, and my power." We thought this quite sufficient; the chief was pleased both with himself for having displayed his "power," and with us for having duly appreciated it; and being anxious to return to the open air, we begged he would excuse our remaining any longer, and, shaking hands with him, we wished him a good morning.

From a conversation with a Nouffie man, who has exiled himself from his native country, and arrived here lately, we learn that these muskets and guns have been procured from the coast in exchange for slaves and ivory. He informs us also that Bornou and Jacoba are at peace, and consequently that the road from Funda to *Kouka*, which is the metropolis of the Bornou empire, is now open and free from danger of any kind. The same individual assures us that a person can travel from one country to the other, by land, in seventeen days; but that to travel by water up the *Tshadda* to Kouka, would be a journey of nineteen days. He likewise reports that Ederesa, the ex-king of Nouffie, had endeavoured to win over the Sultan of Bornou to his cause, and for that purpose had sent him an embassy, with a present of leopards' skins, and a certain number of slaves; but when he left home, it was not generally believed that the monarch of Bornou would interfere in the domestic concerns of Nouffie, or attempt to raise the fallen fortunes of Ederesa, unless he would consent to break off all connexion with the Falátahs, with whom he is on good terms, and promise his aid in their complete extirpation. However, the destiny of Nouffie is already sealed; she is a conquered country in every sense of the word, and a Falátah is her monarch.

Sunday, October 31*st.*—It has been hinted to us that the chief of *Damuggoo* will detain us here longer than will be agreeable, notwithstanding his pledge. At ten in the morning the chief sent for me to visit him, and I immediately obeyed his summons. I found him engaged in earnest conversation with his priests, and he no sooner saw me than he requested me to sit down by his side. He appeared very serious, but did not give me long to speculate on what was coming; for, turning towards me, he said, with a deep-drawn sigh, that the fetish which had been made yesterday for us had not ended in our favour. He was sure, he said, that we should meet with many troubles before we reached the sea. All this was said with a great deal of earnestness, and his countenance was very expressive of sorrow. I desired that he would not feel hurt on our account, telling him that we were not afraid of any thing; that we had done no one any harm in Africa, and we trusted in our God for protection. "It is good," said he; "if my people return from Bocquâ market to-morrow, you shall go in a few days." I thanked him for his kindness, and wished him a good morning

In the course of conversation this morning, the chief said that he cannot think of sending us away in an old leaky canoe such as ours, and unprotected; that such would not be fitting our rank; and he is of opinion that we should meet a thousand difficulties and dangers were we to proceed further down the river without a guide and messenger. He observed that our canoe is what sailors would term not "seaworthy;" for, having been exposed to the heat of the sun, it had split in several places. These considerations had induced him to procure for us a far better canoe than our own; but he expressed his very great sorrow that he could not furnish us with a supply of men till their return from Bocquâ market, whither they had gone in the morning, and would not return for three days to come. We had no remedy, and our only plan was to submit on the ground of expediency, without raising any objection, for we knew that it would be unavailing.

We presented the chief in the forenoon with a musket belonging to one of our men, and my broken watch, which he says he will send to Bonny, to be repaired. We had nothing else to offer him except needles, a pair of bracelets, or our own wearing apparel, which he does not appear to fancy at all. However, we have promised, that should his men take us in safety to Bonny, we would send back something to him which would be more acceptable and of greater value, and which we should be enabled to obtain from the English ships lying there. This intelligence is very gratifying to the chief, and he expresses his thankfulness most profusely. He knows the facility with which European articles are got at the mouth of the river, and he no doubt reckons on a rich present from us. He is certainly deserving of one, for his conduct towards us has been most satisfactory from the commencement. We continue to receive every kindness from him, and he sends us provisions each morning, sufficient for fifty

men for one day, together with palm-wine, rum, cocoanuts, bananas, and numerous other things.

A great part of the population of Damuggoo left
the town this morning for the Bocquâ market. They
take thither powder, muskets, soap, Manchester cottons, and other articles of European manufacture,
and great quantities of rum, or rather of rum and
water; for not more than one-third of it is genuine
spirit, and even that is of the worst quality. These
commodities are exchanged for ivory and slaves,
which are resold to the European traders. The Niger is receding most rapidly; within these two or
three days it has fallen away as many feet, which
confirms us in the supposition that in the interior
the rains are over, though they are only declining
here.

The natives of this part of the country scarcely
ever heard of the religion of Mohammed, and therefore they believe in all manner of gods and demons,
as in Yarriba and other places. They have a variety
of tutelary gods, and others whose business it is to
watch over and protect the public interests. Their
religious dances, and their songs or hymns addressed
to their divinities, differ but slightly from those of
other pagan countries, and the superstitious ceremonies of their faith bear the same close resemblance.
In their belief of the immortality of the soul, and a
future state of rewards and punishments, there is
nothing peculiar or new.

The late occupier of the hut in which we reside
died a few days ago, and was buried; but last night
there was a public declaration that his tutelary god
had resuscitated him, and that he had risen from
the dead. Things of this nature are reported not to
be of rare occurrence, and the rumour was believed,
or rather it was pretended to be believed, by all ranks.
A large procession was therefore formed, attended
by singers and dancers, as usual; and the man who
was said to have undergone so great a change, hav-

ing been placed in the centre, was carried through the
town and exhibited gratis to all who felt a disposition
to see him. After the procession had visited the
chief's house, a messenger was despatched to inquire whether we ourselves felt any inclination to
view the prodigy; but we declined the intended honour, for it would be extremely unpleasant to be sti-
fled in our hut by a multitude of unwashed, half-naked
people. What is to be the final fortune of the man
we know not, but it is generally supposed that he
will die again to-morrow!

It appears to us scarcely credible that the chief,
who is a sensible and intelligent man, should put
any confidence in such egregious nonsense and chicanery; but we rather imagine that he must be aware
of the cheats which are practised upon his credulous
people by their priests, and that, for political considerations, he chooses to connive at and countenance their proceedings; the more so, as he very
recently sent to Nouffie for a Mohammedan priest,
who is now engaged in working Arab charms, &c.
upon his tobe. This man he has intrusted with all
his secrets, and loaded with benefits; but whether
he is a Mohammedan or pagan in heart we are left
to guess. How great soever his confidence in this
mallam may be, yet a white man and a Christian
has far greater claims, he says, to his veneration;
and, as a proof of it, he would request of us a "*mighty
spell,*" which he was convinced it was in our power
alone to give. The virtue of it is to consist chiefly
in making him successful in war. He has a brother,
he says, who is king of a neighbouring and powerful state, with whom he has been at enmity for many
years, and him he wishes to vanquish and bring under subjection, in order to "*plant his foot upon his
neck,*" and reign in his stead. Of this brother, and
of their father, the former king, he related to us the
following story:—

" The late King of *Attà* was a very powerful
II.—O

prince, and one of the most opulent, both as regarded money and slaves, that had ever been known in the whole country. His domestic slaves alone amounted to five hundred; and he had accumulated, by industry, care, and frugality, during a long life, as much money (cowries) as would fill seven or eight ordinary huts. The surrounding nations felt his influence, and trembled at his power; their rulers courted his friendship by voluntary presents, and acknowledged his supremacy by humiliating concessions. The monarch concerned himself greatly in the internal affairs and domestic policy of the kingdom of Funda, whose sovereigns he pulled down and set up again whenever he was influenced by caprice, or spurred on by resentment.

" Now it happened, at length, that this mighty king died, as all great and little sovereigns must do, and he was buried, after the custom of the country, with many public honours, and with all his riches. His eldest son, who was a covetous, worldly-minded prince, succeeded him in his authority; but instead of enjoying the affluence of his venerable parent, he was not worth a single cowrie. The consciousness of his poverty, and the want of consideration and respect among his subjects, caused him to make many moral reflections on the use, value, and purposes of money with mankind, and the penury and wretchedness which the want of it generally occasioned. At length, harassed with doubts and perplexities, he forgot all filial tenderness, and the respect which he owed to his father's memory, and came to the conclusion, that as the money which was buried was of no use whatever to the deceased in the next world, it would be both a charitable and praiseworthy deed to have it dug out of the earth, and put into circulation. And further, to prevent such good-for-nothing practices from being followed in future, he would sentence the body of his father to receive a public punishment. Therefore, with this resolution, he violated the sanctity of the grave, and commanded that the whole of its contents should be disinterred. This done he secured the money, and ordered his slaves to cut off the head of the corpse, and expose it in a conspicuous situation, as a chastisement for the covetous disposition which his father had evinced while living; for the heinous offence which he had consummated when dying of desiring *all* his money to be interred with him, and as a dreadful warning to the people. This want of piety in the new king, his unjustifiable and unnatural action in dishonouring his father's body, and, above all, his contempt for a custom which time had rendered venerable, and which had been sanctioned by the concurrent voice of ages, made a silent, but deep impression on the minds of his subjects; their feelings, which for a long while they had suppressed, broke out at length into passion, the spark was soon kindled into a flame, and a powerful party was soon formed to depose the impious prince. They placed his younger brother at their head, and a sanguinary civil war was the immediate consequence. However, they had suffered the proper time to elapse, and the king was too firmly established to suffer much from their attempts; the rebels were routed in all quarters, and those who could not flee were put to the sword. The Chief of Damuggoo, our host, is the unsuccessful brother; and the chief of Bocquâ, our friend, was one of his principal followers." This accounts for the unwillingness of the latter to send a messenger with us to Attà, and the reasonable apprehensions which he entertained for his safety, which would certainly have been realized.

Tuesday, November 2d.—It is extremely mortifying and vexatious to reflect, that though we are so near our countrymen, and our journey's end, yet we are not suffered to go to them; and it is teasing to think that we are constrained to bend to the will of a man who cannot enter into our feelings, nor share

our hopes and fears, and who deludes us with hol
low promises day after day. Finding the market
people not yet returned from Bocquâ, as we had been
persuaded, we sent an energetic message to the
king, this morning, expressive of our determination
to hazard every danger rather than be detained
longer at Damuggoo, and also to remind him of his
solemn promise. This produced an immediate answer, that, agreeably to our request, we should leave
the town to-day, if we thought it safe to do so. For
his own part, however, if this were to be our purpose, he could only send and protect us a day's journey down the river, where resides the chief of a very
large country, into whose hands he should be constrained to deliver us; that this monarch would
naturally expect a considerable present, and would,
he had no doubt, prolong our stay with him to severa.
weeks. While, on the other hand, would we consent to wait two days longer for the return of his
people, he should be enabled to forward us to Bonny
without touching at the above place, and indeed
without calling at any important town whatever
during the journey. In a choice of evils, we preferred that which appeared to us the least, and therefore resolved to wait here a day or two longer. The
only circumstance which is capable of reconciling
us to our wretched abode is the continued civility,
generosity, and tenderness of the chief.

The streets of Damuggoo are so muddy, owing to
the nature of the soil, and to the rains which have
recently fallen, that we cannot step outside the door
of our hut without exposing ourselves to the inconvenience of being covered with black, filthy mud, so
that we are obliged to stay within from necessity.
Our hut does not exceed six or seven feet in diame-
ter, and withal it is so very dark and dismal, that we
can see neither to read nor write; added to which
we are invaded, from the first peep of morn till the
close of day, by a host of impudent fellows, who

plant themselves round the doorway, and in the passage, like so many blocks of marble, and remain there in spite of us, to the utter exclusion of every particle of air. The chief, to whom we have made a grievous complaint, tells us seriously to "*cut off their heads ;*" but really we do not relish the idea of human heads, all so black and ghastly, tumbling down at our feet, and so we resort to a milder punishment, but hitherto this has not been attended with any good effect. When evening comes, and the moon shines brilliantly above our heads, like all nature, we seek the comforts of repose; but who can sleep when legions of mosquitoes come singing in your face, to tease and worry you without mercy? It is a fact,-that the chief and his people are frequently driven, in the dead of night, to seek shelter from the attacks of these tormenting insects in the open air, or under the trees; but we cannot resort to the same expedient, and are therefore obliged, because "idleness is the parent of many vices," to employ the watchful hours of the night in slaughtering our inveterate persecutors, nor do we cease till morning dawns.

· *Wednesday, November 3d.*—The inhabitants of this town dress, generally speaking, in Manchester cottons (if a cloth confined to the waist, and extending below the knee, may be styled a dress). The neat and becoming tobe or shirt of the interior is worn only by the king and a few of the principal inhabitants. Indeed the people appear to have little communication with the natives of the more inland provinces, and we have found the progress of civilization to be rapidly diminishing the nearer we approach the coast. The women are fond of beads, but esteem only the more costly kind; these are the only personal decorations which they wear. Damuggoo is a considerably large and populous town, but abominably dirty: the huts are round, and constructed much after the same manner as those of Zagōzhi.

being built of mud and loam, strengthened and sup
ported by props and ribs of wood. They have all,
without exception, a poor, mean, and extremely
wretched appearance.

Those of the inhabitants who are not engaged in
trading transactions employ themselves in cultivating the soil. Yams and Indian corn form,
we believe, the principal, if not the only vegetable
food of the poorer classes, and they rarely eat
any thing else. The plantain and banana are imported from a neighbouring state; but these are
beyond their reach, on account of expense; and
form, in fact, with the exception of the cocoanut, the only fruits and vegetables with which they
seem to be acquainted. Rice, which is grown so
generally, and in such abundance, almost in their
immediate neighbourhood, they have never seen;
and as to the different kinds of grain, which are cultivated to a considerable extent so near as Funda
and Nouffie, they have either no knowledge of
them, or, which is more likely, they consider the labour which is required in their culture, and the attention which the rising crops would demand, to
counterbalance the good that might result to themselves by the introduction into their country of different varieties of corn. Therefore, they confine
their agricultural labours to cultivating maize, which
is the hardiest of all grain, and the yam. The inhabitants of Damuggoo never saw a horse, nor have
they the most distant idea of such an animal. Their
domestic animals are the dog, the sheep, the goat,
and the common fowl; the cow cannot be classed
among the number. Goats and fowls are plentiful,
but few sheep are to be seen; and even these are
greatly inferior to those of the more interior parts.
Abundance of excellent fish are caught in the river,
which compensates, in a great degree, for the
scarcity of other animal food.

The king paid us a visit this forenoon, dressed very

appropriately in a handsome tobe of silk and cotton, of the manufacture of Nouffie. He repeated his assurances that we shall leave to-morrow, and though the men are not yet returned from the market, yet they are confidently expected this evening. He behaved with so much native politeness, and promised that we should be detained no longer with so much seriousness and apparent sincerity, that we are induced to believe him.

The Chief of Damuggoo, benevolent as are his looks, and dignified as is his deportment, is always severe in his punishments; and is oftentimes so wantonly cruel as to deprive his subjects of their heads for very trifling offences. An information was this morning laid against a very respectable lad, who is nearly related to the king, if not actually his own son, for having purloined a piece of Manchester cotton from his sovereign. Death was instantly pronounced against the culprit after a confession of his crime, and the sentence was to have been carried into execution this evening; but he implored us, in English, in the most piteous manner, to intercede for his life, affirming, that if all the inhabitants of the town were to come forward in his behalf, their remonstrances and petitions would be unavailing, but that a white man's solicitation would be irresistible. At first we sent Pascoe to the chief, to express the obligation we should feel, if he would, on our account, pardon the delinquent, or at least commute his punishment to a severe flogging; but the stern judge was not to be moved from his purpose by a messenger; his answer was characteristic:—" Tell the white men," said he, " that a black man's request would be useless and vain, I would not grant him so considerable a favour; but if both, or either of them, will intercede in the boy's behalf, personally, and in a formal manner, I may perhaps be induced to forgive him." My brother accordingly took the hint, flattered the vanity of the chief by a per-

sonal application, and thus obtained the boy's pardon, and saved his life with little difficulty. The
gratitude of the youth was apparently sincere.

At five in the afternoon the people returned from
Bocquâ market, and the chief sent us word to be
ready for leaving Damuggoo to-morrow ev ning.
He continues to be very kind to us, and has allowed
us to want nothing which his village could supply.
His people had been very unsuccessful in obtaining
slaves, the demand for them having been so great
that a few only were to be had. Their chief object
had been to procure slaves, but they had also gone
for other purposes of trade.

Thursday, November 4th.—Our departure and future
fate have occupied the whole attention of the chief
and his pagan priests nearly all day. The fetísh
which has been already made has proved unfavourable, and in hopes of still finding some signs of a
propitious nature towards our proceeding to Bonny,
and also to ascertain whether or not we are to proceed on our voyage to-day, the chief and his priests
have been diligently employed in consulting the en-
trails of fowls, but to both of these the omens were
pronounced to be very inauspicious. Our determination of departing, however, was not to be shaken
by such means. By the chief's own arrangement
our people were to embark in the leaky canoe, with
the heaviest of the luggage; whereas my brother
and I were to travel in one of his own canoes, and
to take along with us whatever was of most consequence. To this regulation we could raise no plausible objection, because our old canoe had been partially repaired.

A little after four in the afternoon we conveyed
our luggage to the river-side, and proceeded to load
our canoes. Long before five o'clock, every thing,
on our parts, had been got in readiness for quitting
the town, and we sat in the canoe till after sunset,
waiting the arrival of the boatmen, who did not seem

at all disposed to hurry themselves in making their appearance. We began at length to be wearied with anxiety, and impatient to be stirring. Hundreds of people had been gazing at us for a long while, many of whom had taken the pains to come from different parts of the town in boats for that purpose, and the curiosity of all having been amply indulged, they were moving off in all directions, so that we were almost deserted. The chief could not be spoken with, because he was engaged in a religious rite with his priests, and we were left for awhile to our own reflections, which were far from being of the kindest nature.

At length, when our uneasiness was at its height, we saw him coming towards us with a train of followers. The mallam and all his principal people were with him, bringing numerous jars of palm wine. A mat was spread near the water-side, whereon the chief sat himself, and we were instantly desired to place ourselves one on each side of his person. The palm wine and some rum were then produced; and as we were about to take a long farewell of our hospitable host, we drank of his offering, rather than give offence by a refusal. The palm wine circulated freely in the bowls, and the natives of the village, who witnessed all our proceedings with no little anxiety, seemed to be greatly delighted at seeing their chief and the priests so familiar with white men. Meanwhile several elephants' tusks, and a number of slaves and goats, were put into the canoe as presents to the chief of Bonny. A fatted goat was given us as a parting gift, and a small decanter of rum was thrust in my brother's bosom as a cordial during the night. We drank and chatted away until half-past six in the evening, when we sent Pascoe on before us in charge of our old canoe, telling him that we should soon overtake him.

To our great mortification, we were unable to follow him till eight in the evening, being detained by another fetish ceremony. The Mohammedan priest then gave us the dimensions and shape of a large mirror, a handsome sword, and other articles, which he begged of us to procure for him in England; and then we arose to take our leave of the king, expressing our acknowledgments to him with sincerity and heartiness for the cordial and generous reception we had met with. Our own canoe and people had departed long before, and it was dark when we jumped into the chief's canoe, which was waiting for us, and launched out into the stream. We lay off at a short distance from the bank, when all the fetish people walked knee-deep into the river, and muttered a long prayer, after which they splashed the water towards our canoe with each foot, and we proceeded on. Damuggoo is a long straggling town, and is formed indeed by a collection of villages, which are scattered along the western bank. Touching at one of these, which is rather remote from the starting-place, a number of individuals leaped from the shore into the water, by the side of our canoe, and began pattering about, in order to appease the anger of their deities, and ensure us a favourable voyage.

The natives do every thing by halves; on arriving at the village, it was found that we had not taken a sufficient number of canoe-men for the occasion; and they loitered about the place, bawling for assistance till they were joined by two companions. Every time the canoe stopped for any purpose, the canoe-men muttered some sentences in a low tone to the fetish, invoking the aid of their deity towards a safe passage. All having got into the canoe, we glided down the stream with delightful rapidity, without stopping anywhere, or meeting with further hinderances till midnight. The canoe-men entertained us with their native songs, keeping time with their paddies, and every thing contributed to render the passage pleasant, had we not been uneasy at our canoe with Pascoe being so far before us, without any messenger or guide. This made me determine not to send him on again without either my brother or self accompanying him.

We are inclined to attribute the good reception we met with from the chief of Damuggoo entirely to the influence of the mallam. It is the character of the Nouffie people to speak in good terms of us wherever we have met with them, and it was no doubt the representation of this old man that operated so powerfully in our favour with the chief. We regretted very much that we had nothing better to give him than a few needles for his services to us during our stay, as he had been our interpreter on all occasions.

Friday, November 5th.—We continued on our way down the river until two in the morning, when we arrived at a halting-place, near a considerable village, the name of which we could not ascertain. Here our people landed to repose awhile under the branches of trees, and await the coming of our own canoe, which we had not seen during the night. Our lodgings were very far from agreeable; we were crammed comparatively, into a small canoe, with a dozen people as companions, besides a number of goats, and six slaves, consisting of three women, two men, and a pretty little boy. Neither of these slaves seem to bestow a moment's regret on leaving their native country, though they know they are to be sold on the coast, and conveyed to a foreign and distant land, if we may except a troublesome female, who screamed by starts during the night; but her sorrow was evidently assumed, her object being to disturb her associates in misfortune, and give trouble to her keepers, rather than to give vent to her own feelings. The noise of this unsociable companion was silenced occasionally by a few hearty cuffs on the head by one of the canoe-men. It was impossible for the slaves to lie down, so they sat in the bottom of the canoe, with the goats, and there they slept soundly, though the water which was admitted into the canoe was continually washing and splashing against their naked sides.   The little boy above mentioned is intended as a present from the chief of Damuggoo to the king of Bonny; he is not placed on a similar footing to his companions, but is treated with tenderness.   The men and women slaves are fettered in the day-time, but their irons are taken off at night.   These have been all free people ; but having been found guilty of minor offences at Damuggoo, they are sentenced to perpetual slavery and banishment.

A market is to be held to-morrow in the village near which we are stopping, and several large canoes filled with people and goods are lying alongside of us, for their owners to commence trafficking as soon as the morning shall dawn.   Others are constantly arriving from various quarters for the same purpose, so that we are now (four in the morning) surrounded by a large squadron of native canoes.   Ours, with Pascoe and his companions, has just entered the creek.   It is a heavy and clumsy vessel, and therefore greatly inferior to the light canoes of the natives. Pascoe told us he had hailed a great many canoes thinking they were ours, and we were so much pleased that he had not been stopped, that we entertained a very good opinion of these people.

The river has run in a westerly and south-westerly direction to-day, with many windings.   The breadth has varied from one to three or four miles, and the current has run very rapidly.   The banks were low and swampy, and covered with a thick underwood interspersed with palm trees.

We endeavoured to obtain a little rest, but found it quite impossible, and at five in the morning we arose wearied and fatigued.   The heavy dew which had fallen wetted us completely through.   At sunrise I joined our people in the old canoe, which contained the whole of our luggage, for the purpose of encouraging them to greater exertion, otherwise they would not keep up with the men of Damuggoo, and might loiter behind and lose themselves; and as my brother's canoe could easily overtake me, I proceeded onward at five A. M., leaving him behind with the other.

The village is famous for palm-oil, which it produces in abundance, and the buyers of that commodity were exceedingly numerous. The bank was lined with many hundreds of people whose curiosity to see a white man was irresistible; so that in order to prevent unpleasant consequences after I had left them, my brother's canoe-men, who had been engaged in purchasing provisions, pushed off the shore between seven and eight in the morning, and continued down the river, following my track.

I had left one trunk and one medicine-chest in my brother's canoe, and a couple of muskets, in case he might want them, and being very anxious to get down the river had started without breakfast, at which my people were very much dissatisfied. They complained of being tired very soon, and asked for their breakfast. I cheered them up all I could with the hopes of getting them on further before we stopped; and, taking the paddle myself, I set them the example in using it, at the same time singing "Rule Britannia" to them, and telling them that in six or seven days we should reach the sea, when I would reward them all well. This had the desired effect, and although I could not but think that the poor fellows complained very justly, we continued on very pleasantly.

At six A. M. we were passing rather close to a point in the river, round which it takes an abrupt turn, and the current being very rapid we were carried into an eddy before we were aware of it. It was with considerable difficulty that we got clear of it, but had we been two yards nearer to the shore our canoe would have been dashed into pieces. These dangers will always be avoided by the pre-

caution of keeping in the middle of the river. At
seven A. M. we saw a small river enter the Niger
from the eastward, the banks of which, as well as
those of the Niger, were elevated and fertile. Shortly
after we observed a branch of the river running off
to the westward, about the same size as that from
the eastward. On the right bank of this river,
close also to the bank of the Niger, we observed a
large market, which I was informed is Kirree; and
that the river, flowing to the westward past it, runs
to Benin. A great number of canoes were lying
near the bank. They appeared to be very large, and
had flags flying on long bamboo canes. We took
no notice of them, but passed on, and in a short
time afterward we saw about fifty canoes before us,
coming up the river. They appeared to be very
large and full of men, and the appearance of them
at a distance was very pleasing. They had each
three long bamboo canes, with flags flying from
them, one fixed at each end of the canoe, and the
other in the middle. As we approached each other
I observed the British Union flag in several, while
others, which were white, had figures on them of
a man's leg, chairs, tables, decanters, glasses, and all
kinds of such devices. The people in them, who
were very numerous, were dressed in European
clothing, with the exception of trousers.

I felt quite overjoyed by the sight of these people,
more particularly so when I saw our flag and European apparel among them, and congratulated myself
that they were from the seacoast. But all my fond
anticipations vanished in a moment as the first canoe
met us. A great stout fellow, of a most forbidding
countenance, beckoned to me to come to him, but
seeing him and all his people so well armed I was
not much inclined to trust myself among them, and
paid no attention to him. The next moment I heard
the sound of a drum, and in an instant several men
mounted a platform and levelled their muskets at

us.   There was nothing to be done now but to obey
as for running away it was out of the question, our
square loaded canoe was incapable of it; and to fight
with fifty war canoes, for such we found them, containing each above forty people, most of whom were
as well armed as ourselves, would have been throwing away my own and my canoe-men's lives very
foolishly.   In addition to the muskets, each canoe
had a long gun in its bow that would carry a shot
of four or six pounds, besides being provided with
a good stock of swords and boarding-pikes.

By this time our canoes were side by side, and
with astonishing rapidity our luggage found its way
into those of our opponents.   This mode of proceeding I did not relish at all; so as my gun was loaded
with two balls and four slugs, I took deliberate aim
at the leader, and he would have paid for his temerity
with his life in one moment more, had not three of
his people sprung on me and forced the gun from
my hands.   My jacket and shoes were as quickly
plundered from me, and observing some other fellows at the same time taking away Pascoe's wife, I
lost all command over myself, and was determined
to sell my life as dearly as I could.   I encouraged
my men to arm themselves with their paddles and
defend themselves to the last.   I instantly seized
hold of Pascoe's wife, and with the assistance of
another of my men dragged her from the fellow's
grasp; Pascoe at the same time levelled a blow at
his head with one of our iron-wood paddles that
sent him reeling backwards, and we saw him no
more.

Our canoe having been so completely relieved of
her cargo, which had consisted only of our luggage,
we had plenty of room in her for battle, and being
each of us provided with a paddle, we determined,
as we had got clear of our adversary, to cut down
the first fellow who should dare to board us.   This
was not attempted; and as none of the other canoes

had offered to interfere, I was in hopes of finding
some friends among them, but at all events was determined to follow the people who had plundered us
to the market, where they seemed to be going. We
accordingly pulled after them as fast as we could.
My men, now that the fray was over, began to think
of their forlorn condition. All their things were
gone, and as they gave up all hopes of regaining
them, or being able to revenge themselves on the
robbers, they gave vent to their rage in tears and
execrations. I desired them to be quiet, and endeavoured all in my power to pacify them by telling
them that if we were spared to reach the sea in
safety, I would pay them for every thing they had
lost.

We were following the canoe that had attacked us
as fast as we possibly could to regain our things, if
possible, when some people hailed us from a large
canoe, which I found afterward belonged to the
New Calebar river. One of the people, who was
apparently a person of consequence, called out lustily
to me, " Holloa, white man, you French, you English?"—"Yes, English," I answered him immediately.
"Come here in my canoe," he said, and our two canoes
approached each other rapidly. I accordingly got
into his canoe, and he put three of his men into mine
to assist in pulling her to the market. The people
of the canoe treated me with much kindness, and
the chief of her who had hailed me gave me a glass
of rum. There were several females also in the
canoe, who appeared to take a great deal of interest
in my safety.

On looking around me I now observed my brother
coming towards us in the Damuggoo canoe, and the
same villain who had plundered me was the first to
pursue him. As we had been absent from each other
all the morning, and the foregoing transactions only
relate to myself, the following narrative of my bro
ther's will give the reader an account of his proceed

ings to the time I saw him, and the disaster which soon after followed.

"My brother left the village nearly two hours before me, and therefore he was far in advance when the Damuggoo canoe, in which I had remained, was pushed off the land. Wishing to overtake him, for he had no guide, the men exerted themselves wonderfully to make amends for the time which they had trifled away, and it was really astonishing to see the rapidity with which the canoe was impelled through the water.

• "The morning was cool, serene, and delightful, and the sun had just emerged from a mass of dense clouds, which were fringed with a silvery light. On each side of the river, gentle and undulating hills rose one behind the other, covered with verdure, and here and there varied by groves of dark green trees, which served to render the prospect yet more agreeable. The smooth, transparent surface of the river, disturbed only by the motions of our paddles, so calm, so peaceful in its gentle course, reflected with unerring truth the enchanting landscape from either side, and lent its friendly aid to hasten us to our long-wished-for destination.

"After we had been in the canoe perhaps an hour, one of the men who happened to be standing in the bow fancied that he could descry, in another canoe, then at a considerable distance before us, a sheep and goat which my brother had taken away with him in the morning. All doubt as to the identity of the animals having been removed from his own mind and those of his companions,—though for my own part I must own that my vision was not near keen enough to allow me to agree with them in opinion, —we gave chase to the suspected canoe. The men summoned all their resolution and strength to the task, and, like an arrow from a bow, our narrow vessel darted through the water. We gained rapidly on the chase, and the people, perceiving our object

II.—P

and mistrusting our intentions, kept near the shore, and laboured hard to get away from us. They then entered a branch of the river which was running to the south-west, and sheltered themselves among a number of canoes that were lying alongside a large market-place, situated on the right bank.

"This did not damp the spirit of our men, or deter them from following the pursued: we succeeded in discovering their hiding-place; and at length, after much wrangling and many threats, the robbers (for such they proved to be) were compelled to restore the animals. But how my brother could have suf- fered two men to plunder his canoe puzzled me exceedingly, and I was totally at a loss to account for it. Nothing could exceed my surprise, on ap- proaching the market, to observe, as I thought, large European flags, affixed to poles, and waving over almost every canoe that was there. On a closer examination I discovered them to be imitations only, though they were executed with uncommon skill and neatness. British colours apparently were the most prevalent, and among these the Union flag seemed to be the general favourite. Nor did my former sur- prise diminish in the least when I landed, on finding that the market-people were clad in European appa- rel, though, with the odd fancy which is remarkable among Indians who have any intercourse with Europeans, none of them were dressed in a com- plete suit of clothes. One wore a hat only, with a Manchester cotton, tied round his waist, another a shirt, another a jacket, &c. As all natives, with the exception of kings, are forbidden by law to wear trousers, a common pocket handkerchief was gene- rally substituted for that article of dress. The multitude formed the most motley group that we have ever seen; nothing on earth could be more grotesque or ridiculous. Many of the men had a smattering of the English and French tongues.

"The object for which we had stopped at the

market having been effected to our satisfaction, we pulled out again into the main body of the river, and here we saw several canoes of amazing size coming towards us from the southward. Totally unsuspicious of danger of any kind from this quarter, astonishment at such a sight was the only emotion that entered my mind; and we resolved to pass in the midst of these canoes, that we might more con veniently look on each side of us, for the purpose of ascertaining whether they contained any thing be· longing to us. At the next moment another *squadron* of the same description of vessels came in sight, in one of which I could discover my brother by his white shirt, and I fancied that he was returning to demand restitution of the animals of which he had been plundered, therefore I still felt perfectly easy in my mind.

"When we drew nearer, it was apparent that these were all war-canoes, of prodigious dimensions; immense flags of various colours were displayed in them, a six-pounder was lashed to the bow of each; and they were filled with women, and children, and armed men, whose weapons were in their hands. Such was their size, that each of them was paddled by nearly forty people. In pursuance of our arrangement, we passed through the midst of them, but could see nothing; and we had advanced a few yards, when on looking behind us, we discovered that the war-canoes had been turned round, and were swiftly pursuing us. Appearances were hostile; the apprehension of danger suddenly flashed across my mind; we endeavoured and struggled hard to escape; but fear had taken possession of the minds of my companions, and as they were unable to exert themselves we did not get on: all was vain Our canoe was overtaken in a moment, and nearly sent under water by the violence with which her pursuer dashed against her; a second crash threw two or three of the Damuggoo people overboard,

and by the shock of the third she capsized and sunk,
All this seemed the work of enchantment, so quickly
did events succeed each other; yet, in this interval,
a couple of ill-looking fellows had jumped into our
canoe, and in the confusion which prevailed, began
emptying it of its contents with astonishing celerity.

" On finding myself in the water, my first care was,
very naturally, to get out again; and therefore looking
round on a hundred ruffians, in whose countenances I
could discern not a single trace of gentleness or pity,
I swam to a large canoe, apart from the others, in
which I observed two females and some little ones, .
—for in their breasts, thought I, compassion and
tenderness must surely dwell. Perceiving my design,
a sturdy man of gigantic stature, such as little children dream of, black as a coal, and with a most
hideous countenance, suddenly sprang towards me,
and stooping down, he laid hold of my arm, and
snatched me with a violent jerk out of the water,
letting me fall like a log into the canoe, without
speaking a word.

"I soon recovered, and sat up with my companions,
the women and children, and discovered them wiping
tears from their faces.   In momentary expectation
of a barbarous and painful death, ' for what else,'
said I to myself, ' can all this lead to ?' the scene
around me produced little impression upon my mind ;
my thoughts were wandering far away, and this day
I thought was to be my last.   I was meditating in
this manner, heedless of all that was going on around
me, and reckless of what came next, when I looked
up and saw my brother at a little distance, gazing
steadfastly upon me ; when he saw that I observed
him, he held up his arm with a sorrowful look, and
pointed his finger to the skies.   O ! how distinctly
and eloquently were all the emotions of his soul at
that moment depicted in his countenance !   Who
could not understand him ?   He would have said,

Trust in God!' I was touched with grief. Thoughts of home and friends rushed upon my mind, and almost overpowered me. My heart hovered over the scenes of infancy and boyhood. O how vividly did early impressions return to my soul! But such feelings could be indulged only for a moment. Recollecting myself, I bade them, as I thought, an everlasting adieu; and weaning my heart and thoughts from all worldly associations, with fervour I invoked the God of my life, before whose awful throne I imagined we should shortly appear, for fortitude and consolation in the hour of trial. My heart became subdued and softened; my mind regained its serenity and composure; and though there was nothing but tumult and distraction without, within all was tranquillity and resignation.

"On account of the eagerness and anxiety with which every one endeavoured to get near us in order to share the expected plunder, and the confusion which prevailed in consequence, many of the war canoes clashed against each other with such violence, that three or four of them were upset at one time, and the scene which ensued baffles all description. Men, women, and children, clinging to their floating property, were struggling in the river, and screaming and crying out as loud as they were able, to be saved from drowning. Those that were more fortunate were beating their countrymen off from getting into their canoes, by striking their heads and hands with paddles, as they laid hold of the sides and nearly upset them. When the noise and disorder had in some measure ceased, my brother's canoe and that which I was in were by the side of each other, and he instantly took his shirt from his back and threw it over me, for I was naked. I then stepped into his canoe; for, whatever might be our fate, it would be a mournful kind of pleasure to comfort and console one another in the hour of trial and suffering. But I had no sooner done so, than I was dragged back again by a powerful arm, which I could not resist, and commanded by furious gestures to sit still on my peril.

"Unwilling to aggravate our condition by obstinacy or bravado, which would have been vain and ridiculous, I made no reply, but did as I was desired, and silently watched the motions of our keepers. Now there were still other canoes passing by on their way to the market-place, and among them was one of extraordinary size. Fancying it to be neutral, and hoping to make a diversion in our favour, I beckoned to those who were in it, and saluted them in the most friendly manner. But their savage bosoms were impenetrable to feeling. Surely they are destitute of all the amiable charities of life. I almost doubted whether they were human beings. Their hideous features were darkened by a terrible scowl; they mocked me, clapped their hands, and thumped upon a sullen drum; then with a loud and scornful laugh, the barbarians dashed their paddles into the water and went their way. This was a severe mortification; I felt confused and abashed; and my heart seemed to shrink within itself. I made no more such trials."

Seeing my brother swimming in the river, and people clinging on to what they could, I endeavoured all in my power to induce the people of my canoe to go to him. But all I could do was in vain. Fearing that those in the water might upset the canoe by getting into her, or that she would be overloaded with them, they kept aloof and let them take their chance. My feelings at that moment were not to be described; I saw my brother nearly exhausted, and could render him no assistance, in addition to our luggage being plundered and sunk; and I had just formed the resolution of jumping into the water after him when I saw him picked up.

The canoes near me, as well as mine, hastened to a small sand island in the river, at a short distance from the market, and my brother arrived soon afterward. In a short time the Damuggoo people made their appearance, and also the Chief of Bonny's messenger, having like ourselves lost every thing they had of their own property as well as their master's. This was in consequence of the confusion which had taken place; for these people, no doubt, had they been recognised, would not have been molested. We were all obliged to remain in our respective canoes, and made rather a sorry appearance in consequence of the treatment we had received, which was increased by the tears and lamentations of our own canoe-men, as well as those of Damuggoo, and neither my brother nor myself were in a condition to offer them any consolation.

We had been laying at the island; but now the war-canoes were all formed into a line and paddled into the market-place before alluded to, which is called *Kirree*, and which likewise was the place of their destination. Here we were informed that a *palàver* would be held, to take the whole affair into consideration; and about ten in the morning a multitude of men landed from the canoes, to " hold a council of war," if it may be so termed. For our parts we were not suffered to go on shore; but constrained to remain in the canoes, without a covering for the head, and exposed to the heat of a burning sun. A person in a Mohammedan dress, who we learned afterward was a native of a place near Funda, came to us, and endeavoured to cheer us, by saying that our hearts must not be sore,—that at the palàver which would be held, we had plenty of friends to speak for us. That all the people in the Mohammedan dresses who had come from Funda to attend the market were our friends, besides a great number of females who were well dressed in silk of different colours. These women wore large ivory anklets of about four or five pounds weight, and bracelets of the same material, but not so

large. About twenty canoes full of Damuggoo
people had arrived from the various towns near Damuggoo. These persons, having heard how we had
been treated, also became our friends, so that we
now began to think there was a chance of our escaping, and this intelligence put us into better spirits.

A short time before noon, the river being pretty
clear, several guns were fired as a signal for all the
canoes to repair to the market and attend the palàver. Eager to learn the result of the discussion
at the assembly, in which we were so intimately
concerned, but without the means of gaining any
intelligence, we passed the hours in fearful suspense,
yielding by turns to the pleasing illusions of hope,
and the gloomy forebodings of despair.

The heat of the sun, to which we were exposed,
was excessive, and having no shirt on even to protect my shoulders from the scorching rays, I con-
trived to borrow an old cloth from one of the canoe-
men, who spoke a little English. Some of the
market-women came down to our canoe, and looked
on us with much concern and pity, spreading their
hands out, as much as to say, God has saved you
from a cruel death. They then retired, and in a
few minutes afterward returned, bringing with them
a bunch of plantains and two cocoanuts. This was
an acceptable offering, and we gladly took it and
divided it among our people and ourselves.

A stir was now made in the market, and a search
commenced through all the canoes for our goods,
some of which were found, although the greater
part of them were at the bottom of the river. These
were landed and placed in the middle of the market-
place. We were now invited by the mallams to
land, and told to look at our goods and see if they
were all there. To my great satisfaction I imme
diately recognised the box containing our books,
and one of my brother's journals. The medicine-
chest was by its side, but both were filled with

water. A large carpet bag, containing all our wearing apparel, was lying cut open, and deprived of its contents, with the exception of a shirt, a pair of trousers, and a waistcoat. Many valuable articles which it had contained were gone. The whole of my journal, with the exception of a note-book with remarks from Rabba to this place, was lost. Four guns, one of which had been the property of the late Mr. Park, four cutlasses, and two pistols were gone. Nine elephant's tusks, the finest I had seen in the country, which had been given me by the Kings of Wowow and Boossà, a quantity of ostrich feathers, some handsome leopard-skins, a great variety of seeds, all our buttons, cowries, and needles, which were necessary for us to purchase provisions with,—all were missing, and said to have been sunk in the river. The two boxes and the bag were all that could be found.

We had been desired to seat ourselves, which, as soon as we had done, a circle gathered round us, and began questioning us; but at that moment the sound of screams and the clashing of arms reached the spot; and the multitude, catching fire at the noise, drew their swords, and leaving us to ourselves they ran away to the place whence it proceeded. The poor women were hurrying with their little property towards the river from all directions, and imagining that we ourselves might be trampled under foot, were we to remain longer sitting on the ground, we joined the flying fugitives, and all rushing into the water, sprang into canoes, and pushed off the land, whither our pursuers dared not follow us. The origin of all this was a desire for more plunder on the part of the Eboe people. Seeing the few things of ours in the market-place which had been taken from their canoes, they made a rush to the place to recover them. The natives, who were Kirree people, stood ready for them, armed with swords, daggers, and guns; and the savage Eboes,

finding themselves foiled in the attempt, retreated
to their canoes without risking an attack, although
we fully expected to have been spectators of a
furious and bloody battle. The noise and uproar
which this produced were dreadful, and beyond all
description.

This after all was a fortunate circumstance, inasmuch as my brother and I, having unconsciously
jumped into the same canoe, found ourselves in each
other's company, and were thus afforded, for a
short time at least, the pleasure of conversing without interruption; and he then related to me all that
had happened to him since the morning. Like me,
he had no foresight of mischief, or apprehensions
of danger, and therefore he took no means whatever
of shunning the immense canoes which he perceived
were approaching him with their large flags. But,
on the contrary, these striking and uncommon ap-
pendages, to which neither of us had been accustomed, served to excite his curiosity and win his
admiration rather than awaken any fear or suspicion
of danger.

The palàver not having yet concluded, we had
full leisure to contemplate the scene around us.
We had moored a little way from the banks of the
river: in front of us was the market-place, which
was crammed with people, from all parts of the
neighbouring country, of different tribes,—a great
multitude of wild men, of ferocious aspect, and
savage uncouth manners. To these belonged the
choice, either of giving us life and liberty, or doom-
ing us to slavery and death. In the latter determination their minds might be swayed by suspicion
or caprice, or influenced by hatred; in the former
they might be guided by the hopes of gain, or biassed
by the fears of punishment,—for many of them had
come from the seacoast, and such an adventure as
ours could not long remain concealed from the
knowledge of our countrymen. The shore for a

long way was lined with their canoes, having the colours of various European nations waving from long poles, which were fastened to the seats. Several of these had as many as three flags in each; they were all of immense size, and fringed with blue cotton (baft) cut into scallops. Besides these there were others of the strangest and most grotesque patterns, such as representations of wild beasts, men's legs, wine glasses, decanters, and things of still more whimsical shapes. Whence the barbarians procured these emblematical banners we cannot tell; but we understand that each tribe has its own peculiar flags, which are unfurled whenever they undertake any enterprise of importance. Canoes were likewise stationed near an island or sandbank in the middle of the river, which we considered to be neutral, as their owners did not seem to interfere with the proceedings of the day. But there happened to be among the savages a few well-dressed Mohammedan priests, who had come late to the market from the northward. These were decidedly our friends. Many times they blessed us with uplifted hands and compassionate countenances, exclaiming " *Alla Sullikee !*" (God is King !) Nor did they confine themselves to simple expressions of pity or concern; but, as we subsequently learned, they joined the assembly, and spoke in our favour with warmth and energy, taxing those who had assaulted us with cowardice, cruelty, and wrong, and proposing to have them beheaded on the spot as a just punishment for their crime. This was bold language, but it produced a salutary effect on the minds of the hearers.

The women and children took charge of the canoes while their husbands and fathers were on shore. From the former we received little presents of bananas and cocoanuts, which were our only food during the day, but with the latter we had little communication. Both men and women wore immensely-large ivory rings on their legs and arms, which were at least an inch in thickness, and six inches in depth; and these ornaments were so heavy and inconvenient, that when the females walked, they appeared the most awkward and ungraceful creatures in the world; in fact they could not walk without producing a collision of these unwieldly rings. The women's necks and bosoms were likewise decorated with strings of coral and other beads, but their dress was confined to a piece of figured cotton, encircling the waists and extending halfway down the leg.

At about three in the afternoon we were ordered to return to the small island from whence we had come, and the setting of the sun being the signal for the council to dissolve, we were again sent for to the market. The people had been engaged in deliberation and discussion during the whole of the day, and with throbbing hearts we received their resolution in nearly the following words :—" That the king of the country being absent, they had taken upon themselves to consider the occurrence which had taken place in the morning, and to give judgment accordingly. Those of our things which had been saved from the water should be restored to us, and the person that had first commenced the attack on my brother should lose his head, as a just retribution for his offence, having acted without his chief's permission; that with regard to us, we must consider ourselves as prisoners, and consent to be conducted on the following morning to *Obie*, king of the *Eboe* country, before whom we should undergo an examination, and whose will and pleasure concerning our persons would then be explained." We received the intelligence with feelings of rapture, and with bursting hearts we offered up thanks to our Divine Creator for his signal preservation of us throughout this disastrous day.

It was, perhaps, fortunate for us that we had no article of value which the natives were at all solicit-

ous about; and to this circumstance, added to the
envy of those who had joined in the conquest, but
who had not shared the plunder, may chiefly be attributed, under Providence, the preservation of our
lives.   Our medicine-chest, and a trunk containing
books, &c., which were all spoiled by the water,
were subsequently restored to us; but our wearing
apparel, Mr. Park's double-barrelled gun, the loss of
which we particularly regretted, and all our muskets,
swords, and pistols, with those of our men, were
sunk or missing.   We likewise lost the elephant's
teeth given us by the kings of Boossà and Wowow,
a few natural curiosities, our compass and thermom-
eters, my own journal, my brother's memorandum,
note, and sketch-books, with a small part of his journal
and other books which were open in the canoe, besides all our cowries and needles, so that we are left
completely destitute, to the mercy of we know not
whom.   –

The object of the barbarians in coming so far from
home was never correctly explained to us; but we
have no doubt that it was from motives of punder,
which had our party been larger was to have been
carried into effect on an extensive scale.   But the
capture of two white men, supposed to have valuable
goods with them, seems to have disconcerted all
their plans for the present by producing division and
distrust among them.   However, it was apparent to
us that all these savage warriors had left their country
not only to plunder whatever might happen to fall in
their way, but likewise to attend two or three markets
near *Kirree*, for the purpose of trading with the natives whenever they might fancy themselves not sufficiently powerful to take away their property without fighting and bloodshed.   For this purpose they
were amply furnished with various commodities,
such as powder, muskets, cutlasses, knives, cotton
cloths, earthenware, skins of wild animals, mats,
sweet potatoes. cassada root, and a very large kind

of straw hat which they would exchange for slaves,
ivory, yams, and palm-oil. It was evident also at
Kirree that more than one party of these robbers
had made several attempts at plunder, and it was
equally notorious that they had been many times re-
pulsed. Hence the dreadful screaming at the market,
and the state of hurry, tumult, and alarm that prevailed therein during the whole of the day.

In the evening, when every thing was quiet, fires
were kindled in all the canoes for dressing provisions, and there being a vast number of them, the
Niger was illuminated by streams of yellow light,
which produced a highly romantic but melancholy
effect. It was a time fitted for adoration and thanksgiving to the beneficent Creator and Monarch of all.
But, alas! how few hereabouts are bending the knee
to him; how few are lifting up their hearts to his
mercy-seat!

The Kirree people are a savage-looking race.
They are amazingly strong and athletic, and are also
well-proportioned. Their only clothing is the skin
either of a leopard or tiger fastened round their
waist. Their hair is plaited, and plastered with red
clay in abundance, and their face is full of incisions
in every part of it; these are cut into the flesh so as
to produce deep furrows, each incision being about a
quarter of an inch long, and died with indigo. It is
scarcely possible to make out a feature of their face,
and I have never seen Indians more disfigured. The
Eboe women have handsome features, and we could
not help thinking it a pity that such savage-looking
fellows as the men should be blessed with so handsome a race of females. The mark of the Eboe
people is the point of an arrow pricked in each temple, the end being next to the eye. We are informed
that the leading man, who commanded the first
canoe that attacked us in the river this morning, is
confined in double irons, and condemned to die by
the people who are friends at this place. It is said

they have taken our treatment up with so much determination to do us justice, that if the king of Eboe, whose subject he is, refuses to put him to death, no more of his canoes will be allowed to come to this country to trade. His wives have been crying round him and making great lamentation.

About seven in the evening large heavy clouds, ascending from the horizon, covered the stars like a shroud; a total darkness prevailed, and we were presently visited by a storm, which generally follows a very sultry day; but although it was violent, it was short. The rain descended in torrents, the wind howled through the trees, and all the fires were extinguished in a moment. Our canoe was half filled with water, and ourselves completely drenched; but notwithstanding these inconveniencies and discouragements, we lay down as well as we could to sleep till morning, for nature was wearied out with a long day of anxiety and fatigue.

CHAPTER XIX.

Departure from Kirree—Method of Trading—Character of the Natives —An unhappy Slave—Superstitions of the Canoe-men respecting the Travellers—Stopped by Fog—Pass through a Lake—Arrival at Eboe Town—The King's Palace—Description of King Obie—Interview with him—The Eboe People—Trade of Eboe Town—Disputes of the Natives respecting the Travellers—Decision of King Obie respecting them—Their Disappointment—An Eboe Lady—Arrangements for leaving Eboe.

Saturday, November 6th.—My brother felt quite feverish this morning, and I was very unwell, yet we had nothing to eat, nor any thing to purchase it with. At sunrise our canoe was taken from before Kirree market-place, to the little sandbank or island in the middle of the river, where we waited till nine o'clock for the coming of two war-canoes which it had been resolved should convoy us to the Eboe country which we understand is situated three days' journey hence down the Niger. A head-man from one of them stepped into ours, though as it was we had scarcely room enough to move a limb. The sunken canoe had been got up again; the Damuggoo people had regained their slaves, having lost only cloth and ivory, for which they are told they will be recompensed by the king of the Eboe country on arriving there; so that this circumstance seemed to have revived their hopes a little, and to have inspired them with fresh life and spirits, which one could scarcely expect from individuals that had so recently been half drowned, beaten, and otherwise ill-used. Nevertheless, though our loss far exceeded theirs, we were as cheerful as they. Our minds had been relieved from a painful state of anxiety; we now looked forward to our journey down the river with the most pleasing anticipations; and even in our forlorn condition we profited by the lesson we had received, and rejoiced that our situation was no worse. Our thoughts were once more turned on home; we quickly resumed our former cheerfulness; the freshness of the morning gave us new vigour, and we ardently wished to set out.

At seven in the morning we bade adieu to Kirree, the scene of all our sorrows, accompanied by six large war-canoes, and again took our station with the Damuggoo people. The canoe once more darted along at a great rate, the men, as they applied their whole strength to their paddles, gave us a song of their country, which seemed to animate them to still greater exertion. Our minds were well prepared to enjoy it; and in no part of the country have we listened to a native song with so much pleasure and gratification.

At nine in the morning we passed two beautiful islands, not far from the place where we had been attacked. These were uninhabited and nearly in the middle of the river, which is about three miles broad. The direction of it seemed to be about south-west, or rather more westerly, but having lost our compass with the rest of our things yesterday, we are now quite at a loss for the direction of the river, and can only form an opinion from the place of the sun. At intervals of two or three miles we observed large towns and villages on the banks, which at a short distance from the river became high.   Our canoe people being afraid, I suppose, of the inhabitants, and perhaps being at war with them, would not go near them, although they were in want of yams.

At eleven A. M. the people laid in their paddles, and allowed the canoe to drift down the river, while they took their breakfast.

Besides our convoy, we had a *sumpter-canoe* in company, belonging to the Eboe people, from which the others were supplied with dressed provisions. For our own part, we had neither money nor needles, nor indeed any thing to purchase a meal; and knowing this to be the case, our sable guardians neglected to take into consideration the state of our stomachs. However, we felt no very strong inclination to join them in their repast, though on one occasion we were invited to do so, for we felt an invincible disgust to it, from the filthy manner in which it had been prepared.   Yams were first boiled, and then skinned and mashed into a paste, with the addition of a little water, by hands that were far from being clean.   As this part of the business requires great personal exertion, the man on whom it devolved perspired very copiously, and the consequences may easily be guessed at.   This was the reason for the unconquerable aversion we felt to partake of their food. The natives, however, are not equally squeamish about such trifles, and compassionate our want of taste in not relishing their savoury banquet.   With their yams they generally have a little fish, either smoked and dried, or fresh from the stream : but on

II.—Q

very particular occasions, instead of fish, a young kid, roasted with its skin and hair, is substituted. In eating, they use the fingers only, and every one dips his hand into the same dish. This custom is universal. It is the same among the Moors in Barbary, and the Arabs and Mohammedans in India, and perhaps in many other countries in the world.

Had it not been for the above filthy method of preparing their repast, we should not have hesitated in joining them, having eaten nothing either to-day or yesterday but a small piece of a banana. Half an hour was thus passed, when the men took their paddles again, and the canoes moved on at a swift rate. The river became more winding in its course, and the banks were covered with large trees which hung over the water.

At four in the afternoon we halted to purchase yams at a town on the bank of the river, which was nearly hid from our sight amid the trees and thick underwood. The canoes having reached the bank, five of the canoe-men landed well armed, and proceeded to the town. They had been absent an hour, when they again made their appearance, followed by a great many people carrying bundles. They were also accompanied by one old woman, who appeared to be a person of consequence. It appears that the natives in this part of the river are such outrageous and lawless fellows, that they are mistrustful of each other even in the smallest communication, and we had an opportunity of seeing how far this was carried.

The object of our visit was to purchase yams, and our people had succeeded in getting the villagers to bring some down to the canoes. These people, however, had armed themselves either with a gun or sword as well as our own, and had no women among them excepting the old one above mentioned. Having arrived at the bank of the river, the old woman directed all the yams to be placed in a row before

our people, and in distinct or separate bundles, and
the owners to retire to a short distance, which order
was implicitly obeyed. The purchaser now inspected
the bundles, and having selected one to his satisfaction, which might contain the finest yams, placed
what he considered to be its value by the side of it,
consisting of cloth, flints, &c. The old lady, looking
on all the time, if in her opinion it was sufficient to
give, takes up the cloth and gives it to the owner of
the bundle, and the purchaser likewise takes away
the yams. But on the contrary, if the cloth, or
whatever was thus offered by the purchaser, is not
considered sufficient by the old woman, she allows
it to remain a short time to give him an opportunity
of adding something else to his offer. If this were
not done, the owner of the yams was directed by
the old woman to take them and move them back
out of the way, leaving what had been offered for
them to be taken away also. All this was carried
on without a word passing between the parties, and
the purchase of a sufficient number of yams by our
people occupied three hours. It was something
quite novel to see two large parties of people bartering commodities in this manner; and the apparent
unconcern and determination with which the old
woman held out, when she considered the price
offered for the yams not sufficient, was quite amusing. She knew our men must have yams; and with
an ill grace they added any thing to what they had
already offered. The scene before us was altogether
extraordinary. Many of the people belonging to
the canoes were standing in a group on the bank of
the river near them with muskets, swords, and
spears in their hands; some with the articles with
which they were about to make a purchase. A
quantity of yams, arranged in large bundles, placed
in a row, separated them from another group, consisting of the villagers also armed, and both parties
standing at a short distance from them, leaving a

considerable space between. Here was stationed
the old woman, who, with no little consequence,
directed the whole affair by signs, either to her own
party or ours, not a word being spoken by any one.

We could not help thinking, that every thing, in
the largest market we have seen, might have been
disposed of in the time required for purchasing these
yams, and that only ten days' journey up the river
such a market would be found. This method of
trading must have arisen either from the fear of
quarrelling, or from not understanding each other's
language, which is difficult to suppose; but it seems
to have been instituted by mutual agreement, for
both parties quite understood how they were to act.
This is the first time we have witnessed it. The
villagers have a wild appearance; rather resembling
the Kirree people, but we observed no marks on the
face, nor on any part of the person. We did not
understand their language, and therefore could not
inform ourselves of the name of the people or their
village; and at seven in the evening again proceeded
on our journey.

It was ten at night when we came abreast of a
small town where we stopped. Instead of making the
canoes fast to the bank and landing, we lay out in
the river at a short distance from it, in case of an
alarm by strange canoes. It was long since we had
tasted food, and we had suffered from hunger the
whole day without being able to obtain any thing.
Soon after we had stopped for the night, our guards
gave us each a piece of roasted yam, and our poor
people had the good fortune to get some also, being
the first they have had since leaving Damuggoo.
The roasted yam, washed down with a little water
was to us as joyful a meal as if we had been treated
with the most sumptuous fare, and we laid ourselves
down in the canoe to sleep in content.

The course of the river, according to the best of
our judgment, has been about south-west

Sunday, November 7th.—At the dawn of day, our canoe-men were busily employed in making preparations for departure. We had been unable to get much sleep, from having nothing to protect us from the cold and the heavy dew, which had wetted us completely through. The morning was calm, and beautifully fine; and the clear, shrill whistle of the cheerful parrot echoed through the woods, breaking the stillness which had prevailed around, as we took a hasty leave of the few villagers who had assembled out of curiosity to see us, and pursued our course down the stream. The banks of the river have altered decidedly within these two days; its course is not so serpentine as it has been; the banks are so low and regular, that not even a simple rising can anywhere be distinguished to break their uniformity; and, for the first time, we have seen the fibrous mangrove interspersed among the other trees of the forest. Indeed they are beginning to present a degree of sameness little different from that which prevails on many parts of the seacoast. Both banks, however, are pretty thickly inhabited, and villages are scattered every here and there; for though they are embosomed in trees, and invisible from the river, yet their situation might easily be known from the number of their inhabitants which appeared on the beach to trade with the canoe-men. Plantains, bananas, and yams are cultivated by these villagers to an almost incredible extent. They form, in fact, with the addition of the fish which they may happen to catch, their sole support, and the only articles of export. Many of them, though poor and wretched, are mild, and even timorous in their manners, and are said to be honest and upright in their dealings; but others again are bold, cruel, and rapacious, and are dreaded and shunned not only by their neighbours, but also by those whom business may lead this way, unless they go in large, strong, and well-armed parties. Ours was certainly one of this description; yet men were constantly appointed to keep a watchful eye on the bank, when we were compelled to pass it close, by keeping the channel, in order to guard against surprise by an ambuscade. For this purpose, two or three men stood up in the canoe for several hours at a time, with a musket and cutlass in each hand, to intimidate the natives, by convincing them that we were fully prepared for an attack. The singular method of trading we had witnessed yesterday, or something similar to it, was formerly in use, we believe, between natives and Europeans on various parts of the seacoast; and if we are not mistaken, the same custom is observed to this day, not only in Africa, but in many other parts of the globe likewise.

Among the Damuggoo slaves is a middle-aged, short, fat woman, having a broad, mournful kind of countenance; in fact, there were two of them, so very much alike in all respects, that they might be taken for sisters. As she sat with the goats, whose society, by-the-by, was extremely disagreeable to her, inasmuch as they committed various misdemeanours, to her great annoyance, she fetched one of the deepest and most dismal sighs that I ever heard. This attracted my attention, for she was seated so near me, that from the motion of the canoe, I was not unfrequently jostled against her naked person, which was by no means agreeable, for she was a dirty woman. She had been slowly masticating, with apparent disrelish, part of a boiled yam, which appeared to be cold and dry, and which was now laid aside. She was in deep meditation; tear-drops were in her eyes, ready to fall as she gazed earnestly at a spot of land on the eastern bank, which was fast receding from her view. Her closed lips, slightly upturned, and quivering with emotion, the usual prelude to more violent grief, gave an expression of sadness and silent sorrow to her countenance, which language can but ill express. Nothing could be more touching than this tranquil face of wo. Loud bursts of lamentation, and other vehement expressions of passion, would not be half so eloquent. I imagined that the poor creature was bewailing her hard fate in the ill-usage which she had received from her guardians, one of whom had not long before applied a paddle to her head and shoulders; or she might, I thought, be in want of water, which was beyond her reach; but to satisfy my doubts, I addressed her, and demanded the cause of her emotion. On this she turned round her head, and bestowing a violent thump on the nose of a goat which had discovered her broken yam, and was nibbling it fast away, she replied, pointing with her finger to the spot on which she had been so anxiously gazing, —" *There I was born.*" The chord was touched; she had striven to repress her feelings before, but she could no longer command them; she became more agitated, and wept bitterly as she faltered out, " *That is my country!*" I was softened and moved at the woman's distress, and should doubtless have felt still stronger compassion, if I had not observed her, in the midst of her tears, inflicting the most rigorous chastisement on her brute companions, in the most unmerciful manner. The kids and goats had, in their playfulness, been gamboling about her feet and legs, and bespattered them with a little dirty water from the bottom of the canoe; and I thought to myself, that if a female could behave with cruelty to a companion, being herself in distress, that little pity or gentleness could dwell in her bosom. However, be this as it may, she was greatly afflicted. She might have recalled to her mind, as she was borne past the place where she had received her being, and where her childhood had been spent, the pastimes and amusements of that innocent and happy period of life; and this reflection, bringing along with it a train of pleasing associations, had produced her grief, which was no doubt increased by

comparing the freedom which she once enjoyed with
her present miserable condition of bondage.   It may
appear strange that I should dwell so long on this
subject, for it seems quite natural that every one,
even the most thoughtless barbarian, would feel at
least some slight emotion on being exiled from his
native country, and enslaved.   But so far is this
from being the case, that Africans, generally speaking, betray the most perfect indifference on losing
their liberty, and being deprived of their relatives;
while love of country is seemingly as great a stranger to their breasts, as social tenderness and domestic
affection.   We have seen many thousands of slaves,
some of them more intelligent than others; but the
poor little fat woman whom I have mentioned,—the
associate of beasts, and wallowing in filth, whose
countenance would seem to indicate only listless-
ness, stupidity, and perhaps idiotism, without the
smallest symptom of intelligence,—she alone has
shown any thing like regret on gazing at her native
land for the last time.   "There I was born," said
she, as she was passing by it, weeping,—"that is
my country!"

At eleven o'clock at night we arrived at a spot
which had been chosen as a place of rendezvous for
the whole party, and here we slept in our canoes.
The river has run to-day rather to the southward of
west, varying but slightly from yesterday's course.

Monday, Nov. 8th.—Long before sunrise, though
it was excessively dark, the canoes were put in motion; for as the "Eboe" country is said to be at no
great distance, the Eboe people with us were desirous of arriving there as early in the day as possible.   It proved to be a dull hazy morning, but at
seven o'clock A. M. the fog had become so dense,
that no object, however large, could be distinguished
at a greater distance than a few yards.   This created
considerable confusion; and the men fearing, as
they expressed it, to lose themselves, tied one canoe

to another, thus forming double canoes, and all proceeded together in close company. However, we had gone but a little way after this arrangement, when the men fancied that they had departed from the proper track, and therefore they determined to pull ashore, and wait there till the mist should be dispelled; yet they toiled a full hour before their object was effected. We wished to be more particular in our observations of this interesting part of our journey; but were constrained to forego this gratification, on account of the superstitious prejudices of the natives, who were so infatuated as to imagine, that we had not only occasioned the fog, but that, if we did not sit or lie down in the canoe (for we had been standing), it would inevitably cause the destruction of the whole party;—and the reason which they assigned was, "that the river had never beheld a white man before," and, therefore, they dreaded the consequences of our rashness and presumption in regarding its waters so attentively. This and similar nonsense was delivered with such determination and earnestness, that we reluctantly lay down and allowed ourselves to be covered with mats, in order to quiet their apprehensions; for we did not forget that we were prisoners, and that a perseverance in standing up would have exposed us to the mortification of being put down by force.

We hung on by the shore till the fog had dispersed, when we were again allowed to see the river. We now found ourselves on an immense body of water, like a lake, having gone a little out of the road, and at the mouth of a very considerable river, flowing to the westward, it being an important branch of the Niger; another branch also ran from hence to the south-east, while our course was in a south-westerly direction on the main body; the whole forming, in fact, *three* rivers of considerable magnitude. The banks were all low and swampy, and completely covered with palm-trees.

II.—R

An hour or two after this, or about midday, one of the Eboe men in our canoe exclaimed, "There is my country!" pointing to a clump of very high trees, which was yet at some distance before us; and after passing a low fertile island, we quickly came to it. Here we observed a few fishing-canoes, but their owners appeared suspicious and fearful, and would not come near us, though their national flag, which is a British Union, sewed on a large piece of plain white cotton with scallops of blue, was streaming from a long staff in the bow. The town was yet, we were told, a good way down the river. In a short time, however, we came to an extensive morass, intersected by little channels in every direction, and by one of these we got into clear water, in front of the Eboe town. Here we found hundreds of canoes, some of them even larger than any we had previously met with. They are furnished with sheds and awnings, and afford commodious habitations for a vast number of people, who constantly reside in them; perhaps one of these canoes, which is made of a single trunk, contains as many as seventy individuals.

The little we could see of the houses with which the shore is interspersed gave us a very favourable impression of the judgment and cleanliness of the inhabitants of the town. They are neatly built of yellow clay, plastered over, and thatched with palm-leaves; yards sprucely fenced are annexed to each of them, in which plantains, bananas, and cocoa-trees grow, exhibiting a pleasing sight, and affording a delightful shade. When we came alongside the large canoes already spoken of, two or three huge brawny fellows, in broken English, asked how we did, in a tone which Stentor might have envied; and the shaking of hands with our powerful friends was really a punishment, on account of the violent squeezes which we were compelled to suffer. The chief of these men calls himself *Gun*, though *Blun-*

derbuss, or *Thunder,* would have been as appropriate a name; and without solicitation he informed us that though he was not a great man, yet he was " a little military king;" that his brother's name was King *Boy,* and his father's King *Forday,* who with " King *Jacket,*" governed all the *Brass* country. But what was infinitely more interesting to us than this ridiculous list of kings, was the information he gave us, that, besides a Spanish schooner, an English vessel, called the " Thomas, of Liverpool," was also lying in the *first Brass river,* which Mr. Gun said was frequented by Liverpool traders for palm-oil.

Full of joy at this intelligence, we passed on to a little artificial creek, so narrow that our canoes could scarcely be pulled along, and here we were desired to wait till the king's pleasure respecting us should be known. On the return of the messenger, we were drawn in the canoe over ooze and mud to a considerable distance, when we got out and walked to a house, similar to those which we have already mentioned as having seen from the river. There was a little verandah supported by wooden columns in front, and on the floor mats had been placed for our accommodation. Indeed its whole appearance was so clean and comfortable, and it likewise had such an appearance of neatness and simplicity about it, differing entirely from any thing of the kind which we had seen for a long time, that we were quite pleased with our new abode; and if the countenance of our host had been at all in unison with the agreeableness of his dwelling, we imagined that we could live at ease in it for a few days at least. But it was not so. The harshness of this man's manners corresponded with his sulky, ill-natured face, and deprived us of a good deal of pleasure which we should have enjoyed in reposing at full length on dry, soft mats, after having been cramped up for three days in a small canoe with slaves and goats, and exposed to the dews by night and the sun by day.

An hour or two of rest invigorated and refreshed us extremely; and we then received a message from the king, that he was in waiting to see and converse with us.   Having little to adjust in regard to our dress, we rose up, and followed the man immediately.   Passing near the outskirts of the town, the man conducted us by paths little frequented to the outward yard of the palace, before the door of which was placed the statue of a woman in a sitting posture, and made of clay, very rude of course and very ugly.   Having crossed the yard, in which we saw nothing remarkable, we entered by a wooden door into another which was far superior.   This formed an oblong square; it was cleanly swept and had a very spruce appearance, and each of its sides was furnished with an excellent portico.   Near the door-way we saw, with surprise, a large heavy cannon lying on the ground.   From this enclosure we were led into a third, which, like the former, had its porti coes, and in one of them a number of women were employed in manufacturing a kind of cloth of cotton and dried grass, which they wove together.   Oppo site the entrance is a low clay platform, about three feet from the ground, which was overlaid with mats of various colours, a large piece of coarse red cloth covering the whole, and at each of its corners we observed a little squat figure, also of clay; but whe ther these were intended to represent males or fe· males it is impossible to conjecture.   Here we were desired to place ourselves among a crowd of half-dressed armed men, who were huddled together on the left of the platform, some sitting and others standing, and awaiting the coming of the prince. Our friend Gun was with them, and he immediately claimed priority of acquaintance with us.   He chatted with amazing volubility, and in less than two minutes he was on the most familiar footing, slapping us with no small force just above the knee, to give weight to his observations, and to rivet our attention to his remarks. Then, while we spoke, he would rest his heavy arms on our shoulders, and laugh aloud at every word we said ; look very knowingly, and occasionally apply the palm of his hand to our backs with the most *feeling* energy, as a token of his encouragement and approbation. We wished him to answer questions which concerned us nearly, but the only satisfaction which we received was contained in the expression, " O yes, to be sure !" and this was repeated so often, with an emphasis so peculiar, and with a grin so irresistibly ludicrous, that in spite of our disappointment we were vastly entertained with him.

In this manner was the time beguiled, till we heard a door suddenly opened on our right, and the dreaded *Obie*, King of the Eboe country, stood before us ! And yet there was nothing so very dreadful in his appearance, after all, for he is a sprightly young man, with a mild open countenance, and an eye which indicates quickness, intelligence, and good-nature, rather than the ferocity which we had been told he possesses in an eminent degree. He received us with a smile of welcome, and shook hands with infinite cordiality, often complimenting us with the word " yes !" to which his knowledge of English is confined, and which no doubt he had been tutored to pronounce for the occasion. Several attendants followed their sovereign, most of whom were unarmed, and almost naked, and three little boys were likewise in attendance, whose office it was to fan him when desired.

The dress of the King of the Eboe country somewhat resembles that which is worn, *on state occasions*, by the monarch of Yarriba. Its appearance was altogether *brilliant ;* and from the vast profusion of coral ornaments with which he was decorated, Obie might not inappropriately be styled, " the Coral King ;" such an idea at all events entered our minds, as we contemplated the monarch, sitting on his

throne of clay. His head was graced with a cap
shaped like a sugar-loaf, and covered thickly with
strings of coral and pieces of broken looking-glass,
so as to hide the materials of which it was made;
his neck, or rather throat, was encircled with several
strings of the same kind of bead, which were fastened so tightly as in some degree to affect his respiration, and to give his throat and cheeks an inflated
appearance. In opposition to these were four or
five others hanging round his neck, and reaching almost to his knees. He wore a short Spanish sur-
tout of red cloth, which fitted close to his person,
being much too small. It was ornamented with
gold epaulettes, and the front of it was overspread
with gold lace, but which, like the cap, was entirely
concealed, unless on a close examination, owing to
the vast quantity of coral which was fastened to it
in strings. Thirteen or fourteen bracelets (for we
had the curiosity to count them) decorated each
wrist, and to give them full effect, a few inches of
the sleeves of the coat had been cut off purposely.
The beads were fastened to the wrist with old
copper buttons, which formed an odd contrast to
them. The king's trousers, composed of the same
material as his coat, stuck as closely to the skin as
that, and was similarly embroidered, but it reached
no farther than the middle of his legs, the lower part
of it being ornamented like the wrists, and with
precisely the same number of strings of beads; be
sides which, a string of little brass bells encircled
each leg above the ankles, but the feet were naked.
Thus splendidly clothed, Obie, smiling at his own
magnificence, vain of the admiration which was paid
him by his attendants, and flattered without doubt by
the presence of white men, who he imagined were
struck with amazement at the splendour of his appearance, shook his feet for the bells to tinkle, sat
down with the utmost self-complacency, and looked
around him.

Our story was related to the king in full by the
Bonny messenger who had accompanied us from
Damuggoo, who also dwelt upon the losses which
the people of that place and his own had met with
at Kirree; and if we may be allowed to form an
opinion, it was a fine piece of savage eloquence.
The man's looks and gestures were natural, animated, and forcible, and strictly in keeping with the
feeling, power, and energy with which his expressions were poured forth. The inflections of his
voice, also, were truly admirable. This singular
speech lasted, as near as we could guess, two whole
hours, and produced a visible effect upon all present.
As soon as it was over we were invited by Obie to
take some refreshment; being in truth extremely
hungry at the time, we thankfully accepted the offer,
and fish and yams, swimming in oil, were forthwith
brought us on English plates, the king retiring in the
mean while from motives of delicacy.

The oil was the commonest kind used in the lamps
of warehouses in England, extremely unpalatable,
and emitted so unsavoury a smell that we found it
impossible to partake of it, so great was our disgust:
Gun was of a different opinion, and declaring it to be
the best Liverpool beef fat that he had seen for a
long time, he soon made away with it. When Obie
returned, a general conversation ensued, and he was
engaged in talking promiscuously to those around
him till evening, when the "great palàver," as it is
called, was formally prorogued till the morrow, and
presently after the chief bade us good night, and retired. We conceive it somewhat strange, that though
the palàver was chiefly on our account, not a single
question was put to us while it lasted, nor did we
understand a single sentence that was uttered.
Nevertheless we are led to believe, from the flatter-
ing and gracious manner in which we have been received, and other corresponding circumstances, that

every thing is proceeding favourably to our wishes, and that the palàver will have a happy termination. But *nous verrons!*

The path to Obie's house is in a westerly direction from the creek where we landed, distant about a quarter of a mile, between two lines of neat little huts. In the third, or inner yard of his palace, we also observed a large iron tank, which we were told was used by the king as a bath. The people, with whom we had to wait the arrival of the king, pestered us with all manner of questions before he made his appearance. In answer to their interrogations, I told them we had come from a country called Yàoorie, and another called Boossà, where we had been to obtain the books of one of our countrymen who had been killed a long time ago by the people of the latter place. This answer was quickly followed by a question whether he went there in a ship? and I answered, " No, in a large canoe." " Where is the canoe ?" they asked. "He ran it on the rocks," I replied, " and broke it." They did not, however, seem to comprehend me, and imagined that I was speaking of a ship that was lost at sea, on the other side of the land. The *little military king* of Brass town told us that he had come here for the purpose of buying slaves for a Spanish vessel. When Obie entered he was followed by a man carrying a little brass figure of a deity, which, when he had seated himself, was placed on his right hand.

The poor Damuggoo people were in tears all the time their chief was relating the account of the attack at Kirree : they had lost every thing they had; not only their master's property, but their own also, with the exception of the slaves. They had no means of obtaining provisions, having nothing with which to purchase them, so that the poor fellows are in a starving condition. Obie made them a long speech, and seemed to feel for their destitute condition; he gave them ten yams, and desired them to go to their house, promising to hear the remainder of their story on the moirow.

Our hut is so small that we have scarcely room to lie down, but little as it is we feel ourselves far better off than in our canoe. The mats were comfortable, and we were well inclined to enjoy a good rest. We had not retired long before a boy arrived from the king, bringing with him five yams and one small fowl. This was a poor supply for eight per sons, which our party amounted to, besides ourselves, and would scarcely keep us from starving. At seven in the evening we made a slight supper off a piece of the boiled fowl, with part of a yam, and laid ourselves down to rest. Tired as we were, and much as we needed sleep, we could get none. Our sulky old landlord annoyed us beyond measure, by introducing his friends to see us, and all our endeavours to make him understand that we did not like their intrusion, and wished for rest, were fruitless; there was no getting rid of them, for no sooner was one party gone than another supplied their place. The first part of the night was thus employed, and in the latter part we were kept awake by the most dreadful screaming we ever heard. The noise proceeded from some unfortunate person who seemed to be suffering the severest agony in a hut hard by our own, so that the cries were distinctly heard. We could not learn the occasion of them; but these people having the name of being the most barbarous in their habits, we concluded that they proceeded from some unhappy victim who was a prisoner of war, suffering some horrible death. Our people slept in the house with us, so that we felt some sort of security from their presence.

Tuesday, November 9th.—Two of our attendants who have accompanied us from Cape Coast Castle, and who, during their lifetime, have spent many years in Ashantee, declare that the buildings of the people here are nowise different from those at Coomassie, the capital of that kingdom, than in their size, which is much smaller. They certainly resemble the houses of the Yarribeans, but they surpass them in neatness, regularity, and cleanliness, and are besides much better secured from the rain. There is not a single round hut in the place. The Eboe people, like most Africans, are extremely indolent, and cultivate yams, Indian corn, and plantains only. They have abundance of goats and fowls, but few sheep are to be seen, and no bullocks. The city, which has no other name than the "Eboe Country," is situated on an open plain; it is immensely large, contains a vast population, and is the capital of a kingdom of the same name. It has, for a series of years, been the principal slave-mart for native traders from the coast, between the Bonny and Old Calebar rivers: and for the production of its palm-oil it has obtained equal celebrity. Hundreds of men from the rivers mentioned above come up for the purpose of trade, and numbers of them are at present residing in canoes in front of the town. Most of the oil purchased by Englishmen at the Bonny and adjacent rivers, is brought from hence, as are nearly all the slaves which are annually exported from those places by the French, Spaniards, and Portuguese. It has been told us by many that the Eboe people are confirmed anthropophagi; and this opinion is more prevalent among the tribes bordering on that kingdom than with the natives of more remote districts; but whether it be well or ill-founded, we have as yet no means of ascertaining. Certainly, with the solitary exception of their monarch, the Eboes bear on their countenances strong indications of a brutal, unyielding, and ferocious temper, but so likewise do many other people of different countries, who detest cannibalism, and speak of it with horror.

We were visited this morning by numbers of the

inhabitants, who broke through every restraint to gratify their desire of seeing us. This was what we naturally expected; yet after all they were much better behaved, and less impatient, than we had any reason to apprehend, and they departed with little importunity, considering that they had not been in the habit of bending to the will of prisoners and slaves,—for such we are.

About noon we were informed that our attendance was required at the king's house, Obie being fully prepared, it was said, to resume the hearing of our case, and examine the deposition of the Bonny messenger and the Damuggoo people. On entering the principal yard or court, in which we were yesterday introduced to the king, we found two little ugly clay figures, by the side of their companions, near the platform, and round them "magical characters," as a fortune-teller in Europe would call them, were chalked on the ground. We did not remain here long to admire this strange contrivance, but were presently ordered to return to the middle yard, and there wait under the eastern portico, till Obie should make his appearance. A common English chair, covered with inferior red cloth, had been previously placed there for his use.

It is plain, that the king, for some reason, is very unwilling to introduce us into the interior of his dwelling; as yet we have seen nothing but his yards. The chair alluded to above was placed between two wooden pillars which support the roof of the verandah, and a great number of images are carved on them, very much after the manner of Yarriba. Indeed the difference between the productions of both countries, in this branch of the arts, is scarcely, if at all, to be perceived. On the left of the empty chair stood about fifty of the king's attendants, and to the right of it the Bonny, Brass, and Damuggoo people, with our own, were assembled. In less than half an hour, the men having in the mean time been regaled with a large quantity of palm-wine, the monarch, dressed in every respect as yesterday, entered the yard. His fat, round cheeks were swelling with good-humour, real or assumed, as he shook our hands with a sprightly air, when he instantly sat himself down in his chair to receive the prostrations and addresses of his subjects and others.

The business of the day was entered into with spirit, and a violent altercation soon arose between the Brass and Bonny people, but scarcely any part of the conversation was interpreted to us. Sufficient, however, was explained to put us in a very bad humour; for notwithstanding the opinion we had entertained of the benevolence of the chief, from his pleasing countenance joined to a mild and affable demeanour, we are assured that we shall never leave this country· unless ransomed at a high price! No doubt Obie has been induced to adopt this line of conduct, partly by the instigation of his minions, and partly from the eagerness which has been displayed by the Bonny and Brass people to take us to their respective countries; for he imagines that such bitter contentions would not rise among them, as to whither we shall go, had it not been for the expectation of receiving a handsome recompense from our countrymen at those places. Therefore he is determined on his part to make as much of us as he can.

Bonny is now the place of our destination. We have with us a messenger from the present and a son to the late ruler of that state (King *Pepper*), and, as it has already been related, we had engaged some Damuggoo people to accompany and protect us thither. While on the other hand, we know nothing at all of *Brass*, never having heard the name of such a river in our lives before, and equally ignorant are we of the manners of the natives who inhabit its banks; though it is evident that they have some acquaintance with our countrymen, and

some slight knowledge of our language. The former, who say that Obie maintains a friendly intercourse with their monarch, are as anxious as we
ourselves that they should take us to Bonny, and
have remonstrated with the king rather angrily to
this effect. But the latter are by far the most
numerous and influential party, owing most likely to
their very recent arrival from Brass, with a fresh
stock of European goods, with part of which, it i
said, they have already bribed Obie to give them the
preference.

The discussion was violent and stormy, and the
council did not break up till a late hour in the afternoon. They came to no decision, but will meet
again to-morrow morning. The Brass people affirm
that the " Bonny creek," which is a small branch of
the Niger, is dried up, and that the main river which
runs to Brass belongs to King *Jacket*, who will permit
no foreigners whatever to pass up or down the Niger,
without exacting the accustomed fees or duties.
They will therefore have a very plausible reason
for taking us entirely out of the hands of Obie and
the Damuggoo people. We returned to our dwelling
rather saddened than otherwise at the result of this
day's proceedings.

I asked King Obie permission to allow us to proceed on our journey, and to send one of his canoes
to accompany us to Bonny, and was surprised at hearing that the creek was dried up. We must go down
the large river, he said, to Brass, from whence we
might get to Bonny, as there is a branch of the river
which communicates with the two places. We are
much annoyed by our interpreter. This fellow had
told us that the branch leading to Bonny is the principal, whereas it is evident that it is that leading to
Brass town. This man, whose name is Antonio, is
a native of Bonny, and never tells us exactly what
the king says, so that we are a good deal in the dark
as to what is going on concerning ourselves, and in

fact he is the most useless fellow I ever knew. We were the subject of conversation two hours to-day between the kings; and could not learn what was said, and we went away without knowing for certain what was to become of us.

In the evening Antonio and five other Bonny people came to our hut with tears in their eyes. On asking them what was the matter, " The chief," they said, " is determined to sell you to the Brass people, but we will fight for you and die rather than see you sold." " How many of you Bonny people are there ?" I asked. " Only six," was the reply. "And can you fight with two hundred Brass people ?" I said. " We can kill some of them," they answered, " and your people can assist." I then asked Antonio the reason why he did not interpret what was going forward to-day at the king's house ? He said that he was afraid it would have made our hearts sore,—that it was " a bad palàver." " We have all been to the chief," he added, " crying to him, and telling him that black man cannot sell white man; but he will not listen to us; he said he would sell you to the Brass people." Our poor canoemen on hearing this began to sob aloud, and continued lamenting their fate nearly all night. My brother and I felt much hurt at our situation, for we did not expect it would be so bad as this; but we have made our minds up to prepare ourselves for the worst, for it is impossible to foresee the lengths to which these savages will go. We saw a Funda man at the chief's house, with whom we could have communicated in the Haussà language, but for some reason or other we were not permitted to speak to him.

Wednesday, November 10*th.*—Being taken very unwell with fever this morning, I was unable to attend the summons to the king's house, and requested my brother to go in my stead. The following is his account of what took place.

" On arriving there this morning, to my infinite

surprise I found *King Boy* (Gun's eldest brother) with a number of his attendants already assembled. He was dressed in a style far superior to any of his countrymen, and wore a jacket and waistcoat over a neat shirt of striped cotton, to which was annexed a silk pocket-handkerchief, which extended below the knees. Trousers, as we have already said, I believe are not permitted to be worn, either by natives or strangers of the same hue as themselves, the king alone being an exception to this rule. Strings of coral and other beads encircled his neck, and a pretty little crucifix of seed beads hung on his bosom. This latter ornament, which has probably been given him by a slave captain, had by no means an unbecoming appearance. King Boy introduced himself to me with the air of a person who bestows a favour, rather than soliciting acquaintance, and indeed his vanity in other respects was infinitely amusing. He would not suffer any one to sit between him and the platform, but squatted himself down nearest the king's seat, which as a mark of honour had previously been assigned to us; and with a volubility scarcely imaginable, he commenced a long narrative of his greatness, power, and dignity, in which he excelled all his neighbours; and to this I was constrained to listen, with assumed composure and attention, for a considerable time. To convince me of his veracity, he produced a pocket-book, containing a great number of recommendatory notes, or 'characters,' as a domestic would call them, written in the English, French, Spanish, and Portuguese languages, and which had been given him by the various European traders who had visited the Brass River. This practice of giving written characters, which has for some time been adopted by Europeans, is both praiseworthy and useful, and it is become almost universal on the western coast; because it is not to be supposed that the natives themselves can understand these documents, and strangers are made

acquainted with their good or bad qualities by them,
and taught to discriminate the honest from the un-
faithful and malicious. Boy's letters mention certain
dealings which their authors have had with him, and
they likewise bear testimony to his own character,
and the manners of his countrymen. Among others
is one from a 'James Dow,' master of the brig
Susan, from Liverpool, and dated ' *Brass First River,*
Sept. — 1830,' which runs as follows :—' Captain
Dow states, that he never met with a set of greater
scoundrels than the natives generally, and the pilots
in particular.' These he anathematized as d——d
rascals, who had endeavoured to steer his vessel
among the breakers at the mouth of the river, that
they might share the plunder of its wreck. *King*
Jacket, who claims the sovereignty of the river, is
declared to be a more confirmed knave, if possible,
than they, and to have cheated him of a good deal
of property. The writer describes *King Forday* as
a man rather advanced in years, less fraudulent, but
more dilatory. *King Boy,* his son, alone deserved
his confidence, for he had not abused it, and possessed more honesty and integrity than either of his
countrymen. These are the rulers of the Brass
country, and pretty fellows they are, truly. Mr.
Dow observes further, that the river is extremely
unhealthy, and that his first and second mates, three
coopers, and five seamen had already died of fever,
and that he himself had had several narrow escapes
from the same disorder. He concludes by caution-
ing traders against the treachery of the natives
generally, and gives them certain directions concerning the ' dreadful bar,' at the mouth of the river,
on which he had nearly perished. Another of Boy's
papers informs us that the writer's name is ' Thomas
Lake, and that he is master of the brig *Thomas,* of
Liverpool,' which is now lying in Brass River.

" This business had been no sooner settled than
Obie entered the yard attended as usual. but clad

differently in loose silks. After the customary salutations, Boy directed the monarch to appeal to me, that he might be satisfied in what estimation he was held by white men. Of course, I said a variety of fine things in his favour, which were received with a very good grace indeed: but that a piece of paper, simply, which could neither hear, speak, nor understand, should impart such information, was a source of astonishment and wonder to Obie and his train, who testified their emotion in no other manner than by looks of silly amazement, and repeated bursts of laughter.

" The king then said, with a serious countenance, ' that there was no necessity for further discussion respecting the white men, his mind was already made up on the subject;' and, for the first time, he briefly explained himself to this effect:—' That circumstances having thrown us in the way of his subjects, by the laws and usages of the country he was not only entitled to our own persons, but had equal right to those of our attendants; that he should take no further advantage of his good fortune than by exchanging us for as much English goods as would amount in value to twenty slaves. In order to have the matter fairly arranged and settled, he should, of his own accord, prevent our leaving the town, till such time as our countrymen at Brass or Bonny should pay for our ransom, having understood from ourselves that the English at either of those rivers would afford us whatever assistance we might require, with cheerfulness and alacrity. Concerning the goods of which we had been robbed at Kirree, he assured us that he would use his utmost exertions to get them restored. He lamented that circumstance more than any one, but he denied that a single subject of his had any thing to do with it, and attributed the whole of that unfortunate affair to the rashness and brutality of a certain people that inhabited a country nearly opposite to his own.

II.—S

whose monarch was his particular friend, therefore
he apprehended little difficulty in seeing justice done
us; but then,' said he, 'it is necessary that you
should wait here for an indefinite time till a council
of that nation be held, when the plunderers will be
examined, and your claims established. The Damuggoo people that have come with you have, like
yourselves, suffered much loss; for my own part I
shall make them a present of a slave or two as a
compensation, and they have my permission to go
along with you for the present, which I understand
you have promised their monarch ; but you must not
expect them to be your guide to the sea, for their
responsibility ends here.' "

" When all this was interpreted to me by Antonio,
I was thunderstruck. It was in vain that I assured
Obie that there was not the slightest necessity for
our detention in the town, that our countrymen
would redeem us the moment they should see us,
but not before; and equally unavailing were my
solicitations for him to alter this arrangement and
suffer us to depart; but the fears of his subjects,
and the representations of the men of Brass, had
made too deep an impression on his mind to be
so easily eradicated : we found it too late either to
implore or remonstrate.

" This final decision of the king is a bitter stroke
to us ; for we fondly indulged the hope of a more
favourable result from the deliberations of the savage
council, at whose dissolution we expected to be sent
to the seacoast without being perplexed with further embarrassments. We have now to await the
return of a messenger from thence, who has not
yet been sent on his errand, and he is to bring back
with him the value of twenty slaves ere we obtain
our freedom. Heaven only knows whether the
masters of English vessels at Bonny or Brass have
the ability or will feel a disposition to ransom us.
We only know that if disposed of at all, we shall
be sold for infinitely more than we are worth."

" As may naturally be supposed, I returned home much depressed and afflicted, to inform my brother of the result of the palàver, and he was as greatly surprised and affected as myself at the intelligence. But though we are full of trouble and uneasiness at our gloomy situation, yet we do not repine at the divine dispensations of that Almighty Providence which has comforted us in the hour of adversity, and relieved us in times of pain and distress,—which has rescued us from the lap of danger, and snatched us from the jaws of death."

Thursday, November 11*th.*—This morning my brother felt himself extremely unwell, but I am rather better. In truth we wonder much that our health, generally speaking, has been so good, when we reflect for a moment on the hardships and privations which we have lately undergone, the perplexities in which we have been entangled, and the difficulties with which we have had to contend. After all of them, however, by the blessing and mercy of our God, instead of sorrow and suffering, we have enjoyed a lightness and even levity of spirits, which caused them to make but a feeble and transient impression upon our minds; but nature, though she make extraordinary efforts for a time, will at last be crushed by repeated disappointments, cares, and vexations, unless she be supported by the vigour of health, and encouraged by the excitement of powerful feelings; while hope, that most agreeable but delusive phantom, is oftener sought than found, and will frequently vanish from the desponding bosom when her influence is most required, leaving it for a season a prey to fear and suspicion, and the whole dark and sorrowful train of the depressing passions. Under their baneful influence we are at present, in some degree, labouring; and we occasionally fall into such a state of apathy and quietism, in regard to our present situation and future prospects, as to be perfectly indifferent about them; and I verily believe that if a single struggle could restore us to freedom and happiness, we should scarcely have sufficient animation to make that effort. I blush to say that on these occasions, neither the reflection of *past* deliverances, nor the consciousness that we are still under the protection of the same beneficent and indulgent Being that has ever been our refuge and guardian, can restore entirely our confidence in his mercies, or teach us to be resigned to his divine will.

During the few days that we have spent in this place, we have been sadly perplexed for want of provisions; and our people, who for the first day bore this privation in silence, have since then been loud in their complaints. The constant fear which they entertain of being taken away and sold has now, however, changed this lively feeling of discontent into sullenness and despondency. What makes the matter still worse is the fact that having lost our needles and cowries at Kirree, we have not the means of purchasing any thing, although the cowry shell is not current here. Poverty is in most places, I believe, considered one of the greatest of evils, but it is more particularly so here where it is tantamount to a curse (or at least it is reckoned so in us); and where the virtues of benevolence and humanity, if exercised at all, are never displayed except on extraordinary occasions. Obie has been in the habit of sending us a fowl, or a yam or two every morning; but, as we are ten in number, it makes but a slender meal, and it is barely sufficient to keep us from actual starvation. To stop, if possible, the sullen murmurings of our people, we have been reduced to the painful necessity of begging; but we might as well have addressed our petitions to the stones or trees,—we might have spared ourselves the mortification of a refusal. We never experienced a more stinging sense of our own humbleness and imbecility than on such occasions, and never had we greater need of patience and lowliness of spirit. In most African towns and villages we have been regarded as demigods,. and treated in consequence with universal kindness, civility, and veneration; but here, alas! what a contrast,—we are classed with the most degraded and despicable of mankind, and are become slaves in a land of ignorance and barbarism, whose savage natives have treated us with brutality and contempt. It would be hard to guess whence these unkindly feelings towards us have originated; we feel that we have not deserved them, yet the consciousness of our own insignificance sadly militates against every idea of self-love and self-importance, and teaches us a plain and useful moral lesson! Though we make the most charitable allowances for the Eboe people, we are notwithstanding obliged to consider them the most inhospitable tribe, as well as the most covetous and uncivil, that we are acquainted with. Their monarch and a respectable married female, who has passed the meridian of her days, are the only individuals, among several thousands, that have shown us any thing like civility or kindness, and the latter alone has acted, we are convinced, solely from disinterested motives.

All ranks of people here are passionately fond of palm-wine,· and drink of it to excess whenever they have an opportunity, which often occurs, as great quantities of it are produced in the town and its neighbourhood. It is a very general and favourite custom with them, as soon as the sun goes down, to hold large meetings and form parties in the open air or under the branches of trees, to talk over· the events of the day, and make merry with this exciting beverage. These assemblies are kept up till after midnight; and as the revellers generally contrive to get inebriated very soon after they sit down to drink, the greatest part of the evening is devoted to wrangling and fighting, instead of convivial intercourse, and occasionally the most fearful noises that it is possible for the mind to conceive. Bloodshed and even murder, it is said, not unfrequently terminate these boisterous and savage entertainments. A meeting of this description is held outside the yard of our residence every evening, and the noise which they make is really terrifying, more especially when the women and young people join in the affray, for a quarrel of some sort is sure to ensue. Their cries, groans, and shrieks of agony are dreadful, and would lead a stranger to suppose that these dismal and piercing sounds proceeded from individuals about to be butchered, or that they were extorted by the last pangs of anguish and suffering. We trembled with alarm for the first night or two, imagining from these loud and doleful cries, that a work of bloodshed and slaughter was in progress; and we found it useless to endeavour to sleep, till the impression of the first wild cry that was uttered and the last faint scream had worn away. But now we are in some measure more reconciled to them from the frequency of their occurrence, or rather we feel less apprehension than we did as to their origin,—understanding with surprise that they are only the effects of a simple quarrel, and excite from the inhabitants no more than a casual remark; though they say that, in fits of ungovernable passion, the most heinous crimes are consummated in these frantic revels.

Our matronly female acquaintance, though excessively fat, is of diminutive stature, and by her cheerful pleasantry she has beguiled in some degree the wearisomeness of the long evening hours, and banished that *ennui* which the disagreeableness of our situation has partially induced, simply by her endeavours to do so. For not content with paying us formal visits in the daytime, she comes into our yard every night, instead of joining the orgies of her acquaintance, accompanied by two or three friends of congenial natures, with the very benevolent inten-

tion of pitying our misfortunes, and dissipating our
melancholy. Two or three slaves follow their mistress into the yard, carrying a few bottles of their
favourite "palm-wine," and perhaps with a plate of
bananas also, that the evening may be passed the
more agreeably. .

Our sleeping quarters are in a recess, which is
elevated three or four feet from the ground, and supported by wooden columns. It is without a door, or
indeed any thing answering the same purpose, so that
we enjoy the refreshing coolness of the evening air,
with the disadvantage of being gazed at by whoever
has the curiosity to enter our premises. We generally lie down shortly after sunset, and presently our
fat, jolly little friend, duck-like, waddles into our yard
with her companions and slaves, to offer us the evening salutation, and enter into the usual familiar discourse. This is commonly preceded by a large po-
tation of palm-wine, which is relished with a loud
and peculiar smack, expressive of the pleasure and
satisfaction afforded by so copious a draught, and
betokening also much internal warmth and comfort.
The officious slaves having spread mats for the purpose directly in front of our recess, our lady-visiter
and her associates, together with our ill-natured host,
who has by this time joined the party, squat themselves down in a circle, and under the inspiration of
the fermented juice, maintain a pretty animated conversation till it is all expended, and sleep "weighs
their eyelids down." For ourselves we have little
if any thing to say, because we are pretty nearly as
ignorant of their language as they are of ours; and
interpretation is unfavourable to the contagion of
social felicity. Yet it is highly diverting to watch
the influence of the palm-wine on their looks, language, and ideas. The flushed countenance is invisible in a black lady; but then she has the liquid and
unsettled eye, the proneness to talk with irresistible
garrulity, the gentle simper or the bursting laugh, at

any trifle or at nothing at all; and to wind up the
list of symptoms, she has that complacent idea of her
own good points, and superior qualifications, which
elicit her own approbation without exciting the applauses of her associates, and which distinguish the
inexperienced male reveller in every part of the
globe. All these were observable in our talkative
little friend, as well as in her companions. It is a
relief also to contemplate, from our resting-place,
the peace and harmony of the little party before us
so entirely different from the boisterous one without
because it gives us a comfortable sense of our se
curity, which we should not certainly have entertained had we been left to our own reflections; and
when after a good deal of turning and restlessness
we at length fall into a disagreeable and unrefreshing
doze, and are attacked by that hideous phantom
nightmare, which is often the case,—starting up in
a fright from the assassin's knife, which we can
scarcely persuade ourselves to be unreal,—it is pleasant to fix our eyes upon our comical little visiter,
with her round shining face, and her jolly companions; all apprehension of mischief immediately
vanishes, and a truly pleasing effect is produced upon
our minds and spirits. The breaking up of the party
outside is a signal for our friends also to depart,
when, rising from her mat, the mistress, after shaking
hands, wishes us good night, in a thick tremulous
tone, and waddling out of our yard in a direction
which Hogarth denominates " the line of beauty,"
she returns home to her husband, who is a valetudi-
narian. Thus our evenings are passed, and thus much
of our solitary Eboe friend.

In addition to the value of twenty slaves which the
King of Eboe demands for us, we hear that King
Boy requires the value of fifteen casks of palm oil,
which is the same as fifteen slaves, for himself, and
as payment for the trouble he and his people will
have in conducting us to the English vessel. He

says that he must take three canoes and one hundred and fifty people, and therefore that it is impossible he can do it for less. The chief has said that if I do not consent to give King Boy a *book* for all this money, he shall send us into the interior of the country to be sold, and that we shall never see the sea again. I see clearly that we have no alternative, and I think it best to agree to give him the bill, not intending, however, on our arrival at the sea, to give him more than twenty common trade guns to pay this chief and all other expenses. King Boy was to give Obie five pieces of cloth and one gun, as part payment; the remainder is to be paid on his return from having delivered us up to the brig. Our people are all in high spirits at the prospect of leaving this place and obtaining their freedom, for they have so much faith in the character of the English that they do not doubt that the captain of the brig will redeem us.

The Eboe people have a savage appearance. The custom of marking their temples with indigo, in the shape of an arrow, is general among them, both with the males and females. The women are generally pretty, and wear the same sort of ivory rings round their legs and wrists, to which allusion has been previously made. They are extensive traders, and supply the Brass people entirely with palm-oil, poultry, goats, and yams, &c. The Eboe people are also famous for making large canoes, and all those of the differen. rivers, from Benin to Calebar, are constructed by them. Since the first day of our arrival we have had no fowl, but have been kept on the regular slave allowance of half a yam per day. This may have preserved our health, for it is more than likely that if we had lived well after being nearly starved, and exposed as we had been to the hot sun during the day, and the dews at night, we should have had some dangerous fever.

Last evening, Obie, in his showy coral dress, came

barefooted to our hut, to inspect our books, and examine the contents of our medicine chest. His approach was announced to us by the jingling of the little bells which encircled his feet. He appeared greatly pleased with every thing he saw, and looked aghast when informed of the powerful properties of some of the medicines, which ended in a fit of laughter. He expressed a strong desire to have a little, especially the purgatives; and as we treated the Sultan of Yaoorie and family, so we treated him. Obie was evidently fearful of our books, having been informed that they could " tell all things;" and appeared to shrink with horror at one which was offered him, shaking his head, saying that he must not accept it, for that it was good only for white men, " whose God was not his god!" The visit was of short duration.

We found King Boy in the inner yard of the king's house again to-day, and from his significant physiognomy we conjectured that he had something of consequence to communicate. Obie received us with his usual politeness and jocularity; but instantly directed his attention and discourse to King Boy, who maintained an earnest and pretty animated conversation with him for some time. The Bonny people were in attendance, weeping. As we were frequently pointed out and named, we had no doubt whatever that it was chiefly concerning ourselves, which opinion was soon after confirmed. As if the parties had some secrets to discuss which they did not wish either their attendants or our own to overhear, they retired to the middle court, where having conversed for a time by themselves, they returned with anxious looks to resume the conversation.

This was repeated twice; after which (as we subsequently understood) Obie briefly related in a loud voice the result of this extraordinary conference, and all present, except the men of Bonny, shouted simultaneously the monosyllable " Yah!" as a token of their approbation.

In the mean time, from anxiety to be made acquainted with what had transpired respecting ourselves, we felt rather impatient and uneasy,—the
answer of King Boy to our repeated interrogations
having been only " plenty of bars !" the meaning
whereof we were grievously puzzled to define.
But shortly after the termination of the palàver,
how transported were we to hear the last-men-
tioned individual explain himself in broken English
to this effect : " In the conversation which I have
just had with Obie, I have been induced to offer him
the goods which he demands for your ransom, on
the faith that they be hereafter repaid me by the
master of the brig Thomas, which is now lying in
the First Brass River, and that the value of fifteen
bars or slaves be added thereto in European goods,
and likewise a cask of rum, as a remuneration for
the hazard and trouble which I shall inevitably
incur in transporting you to Brass.   If you consent
to these conditions, and on these only I consent to
redeem you, you will forthwith give me a bill on
Captain Lake for the receipt of articles to the value
of thirty-five bars, after which you will be at liberty
to leave this place, and go along with me whenever
you may think proper, agreeably to the understanding at present existing between Obie and myself."
This was heavenly news indeed ; and we thanked
King Boy over and over again for his generosity and
nobleness ; for we were too much elated at the
time to reflect on the exorbitant demands which he
had imposed upon us.   We immediately gave him
a bill on Mr. Lake : indeed there was nothing which
we would not have done rather than lose the opportunity of getting down to the sea, which seemed
so providentially held out to us.   Obie perceived
by the great and sudden change in our counte
nances the joy which filled our breasts ; and having
asked us whether we were not pleased with his
arrangements, in the fulness of our hearts, he ex-

acted from us a promise that, on returning to England, we would inform our countrymen that he was a good man, and that we would pay him a visit whenever we should come again into the country.

When King Boy came for his *book*, I gave it him, and he wished to send it down to the brig, to know if it was good. This I had expected, so I told him that the *book* would be of no use unless we were sent along with it, and that the captain would not pay it before he had taken us on board the brig, on which he put it into his pocket-book.

We then bade him farewell, and he took leave of us in a kind and cordial manner.

Fearing that something might yet occur to detain us, and ultimately change the king's resolution altogether, we were most eager to get out of the reach of him and his people as quickly as possible. Therefore we lost not a moment, but hastened to our lodgings, and having sent our people on board Boy's canoe, we hurried after them immediately, and embarked at three in the afternoon. And thus terminated four of the most wretched days of our existence. Our own old leaky and shattered canoe we are unable to take with us, as it would detain us very much, from being so heavy to move along; the Damuggoo people will accompany us in their own, and every thing is arranged for our departure at an early hour to-morrow.

The Brass canoe, which is now become our dwelling, is extremely large and heavily laden. It is paddled by forty men and boys, in addition to whom there may be about twenty individuals, or more, including a few slaves and ourselves,—so that the number of human beings will amount to at least sixty Like Obie's war-canoes, it is furnished with a cannon, which is lashed to the bow, a vast number of cutlasses, and a quantity of grape and other shot, besides powder, flints, &c. It contains

a number of large boxes or chests, which are filled
with spirituous liquors, cotton, and silk goods, earthenware, and other articles of European and other
foreign manufactures; besides abundance of provisions for present consumption, and two thousand
yams for the master of a Spanish slaver, which is
now lying in Brass river.   In this canoe three men
might sit with ease abreast of each other, and from
the number of people which it contains, and the immense quantity of articles of various descriptions,
some idea of its size may be formed.   It has been
cut out of a solid trunk of a tree, and draws four feet
and a half water, being more than fifty feet in
length.   But it is so deeply laden that not above
two inches of the canoe is to be seen above the
water's edge.   With its present burden, it would be
impossible for her to sail on any river less smooth
than the Niger, and even as it is, when it comes to
be paddled, there will be danger of its being swamped.
It is really laughable to reflect that the canoe
is supplied with two immense speaking-trumpets,
which, considering the Stentorian lungs of the men
of Brass, are entirely superfluous, and that she is
commanded by regularly appointed officers, with
sounding titles, in imitation of European vessels,
such as captain, mate, boatswain, coxswain, &c.,
besides a cook and his minions.   These distinctions
are encouraged by King Boy, whose vanity and
consequence even in the most trifling concerns is
irresistibly diverting.   We shall sleep in the canoe
to-night, but it is almost unnecessary to say that
want of room, as in former cases, will be an intolerable grievance.

` Before we embarked, we had taken a little boiled
yam with palm-oil at Obie's house, and we remained
two hours lying by the bank.   At seven in the evening we settled ourselves for the night, but found
that we were exceedingly cramped up from want of
room, occasioned by the yams being stowed badly.

CHAPTER XX.

Friday, November 12th.—A GREAT tumult arose
last night between the natives and the men of Brass,
which might have had a serious and fatal termination,
if the latter had not taken timely precaution to convey
their canoe from the beach into the middle of the
stream, whither the natives could not follow them.
The natives had flocked down to the water's edge
in considerable numbers, armed with muskets, spears,
and other offensive weapons, and kept up a dreadful noise, like the howling of wolves, till long after
midnight, when the uproar died away.   During the
night my brother experienced a smart paroxysm of
fever, which left him towards morning very languid
and heartless.   He was prevented from taking medicine, not only from our exposed situation, but likewise from its awkwardness and unpleasantness,
originating from the number of people among whom
we were literally jammed.   King Boy slept on
shore with his wife *Addizetta,* who is Obie's favourite daughter, and on her account we waited till
between seven and eight o'clock in the morning,
when she made her appearance with her husband,
—who we understand has embraced the present opportunity of making an excursion with her to his
native country, to vary her life a little by a change
of air and scene, and to introduce her to his other
wives and relatives residing at Brass.   She has

Vive l'union!

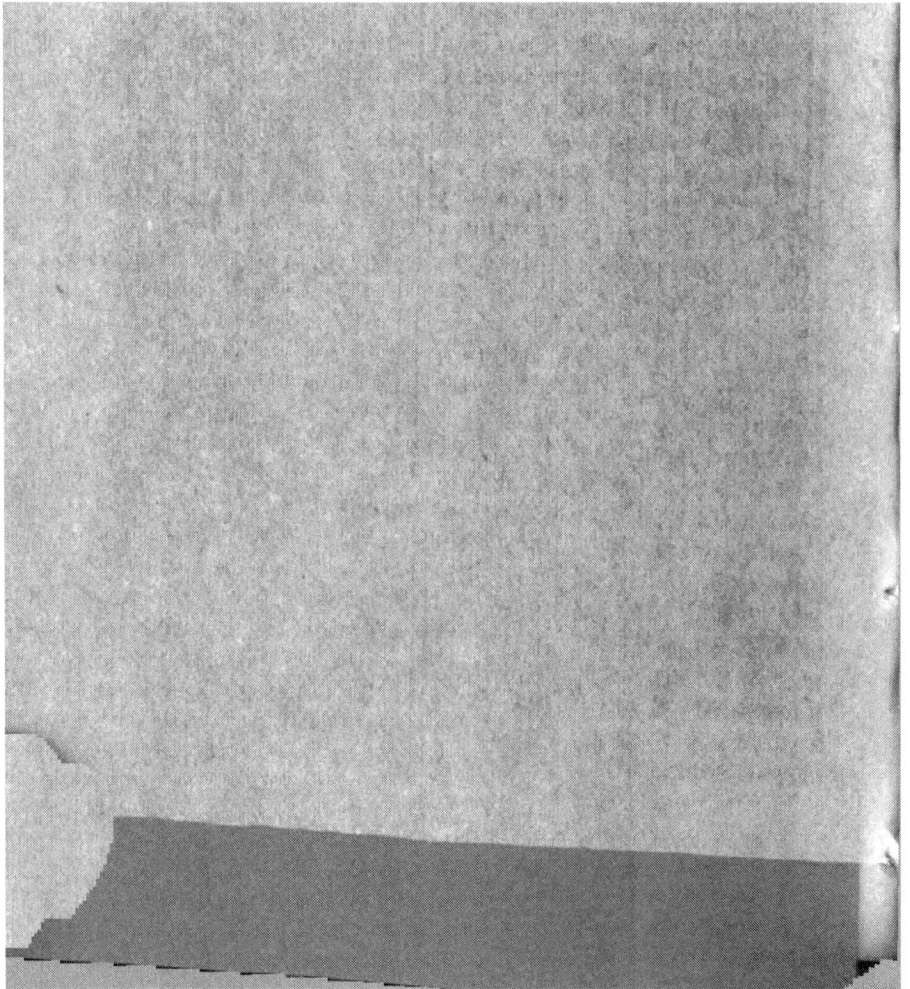

besides expressed a desire to see white men's ships, and it is partly to gratify her curiosity in this particular that she is going with us. On stepping into the canoe, with a spirit of gallantry, Boy handed her to the best seat, which was a box, close to which he himself sat; and which we had relinquished in her favour from motives of delicacy. Her face was towards the bow, while my brother and I sat directly *vis à vis* on a heap of yams; but we were so close to the opposite party, that our legs came continually in contact, which threatened to produce much inconvenience and some confusion. We were still further detained by removing various heavy articles into another canoe which was lying alongside, because ours was pronounced too deeply laden to be safe; but after all she did not appear to be lightened very considerably. This being done, at half-past seven we pushed off the Eboe shore, and for a little while, with forty paddles dashing up the silvery foam at the same moment, we glided through the water with the speed of a dolphin. To us it afforded no small gratification.

The eyes of man are so placed in his head, that it has been frequently observed, whether sitting or standing, he can behold earth and sky at the same moment without inconvenience, which is an advantage, I believe, that no other animal possesses in an equal degree, if he does at all. As I was reflecting on this circumstance, I happened to cast my eyes towards the horizon, to convince myself of its reality, when I found the tall, masculine figure of Obie's favourite daughter intercepted it entirely from my view. Being thus balked for the moment in my intentions, I was instantly diverted from them, and I thought the opportunity favourable for studying the physiognomy and person of King Boy's " ladye-love." Addizetta may be between twenty and thirty years of age, or perhaps younger, for she takes snuff, and females arrive at womanhood in

warm countries much sooner than in cold ones.
Her person is tall, stout, and well proportioned,
though it has not dignity sufficient to be commanding; her countenance is round and open, but dull,
and almost inexpressive; mildness of manners, even
ness of temper, and inactivity of body also, might
notwithstanding, I think, be clearly defined in it,
on the whole she had a perfect virginity of face,
which betrays not the smallest symptom of feeling.
Her forehead is smooth and shining as polished
ebony, but it is rather too low to be noble; her eyes
full, large, and beautiful, though languid; her cheeks
of a Dutch-like breadth and fulness; her nose finely
compressed, but not quite so distinguished a feature
as the negro nose in general; there is a degree of
prettiness about her mouth, the lips not being disa-
greeably large, which is further embellished by a
set of elegant teeth, perfectly even and regular, and
white as the teeth of a greyhound; her chin—but
I am unable to describe a chin; I only know that it
agrees very well with the other features of the face.

Addizetta seldom laughs, but smiles or simpers
most engagingly whenever she is more than ordi-
narily pleased; and she seems not to be unconscious
of the powerful influence which these smiles have
over the mind of her husband. Her dress and personal ornaments may be described in few words;
the former consisting simply of a piece of figured
silk, encircling the waist, and extending as far as
the knees; her woolly hair, which is tastefully
braided, is enclosed in a net, and ends in a peak at
the top; the net is adorned, but not profusely, with
coral beads, strings of which hang from the crown to
the forehead. She wears necklaces of the same
costly bead, copper rings encircle her fingers and
great toes, bracelets of ivory her wrist, and enormous rings, also of elephant's tusks, decorate her
legs, near the ankle, by which she is almost disabled
from walking, on account of their ponderous weight

and immense size. I had almost finished the scrutiny of her person, when Addizetta, observing me regarding her with more than common attention, at length caught my eye, and turned away her head with a triumphant kind of smile, as much as to say, " Ay, white man, you may well admire and adore my person; I perceive you are struck with my beauty, and no wonder neither ;" yet I immediately checked the ill-natured construction which I had put on her looks, and accused myself of injustice. For though, said I to myself, Addizetta, poor simple savage, may be as fond of admiration as her white sisters in more civilized lands; yet her thoughts, for aught I know, might have been very remote from vanity and self-love. However, that she smiled I am quite certain, and very prettily too, for I saw a circling dimple radiating upon her full, round cheek, which terminated in a momentary gleam of animation, and illuminated her dark languishing eye like a flash of light—and what could all this mean? I had forgotten to say that the person of Obie's daughter is tattooed in various parts; but the incisions, or rather lacerations, are irregular and unseemly. Her bosom in particular, bears evident marks of the cutting and gashing which it had received when Addizetta was a child; for the wounds having badly healed, the skin over them is risen a full half inch above the natural surface. By the side of each eye, near the temple vein, a representation of the point of an arrow is alone formed with tolerable accuracy. They look as though indigo had been inserted into the flesh with a needle; and by this peculiarity, with which every female's face is impressed, the Eboe women are distinguished from their neighbours and surrounding tribes.

Before breakfast, Addizetta was employed above an hour in cleaning and polishing her teeth, by rubbing them with the fibrous roots of a certain shrub or tree, which are much esteemed and generally

II.—T

used for the purpose in her own country, as well as in the more interior parts. Great part of the day is consumed by many thousands of individuals in this amusing occupation, and to this cause the brilliant whiteness of their teeth for which Africans, generally speaking, are remarkable, may be attributed.

About ten in the morning a mess of fish, boiled with yams and plantains, was produced for breakfast. As King Boy was fearful that our presence might incommode his lady, we were desired to move farther back, that she might eat with additional confidence and comfort, for alas! we are not placed on an equality with Addizetta and her kingly spouse. When they had breakfasted, and swallowed a calabash of water from the stream, we ourselves were served with a plateful, and afterward the boat's crew and the slaves were likewise regaled with yams and water. In the evening another refreshment, similar to this, was served round to all; and these are the only meals which the men of Brass have during the twenty-four hours. Before eating himself, Boy makes it a practice of offering a small portion of his food to " the spirits of the river," that his voyage may be rendered propitious by conciliating their good-will. Previous also to his drinking a glass of rum or spirits, he pours a few drops of it into the water, invoking the protection of these fanciful beings, by muttering several expressions between his teeth, the tenor of which, of course, we do not understand. This religious observance, we are told, is invariably performed whenever the Brass people have occasion to leave their country by water, or return to it by the same means; it is called a meat and drink offering, and is celebrated at every meal. A custom very similar to this prevails in Yarriba, at Badágry, Cape Coast Castle, and along the western coast generally;—the natives of those places never take a glass of spirits without spilling a quantity of it on the ground, as a "fetish." In the morning we observed a branch of the river running out in a westerly direction, the course of the main body being south-west.

We stopped awhile at various little villages during the day, to purchase yams, bananas, and cocoanuts ; and the curiosity of their poor inhabitants at our appearance was intense. They are chiefly fishermen or husbandmen, and notwithstanding our uncouth and remarkable dress, they behaved to us without rudeness, and even with civility, so that their inquisitiveness was not disagreeable. Speaking-trumpets, we should imagine, are quite a novelty with the men of Brass, by the extraordinary rapture which they display for their music, which certainly is any thing but melodious. Two of these instruments, as we said yesterday, are in the canoe, for the convenience of issuing orders; and they have not been from the mouths of the officers for ten minutes together during the whole day, so great has been the desire of all to breathe through them, and add to the deafening noises made by their constant quarrelling with each other. This is a great annoyance, but we are constrained to submit to it in silence ; besides, it is entirely superfluous, for the voices of the people are of themselves loud and powerful enough for all the common purposes of life ; and when they have a mind to strain their *brazen* lungs, no speaking-trumpet that has ever been made, be it ever so large, could match the quantity of horrid sound which they make—it would drown the roaring of the sea. In addition to the officers and attendants in the canoe that we mentioned yesterday, we have one drummer, the king's steward, and his lady's maid, and two persons to bail out water, besides three captains, to give the necessary directions for the safety of the canoe. The noise made by these fellows as we started, in bawling to their fetish through the trumpet, was beyond all description. Their object was to secure us a safe journey, and most certainly, if noise could do so, we were pretty certain of it. The villages that we passed in the course of the day were very numerous, and distant not more than two or three miles from each other on the banks of the river. They were surrounded by more cultivated land than we have seen this last fortnight; the crops consisting of yams, bananas, plantains, Indian corn, &c. &c., and we have not seen so much since leaving Kacunda. The banks here seem to be well calculated for the growth of rice, and every other grain that we have seen in the interior. The villages had a pleasing appearance from the river. The houses seem to be built of a light-coloured clay, and being thatched with palm branches, they very much resemble our own cottages. They are of a square form, with two windows on each side of the door, but have no upper rooms.

The villagers seem to be equally as distrustful as those above Eboe town in trading with our people, for the men only came down with their yams and fish, and were armed with guns and swords. The fish they brought us consisted of cat-fish and shrimps, which had been smoked over a wood-fire, and when boiled were very palatable. The villagers had no tattoo marks; they wear the grass cloth fastened round their waists, and the better sort wore printed cottons. We engaged two small canoes to carry the yams we had purchased.

In many places we observed that the river had overflowed its banks, and was running between the trees and thick underwood. In the widest part, it did not seem to be more than a mile and a half across. The course of the river has been to-day nearly south-west: its width is sensibly diminishing, indeed it is fast dwindling away into an ordinary stream.

Saturday, November 13th.—Perhaps there cannot be a greater comfort under the sun than sound and

Invigorating sleep to the weary; nor, in our opinion, a greater grievance than the loss of it; because wakefulness, at those hours which nature has destined for repose is, in nine cases out of ten, sure to be the harbinger of peevishness, discontent, and ill-humour, and not unfrequently induces languor, lassitude, and disease. No two individuals in the world have greater reason to complain of disturbed slumbers or nightly watching than ourselves. Heretofore this has been occasioned chiefly by exposure to damps, rains, and dews, mosquito attacks, frightful and piercing noises, and over-fatigue, or apprehension and anxiety of mind. But now, in the absence of most of these causes, we are cramped, painfully cramped, for want of room, insomuch that when we feel drowsy, we find it impossible to place ourselves in a recumbent posture, without having the heavy legs of Mr. and Mrs. Boy, with their prodigious ornaments of ivory, placed either on our faces or on our breasts. From such a situation it requires almost the strength of a rhinoceros to be freed: it is excessively teasing. Last night we were particularly unfortunate in this respect; and a second attack of fever, which came on me in the evening, rendered my condition lamentable indeed, and truly piteous. It would be ridiculous to suppose that one can enjoy the refreshment of sleep, how much soever it may be required, when two or more uncovered legs and feet, huge, black, and rough, are traversing one's face and body, stopping up the passages of respiration, and pressing so heavily upon them at times as to threaten suffocation. I could not long endure so serious an inconvenience, but preferred last night sitting up in the canoe. My brother was indisposed, and, in fact, unable to follow my example and, therefore, I endeavoured if possible to render his situation more tolerable. With this object in view, I pinched the feet of our snoring companions (Mr. and Mrs. Boy) repeatedly, till the pain caused them to awake, and remove them from his face, and this enabled him to draw backwards a few inches, and place his head into a narrow recess which is formed by two boxes. However, this did not allow him liberty to turn it either way, and thus jammed, with no command whatever over his suffering limbs, he passed the hours without sleep, and arose this morning with bruised bones and sore limbs, complaining bitterly of the wretched moments which the legs of Mr. and Mrs. Boy had caused him, with their ivory rings and heaps of yams.

It was not till two o'clock this morning that we arrived at a convenient place for stopping awhile, to give the canoe-men rest from their labour; and at daybreak we launched out again into the river, and paddled down the stream. At seven in the morning, Boy and his wife having landed to trade, I took their place, and slept soundly an hour and a half, which quite refreshed me. Without encountering any thing remarkable, we passed the day in much the same manner as yesterday, stopping occasionally at certain villages which are scattered along the banks, for the purpose of bartering with their inhabitants. Plantains, bananas, and yams are cultivated by them to an extraordinary and almost incredible extent, and for the space of nearly twenty miles scarcely any thing else but plantations of these shrubs and vegetables are to be seen. This circumstance has led us to infer that the country is infinitely more populous than its general appearance would seem to indicate. It is flat, open, varied, and beautiful in many places, and its soil is a rich dark mould or loam. But notwithstanding this extensive cultivated tract, and other large and verdant patches, the useless mangrove-tree (*rhizophera mangle*), with its pendant branches and impenetrable roots, is fast encroaching on every moist situation the nearer we approach the sea.

We continued our course down the river until two

hours after midnight, when we stopped near a small
village on the east side of the river. We made fast
to the shore, and the people settled themselves in
the canoe to sleep. Having sat up the whole of last
night, for the best of all reasons, because I could find
no room to lie down, in consequence of the crowded
state of our canoe, and feeling myself quite unequal
to do the same again, I took my mat and went on
shore, determined, if possible, to sleep on the ground.
Overcome by fatigue and the fear of being attacked
by alligators, or any thing else, I selected a dry
place, and laid myself down on my mat. I had
nearly dropped asleep, when I was roused by several
severe stings, and found myself covered with black
ants. They had got up my trousers, and were tormenting me dreadfully. At first I knew not which
way to get rid of them, and ran about as fast as I
could, with the idea of shaking them off me, but
with all my endeavours it was long before I could
get rid of them. Our men, Paskoe, Sam, and Jowdie, seeing the condition I was in, landed from the
canoe, and made large fires in the form of a ring, and
I laid down in the midst of them and slept till daylight. The sting of a black ant is quite as painful
as that of a wasp.

Sunday, November 14*th.*—This morning at daylight,
when the natives brought their fish and yams to our
people for sale, they did not appear to be at all surprised at seeing our white faces, from which I am
led to believe that they have seen white men at the
seaside. At five in the morning we again resumed
our course down the river. At ten A. M. we passed
a small branch of the river running off east-south-
east.

In the course of the day we passed several sand-
banks in the middle of the river, and our people ran
the canoe aground on them purposely, to get into
the water and to have a wash. The sun was exceedingly powerful, and they appeared to enjoy the water

very much. The channels of the rivei on each side
of the banks appear to be very deep, and the depth
on the banks I concluded to be about three feet.
After our people had taken a good wash, we again
proceeded onwards.

At seven in the evening we departed from the main
river, and took our course up a small branch towards
Brass town, running in a direction about south-east
by east from that which we had left.   The course of
the river has been about south, and continued in the
same direction when we left it.   It has overflowed
its banks in many places that we passed to-day, and is
considerably diminished in its breadth.   The widest
part was not more than a mile and a half across, and
the narrowest about three hundred yards.   We have
seen many villages in the course of the day, and
where the banks were not overflown, there was
much cultivated land.

At half-past eight in the evening, to our great satisfaction, we found ourselves influenced by the tide.
We had previously observed an appearance of foam
on the water, which might have been carried up by
the flood-tide from the mouth of the river; but we
now felt certain of being within its influence.   We
were constantly annoyed by the canoe running
aground on a bank, or sticking fast in the underwood, which delayed our progress considerably, and
the men were obliged to get out to lighten and lift
the canoe off them.   Our track was through a narrow creek arched over by mangroves, so as to form
a complete avenue, which in many places was so
thick as to be totally impenetrable by the light above.
At ten P. M. a heavy shower of rain wetted us thoroughly; and after this was over, the dripping from
the trees which overhung the canoe kept us in constant rain nearly all night.   The smell from decayed
vegetable substances was sickly and exceedingly
disagreeable.

Monday, November 15th.—Through these gloomy

and dismal passages we travelled during the whole
of last night, without stopping, unless for a few
minutes at a time to disengage ourselves from the
pendent shoots of the mangrove and spreading bram-
bles in which we occasionally became entangled.
These luxuriant natives of the soil are so intricately
woven, that it would be next to impossible to eradi-
cate them.   Their roots and branches are the receptacles of ooze, mud, and filth of all kinds, exhaling
a peculiarly offensive odour, which no doubt possesses highly deleterious qualities.   The reason ad-
duced for not resting during the night was the apprehension entertained by King Boy of being unable
to overtake his father and brothers this morning,
they having left the Eboe country the day before us.
A certain spot had previously been fixed on by the
parties for the meeting, and we arrived there about
nine o'clock A. M., and found those individuals in
three large canoes, with their attendants, waiting
our arrival.   Here we stopped, and made our canoes
fast to the trees, to take refreshment, such as it was,
and half an hour's rest; and here we were introduced to the renowned King Forday, who, according to his own account, is monarch of the whole
country.   In one of the canoes sat old King Forday,
in company with several fetish priests; the second
canoe belonged to King Boy, and the third was Mr.
Gun's.   These canoes had come thus far for the
purpose of escorting us into their country.
  King Forday is a complacent, venerable-looking
old man, but was rather shabbily dressed, partly in
the European and partly in the native style.   Like
most savages, his fondness for spirituous liquors is
extreme, and he drank large potations of rum in our
presence, though it produced no visible effect either
upon his manners or conversation. In the jollity of the
moment he attempted to sing, but his weak, piping
voice did not seem to second his inclination, and the
sound died away from very feebleness.   His sub-
  II.—U

jects, however, amounting to nearly two hundred individuals, testified their approbation of the effort by a tremendous "Yah!" shouted simultaneously by every voice, which sounded like the roar of a lion.

During the time we had been at breakfast the tide ebbed and left our canoes lying on the mud. Breakfast being over, the fetish priests commenced their avocations by marking the person of King Boy from head to foot with chalk, in lines, circles, and a variety of fantastic figures, which so completely metamorphosed him as to render his identity rather questionable at the distance of only a few yards. His usual dress had been thrown aside, and he was allowed to wear nothing but a narrow silk handkerchief tied round his waist; on his head a little close cap was placed, made of grass, and ornamented with large feathers. These, we found, were the wing feathers of a black and white buzzard, which is the fetish bird of Brass town. Two huge spears were also chalked and put into his hands, and thus equipped his appearance was wild and grotesque in the extreme. The same operation was performed on the rest of the party, and the fetish priests were chalked in the same manner. Our own people were merely marked in the forehead, and ourselves, perhaps from being already white, although our faces were not a little tanned, were exempted from the ceremony.

At eleven A. M. we were ordered into King Forday's canoe to sit down with him. The old man asked us immediately, in tolerably good English, to take a glass of rum with him, and having seen us wondering at the strange appearance of King Boy and the rest of the party, gave us to understand that n consequence of no man having come down the river as we had, it was done to prevent any thing bad happening to them. We also understood from him that a certain rite would be performed to Djudju, the fetish or domestic god of Brass town, in honour of our coming. The tide was now fast returning, and preparations were made for proceeding to Brass town. For this purpose the canoes were all arranged in a line, that of King Boy taking the lead, ourselves and King Forday in the next, followed by King Boy's brother, Mr. Gun, and the Damuggoo people in others, and in this order we proceeded up the river. Gun is styled the *little military king* of Brass town, from being intrusted with the care of all the arms and ammunition, and on this occasion he gave us frequent opportunities of witnessing his importance and activity, by suddenly passing a short distance before the rest of the canoes and firing off the cannon in the bow of his own, and then dropping behind again.

The whole procession formed one of the most extraordinary sights that can be imagined. The canoes were following each other up the river in tolerable order, each of them displaying three flags. In the first was King Boy, standing erect and conspicuous, his head-dress of feathers waving with the movements of his body, which had been chalked in various fantastic figures, rendered more distinct by its natural colour; his hands were resting on the barbs of two immense spears, which at intervals he darted violently into the bottom of the canoe, as if he were in the act of killing some formidable wild animal under his feet. In the bows of all the other canoes fetish priests were dancing and performing various extraordinary antics, their persons, as well as those of the people in them, being chalked over in the same manner as that of King Boy; and, to crown the whole, Mr. Gun, the little military gentleman, was most actively employed, his canoe now darting before and now dropping behind the rest, adding not a little to the imposing effect of the whole scene by 'he repeated discharges of his cannon.

In this manner we continued on till about noon, when we entered a little bay, and saw before us, on the south side of it, two distinct groups of buildings, one of which is King Forday's town, and the other King Jacket's town. The cannons in all the canoes were now fired off, and the whole of the people were quickly on the look-out to witness our approach. The firing having ceased, the greatest stillness prevailed, and the canoes moved forward very slowly between the two towns to a small island a little to the east of Jacket's town. This island is the abode of the Dju-dju, or grand fetish priest, and his wives, no one else being permitted to reside there. As we passed Forday's town, a salute of seven guns was fired off at a small battery near the water. The canoes stopped near the fetish hut on the island, which is a low insignificant building of clay. The priest, who was chalked over nearly in the same manner as Boy, drew near to the water's edge, and with a peculiar air asked some questions, which appeared to be answered to his satisfaction. Boy then landed, and, preceded by the tall figure of the priest, entered the religious hut. Soon after this the priest came to the water-side, and, looking on us with much earnestness, broke an egg, and poured some liquid into the water, after which he again returned to the hut. The Brass men then rushed on a sudden into the water, and returned in the same hasty manner, which to us appeared equally as mysterious as the rest of the ceremony.

After remaining at the island about an hour, during which time Boy was in the hut with the priest, he rejoined us, and we proceeded to Forday's town and took up our residence at Boy's house. In the extraordinary ceremony which we had just witnessed, it was evident that we were the persons principally concerned; but whether it terminated in our favour or against us—whether the answers of the Dju-dju were propitious or otherwise, we shall be able to ascertain only by the future behaviour of the Brass people towards us.

We saw with emotions of joy a white man on shore while we were in the canoe, waiting the conclusion of the ceremony. It was a cheering and goodly sight to recognise the features of a European in the midst of a crowd of savages. This individual paid us a visit in the evening; his behaviour was perfectly affable, courteous, and obliging, and in the course of a conversation which we had with him, he informed us that he is master of the Spanish schooner which is at present lying in the Brass river for slaves. Six of her crew, who have been ill of fever, and are still indisposed, likewise reside in the town.

Tuesday, Nov. 16th.—Of all the wretched, filthy, and contemptible places in this world of ours, none can present to the eye of a stranger so miserable an appearance, or can offer such disgusting and loathsome sights, as this abominable Brass town. Dogs, goats, and other animals run about the dirty streets, half-starved, whose hungry looks can only be exceeded by the famishing appearance of the men, women, and children, which bespeaks the penury and wretchedness to which they are reduced; while the persons of many of them are covered with odious biles, and their huts are falling to the ground from neglect and decay.

Brass, properly speaking, consists of two towns, of nearly equal size, containing about a thousand inhabitants each, and built on the borders of a kind of basin, which is formed by a number of rivulets, entering it from the Niger through forests of mangrove bushes. One of them is under the domination of a noted scoundrel called *King Jacket,* who has already been spoken of; and the other is governed by a rival chief, named *King Forday.* These towns are situated directly opposite each other, and within the distance of eighty yards; and are built on a marshy ground, which occasions the huts to be always wet. Another place, called "Pilot's town" by Europeans, from the number of pilots that reside in it, is situated nearly at the mouth of the First Brass River (which we understand is the "*Nun*" river of Europeans), and at the distance of sixty or seventy miles from hence. This town acknowledges the authority of both kings, having been originally peopled by settlers from each of their towns. At the ebb of the tide, the basin is left perfectly dry, with the exception of small gutters, and presents a smooth and almost unvaried surface of black mud, which emits an intolerable odour, owing to the decomposition of vegetable substances, and the quantity of filth and nastiness which is thrown into the basin by the inhabitants of both towns. Notwithstanding this nuisance, both children and grown-up persons may be seen sporting in the mud, whenever the tide goes out, all naked, and amusing themselves in the same manner as if they were on shore.

The Brass people grow neither yams nor bananas, nor grain of any kind, cultivating only the plantain as an article of food, which, with the addition of a little fish, forms their principal article of diet. Yams, however, are freely imported from Eboe and other countries by the chief people, who resell great quantities of them to the shipping that may happen to be in the river. They are enabled to do this by the very considerable profits which accrue to them from their trading transactions with people residing farther inland, and from the palm-oil which they themselves manufacture, and which they dispose of to the Liverpool traders. The soil in the vicinity of Brass is for the most part poor and marshy, though it is covered with a rank, luxuriant, and impenetrable vegetation: even in the hands of an active, industrious race, it would offer almost insuperable obstacles to general cultivation; but with its present possessors the mangrove itself can never be extirpated, and the country will, it is likely

enough, maintain its present appearance till the end
of time.

The dwelling in which we reside belongs to King
Boy; it stands on the extreme edge of the basin, and
was constructed not long since by a carpenter, who
came up the river for the purpose from Calebar, of
which place he is a native; he received seven slaves
for his labour. The man must have seen European
dwellings, as this is evidently an attempt to imitate
them. Its form is oblong, and it contains four apartments, which are all on the ground floor, lined with
wood, and furnished with tolerably made doors and
cupboards. This wood bears decided marks of its
having once formed part of a vessel, and is most
likely the remains of one which was wrecked, we
hear, not long ago, on the bar of the river. The
house has recently been converted into a kind of
seraglio by King Boy, because he has, to use his own
expression, "plenty of wives," who require looking
after. It also answers the purpose of a storehouse
for European goods, tobacco, and spirituous liquors.
Its rafters are of bamboo, and its thatch of palm-
leaves. The apartment which we occupy has a
window overlooking the basin, outside which is a
veranda, at present occupied by Pascoe and his
wives. The whole of its furniture consists of an
old oaken table; but it is supplied with seats made
of clay, which are raised about three feet from the
ground. These, together with the floor, which is of
mud, are so soft and wet, as to enable a person to
thrust his hand into any part of them, without any
difficulty whatever. In one corner communicating
with the other apartments is a door, which is destitute of a lock, and kept always ajar, except at night,
when it is closed. One of the sides of the room is
decorated with an old French print representing the
Virgin Mary, with a great number of chubby-faced
angels ministering to her, at whose feet is a prayer

on "Our Lady's good deliverance." The whole group is designed and executed in very bad taste.

When the tide is in, the water flows up to the doors and windows of our house, which may perhaps account for its dampness; it is held in very high estimation by its owner, and called an English house. The houses in general are built of a sort of yellow clay, and the windows are all furnished with shutters. There are several huts opposite the town, where the people make salt, after the rains are over: the water at present is brackish, from the effect of the rains; but in the course of two months, Boy tells us that it will be quite salt, when they will again commence making it. It is an article of trade, and appears to be taken in large quantities to the Eboe market, where it is exchanged for yams, the cowry shell not being circulated lower down the river than Bocquâ. The principal employment of the people consists in making salt, fishing, boiling oil, and trading to the Eboe country, for not a particle of cultivated land is to be seen. They live exclusively on yams and palm-oil, with sometimes a small quantity of fish. They bring poultry from the Eboe country, but rear very little themselves, and what they have are carefully preserved and sold to the ships that frequent the river.

A little palm-oil would be a great luxury to us, but King Boy will not give us any. Our allowance consists of half of a small yam each day; but this evening, King Boy being out of the way, two of his wives brought us half a glass of rum each, and four yams: this was a great treat to us, but a considerable risk to them, for had Boy discovered the theft, it is more than likely he would have had them flogged and sold.

Wet and uncomfortable as is our dwelling, yet it is infinitely more desirable and convenient than our confined quarters in the canoe, for here we have the pleasure of reposing at full length, which is a luxury we could not have purchased on the water at any price. The Spanish captain visited us again this morning, and left the town in the afternoon on his return to his vessel: slaves, he tells us, are very scarce, and obtained with difficulty and expense.

To-day I was requested to visit King Forday, and I accordingly complied with the summons. His house is about a hundred yards distant from that of King Boy, and on entering it I found him sitting half-drunk, with about a dozen of his wives and a number of dogs, in a small filthy room. I was desired to sit down by his side, and to drink a glass of rum. He then gave me to understand, as well as he could, that it was customary for every white man who came to the river, to pay him four bars. I expressed my ignorance and surprise at this, but was soon silenced by his saying, " That is my demand, and I shall not allow you to leave this town until you give me a *book* for that amount." Seeing that I had nothing to do but to comply with his demand, I gave him a bill on Lake, the commander of the English vessel, after which he said, " To-morrow you may go to the brig, take one servant with you: but your mate" (meaning my brother) "must remain here with your seven people, until my son, King Boy, shall bring the goods for himself and me; after this they shall be sent on board without delay." Much as I regretted the necessity of parting with my brother, I was obliged to agree to this arrangement; and with the hopes of profiting by it, I told King Forday that we were all very hungry, and begged him to send us a fowl or two, which he promised to do.

In order that I might make a decent appearance before my countrymen to-morrow, I have been obliged to sit all the afternoon with an old cloth wrapped round me, until my clothes were washed and dried. It is now six in the evening, and the mean old king has sent us neither fowls nor yams.

This is the most starving place that I have yet seen.
Mr. Gun has given us two meals since our arrival
here, consisting of a little pounded yam, and fish
stewed in palm-oil, and for this he has the impudence to demand two muskets in payment. These
fellows, like the rest on the coast, are a set of im
posing rascals, little better than downright savages
We are told that they have absolutely starved three
white men to death lately, who were wrecked in a
slaving vessel, when crossing the bar.

CHAPTER XXI.

Wednesday, November 17th.—I HAD determined that
one of our men should accompany me down the
river; and at ten o'clock, having taken leave of my
brother and the rest of our party, we embarked in
King Boy's canoe, with a light heart and an anxious
mind. Although distant about sixty miles from the
mouth of the river, our journey appeared to me already completed, and all our troubles and difficulties
I considered at an end. Already, in fond anticipation, I was on board of the brig, and had found a
welcome reception from her commander,—had related to him all the hardships and dangers we had
undergone, and had been listened to with commise-
ration,—already had I assured myself of his doing

all he could to enable me to fulfil my engagements with these people, and thought ourselves happy in finding a vessel belonging to our own country in the river at the time of our arrival. These meditations, and a train of others about home and friends, to which they naturally led, occupied my mind, as our canoe passed through the narrow creeks, sometimes winding under avenues of mangrove-trees, and at others expanding into small lakes occasioned by the overflowing of the river. The captain of the canoe, a tall sturdy fellow, was standing up, directing its course, occasionally hallooing, as we came to a turn in the creek, to the fetish, and where an echo was returned, half a glass of rum and a piece of yam and fish were thrown into the water. I had never seen this done before; and on asking Boy the reason why he was throwing away the provisions thus, he asked, " Did you not hear the fetish ?" The captain of the canoe replied, " Yes." " That is for the fetish," said Boy ; " if we do not feed him and do good for him he will kill us, or make us poor and sick." I could not help smiling at the ignorance of the poor creatures, but such is their firm belief.

We had pursued our course in this manner, which had been principally to the west, till about three in the afternoon, when we came to a branch of the river about two hundred yards wide, and seeing a small village a short distance before us, we stopped there for the purpose of obtaining some dried fish. Having supplied our wants and proceeded on, about an hour afterward we again stopped, that our people might eat something. Boy very kindly presented me with a large piece of yam, reserving to himself all the fish we had got at the village, and after making a hearty meal off them, he fell asleep : while he was snoring by my side, the remainder of the fish attracted my notice, and not feeling half satisfied with the yam he had given me, I felt an irresistible inclination to taste them. Conscience acquitted me on the score of hunger, and hinted that such an opportunity should not be lost; and accordingly, I very quickly demolished two small ones.   Although entirely raw, they were delicious, and I do not remember to have enjoyed any thing with a better relish in all my life.

There is scarcely a spot of dry land to be seen anywhere; all is covered with water and mangrove-trees.   After remaining about half an hour here, we again went forward, and at seven in the evening arrived in the Second Brass River, which is a large branch of the Quorra.   We kept our course down it about due south, and half an hour afterward I heard the welcome sound of the surf on the beach. We still continued onward, and at a quarter before eight in the evening we made our canoe fast to a tree for the night, on the west bank of the river.

Thursday, November 18*th.*—This morning I found my clothes as thoroughly wet from the effects of the dew as if I had been lying in the river all night in stead of the canoe.   This was disagreeable enough, but I had gone through as bad before, and a short time, I flattered myself, would put an end to all such trouble.   At five in the morning we let go the rope from the tree, and took our course in a westerly direction up a creek.   At seven we arrived in the main branch of the Quorra, which is called the river Nun, or the First Brass River, having entered it opposite to a large branch, which King Boy informed me runs to Benin.   The direction of the river Nun was here nearly north and south, and we kept on our course down the stream.

About a quarter of an hour after we had entered the river Nun, we descried, at a distance before us, two vessels lying at anchor.   The emotions of delight which the sight of them occasioned are quite beyond my powers of description.   The nearest to us was a schooner, a Spanish slave-vessel, whose captain we had seen at Brass town.   Our canoe

was quickly by her side, and I went on board   The
captain received me very kindly, and invited me to
take some spirits and water with him.   He complained sadly of the sickly state of the crew, asserting that the river was extremely unhealthy, and that
he had only been in it six weeks, in which time he
had lost as many men.   The remainder of his crew,
consisting of thirty persons, were in such a reduced
state, that they were scarcely able to move and
were lying about his decks more resemoing skele-
tons than living persons.   I could do no good here,
so I took my leave of the captain, and returned into
the canoe.

We now directed our course to the English brig,
which was lying about three hundred yards lower
down the river.   Having reached her, with feelings
of delight mingled with doubt, I went on board.
Here I found every thing in as sad a condition as I
had in the schooner; four of the crew had just died
of fever; four more, which completed the whole,
were lying sick in their hammocks, and the captain
appeared to be in the very last stage of illness.   He
had recovered from a severe attack of fever, and
had suffered a relapse in consequence of having
exposed himself too soon, which had nearly been
fatal to him.   I now stated to him who I was, explained my situation to him as fully as I could, and
had my instructions read to him by one of his own
people, that he might see I was not imposing on him.
I then requested that he would redeem us by paying
what had been demanded by King Boy, and assured
him that whatever he might give to him on our
account would certainly be repaid him by the British
government.   To my utter surprise and consternation, he flatly refused to give a single thing, and ill
and weak as he was, made use of the most offensive
and shameful oaths I ever heard.   "If you think,"
said he, " that you have a —— fool to deal with, you
are mistaken; I'll not give a b——y flint for your

bill; I would not give a —— for it." Petrified with
amazement, and horror-struck at such conduct, I
shrunk from him with terror. I could scarcely believe what I had heard, till my ears were assailed by
a repetition of the same. Disappointed beyond
measure by such brutal conduct from one of my
own countrymen, I could not have believed it possible; my feelings totally overpowered me, and I was
ready to sink with grief and shame. I returned to
the canoe, undetermined how to act, or what course
to pursue. Never in my life did I feel such humilia-
tion as at this moment. In our way through the
country we had been treated well; we had been in
the habit of making such presents as had been expected from us; and, above all, we had maintained
our character among the natives, by keeping our
promises. This was now no longer in my power,
as my means were all expended; and when, as a last
and, as I had imagined, a certain resource, I had
promised the price of our ransom should be paid by
the first of our countrymen that we might meet
with, on the best of all securities, to be thus refused
and dishonoured by him would, I know, degrade us
sadly in the opinion of the natives, if it did not les-
sen us in our own.

As there were no hopes that the captain of this
vessel would pay any thing for us, I went on board
again, and told King Boy that he must take us to
Bonny, as plenty of English ships were there. " No,
no," said he, " dis captain no pay, Bonny captain no
pay; I won't take you any further." As this would
not do, I again had recourse to the captain, and implored him to do something for me, telling him that
if he would let me have only ten muskets, Boy might
be content with them, when he found that he could
get nothing else. The only reply I received was,
" I have told you already I will not let you have even
a flint, so bother me no more."—" But I have a brother
and eight people at Brass town," I said to him; " and

If you do not intend to pay King Boy, at least persuade him to bring them here, or else he will poison or starve my brother before I can get any assistance from a man-of-war, and sell all my people." The only answer I received was, "If you can get them on board, I will take them away; but, as I have told you before, you do not get a flint from me." I then endeavoured to persuade Boy to go back for my people, and that he should be paid some time or other. "Yes," said the captain, "make haste and bring them." Boy very naturally required some of his goods before he went, and it was with no small difficulty I prevailed on him afterward to go without them.

The captain of the brig now inquired what men I had; and on my telling him that I had two seamen, and three others who might be useful to him in working his vessel, his tone and manner towards me softened a little. He agreed with me that they might be useful in getting the brig out of the river, as half of his crew were dead, and the other half sick; so I took courage and asked him for a piece of beef to send to my brother, and a small quantity of rum, which he readily gave me. I knew that my brother, as well as myself, much needed a change of linen, but I could not venture to ask such a thing from the captain with much hopes of success; so the cook of the brig appearing to be a respectable sort of man, I applied to him, and he produced me instantly three white shirts. King Boy was now ready to depart, not a little discontented, and I sent my man into his canoe with the few things I had been able to obtain, and a note for my brother. I desired him to give Antonio an order on any English captain that he might find at Bonny, for his wages, and also one for the Damuggoo people, that they might receive the small present I had promised to their good old chief, who had treated us so well. At two in the afternoon King Boy left me, promising to return

with my brother and people in three days, but grumbling at not having been paid his goods.

I now endeavoured to make myself as comfortable as I could in the vessel; and thinking that the
captain might change his behaviour towards me
when he got better, I determined to have as little to
say to him till then as possible.

Friday, November 19th.—This morning Captain
Lake seemed to be much better, and I ventured to
ask him for a change of linen, of which I was in
great want. He readily complied with my request,
and I enjoyed a luxury which I had not experienced
a long time. In the course of the morning I conversed with him about our travels in the country,
and related the whole particulars of the manner in
which we had been attacked and plundered at
Kirree. I explained to him how King Boy had
saved us from slavery in the Eboe country, and
how much we felt indebted to him for it. I endeavoured to impress this on his mind particularly, as I
still hoped to bring him round to pay Boy what I
had promised him. Having laid all before him as
fully as I was able, and pointed out to him the bad
opinion Boy would have of us, and the injurious
tendency towards Englishmen in general that would
result from not keeping our word with him, which
it was in his power to enable us to do, I asked him
to give me ten muskets for my bill on government.
He had listened to my story with attention, but I no
sooner advanced my wants, than with a furious oath
he repeated his refusal, and finding him as determined
as ever he had been, I mentioned it no more. He
moreover told me, in the most unkind and petulant
manner, "If your brother and people are not here
in three days, I go without them." This I believed
he would not do, as the men would be of service to
him, but I had Boy's promise that they should be
with me at that time.

In the middle of the day, the pilot who had

brought the vessel into the river came on board and demanded payment for it, which gave me an opportunity of seeing more of the disposition of Mr. Lake. The pilot had no sooner made his business known than Lake flew into a violent rage, cursing him and abusing him in the most disgusting language he could use; he refused to pay him any thing whatever, and ordered him to go out of the ship immediately. Whether Lake was right or wrong in this· I know not, but I was shocked at his expressions, and the pilot reluctantly went away, threatening that he would sink his vessel if he offered to leave the river without paying him his due. I was rather surprised to hear such language from the pilot, and doubted his meaning, till I found that he had a battery of seven brass guns at the town on the eastern side of the river near its entrance, which, if well managed, might soon produce that effect. This town, as before observed, is named Pilot's town, being the established residence of those who conduct vessels over the bar.

Saturday, November 20*th.*—Captain Lake continues to recover from his illness. This morning I asked him if he would take us to Fernando Po when we left the river. This he refused, saying that the island had been given up, that there was not a single white man on it, and that we could get no assistance there; but that if all my people should arrive by the morning of the 23d, he would land us at *Bimbia,* a small island in the river Cameroons, whither he was going to complete his cargo, and at this island he said I should find a white man, who keeps a store for Captain Smith. I was quite satisfied with this arrangement, feeling assured that I should get every thing I might want from him.

My chief concern was about my brother, and I much feared that the vessel would sail without him, for there was no dependence on the captain, so little did he care for us, or the object of our visiting the

II.—X

country. I took an opportunity of begging him, in the event of my brother and the men not arriving by the 23d, to wait a little longer for them, asserting at the same time that if he went away without them they would be assuredly starved, or sold as slaves, before I could return to them with assistance. I might have just as well addressed myself to the wind. "I can't help it, I shall wait no longer," was the only reply he made me, in a surly, hasty tone, which convinced me that all attempts to reason with him would be fruitless.

In the afternoon the chief mate and three Kroomen were sent away by his direction to sound the bar of the river, in order to know whether there was sufficient depth of water for the vessel to pass over it. The pilot who had been dismissed so peremptorily yesterday was determined to have his revenge, and being naturally on the look-out, had observed the movements of the boat. So favourable an opportunity was not to be lost; and accordingly, watching her, he despatched an armed canoe, and intercepted her return at the mouth of the river. The mate of the brig and one of the Kroomen were quickly made prisoners and conveyed to the Pilot's-town, and the boat with the remainder sent back with a message to the captain, that they would not be given up until the pilotage should be paid. Lake must have felt annoyed at this; but whether he did or not, he treated it with the greatest indifference, saying that he did not čare, he would go to sea without his mate or the Kroomen either, and that he was determined not to pay the pilotage.

Sunday, November 21st.—Nothing remarkable occurred to-day. My thoughts were entirely occupied by my brother, and I felt very anxious for his return.

Monday, November 22d.—My anxiety for my brother's safety made me very unhappy, and I was on the look-out the whole day for him and our men

Lake, observing the distress I was in, told me not to trouble myself any more about them; adding, that he was sure he was dead, and that I need not expect to see him again. "If he had been alive," said Lake, " he would have been here by this time ; to-morrow morning I shall leave the river." Such unfeeling and inhuman conduct from this man only tended to increase my dislike for him, and without paying him any attention I kept looking out for my party. Such was my anxiety, that I was on the look-out long after dark, and could not sleep all night.

Tuesday, November 23d.—This morning, to my great joy and to the mortification of Lake, the sea breeze was so strong that it raised a considerable surf on the bar, and prevented us from getting out. This was an anxious time, and the whole of the day my eyes were riveted to the part of the river where I knew my brother must come, without my seeing any thing of him. The day passed away in tedious watching, and the night was far spent without my seeing him. About midnight I saw several large canoes making their way over to the west bank of the river, in one of which I imagined that I could distinguish my brother. I observed them soon after land, and saw, by the fires which they made, that they had encamped under some mangrove-trees. All my fears and apprehensions vanished in an instant, and I was overjoyed with the thoughts of meeting my brother in the morning.

The captain of the brig, having observed them, suddenly exclaimed, " Now we shall have a little fighting to-morrow; go you and load seventeen muskets, and put five buckshot into each. I will take care that the cannon shall be loaded to the muzzle with balls and flints, and if there is any row, I will give them such a scouring as they never had." He then directed me to place the muskets and cutlasses out of si ht near the stern of the vessel, and

said to me, " The instant that your people come on
board, call them aft, and let them stand by the arms
Tell them, if there is any row, to arm themselves
directly, and drive all the Brass people overboard."
This was summary work with a vengeance, and
every thing betokened that Lake was in earnest.   I
saw clearly that he was resolved on adopting severe
measures, and he appeared to possess all the determination necessary to carry them through.

I could not help feeling otherwise than distressed
and ashamed of leaving the Brass people in this
manner, but I had no alternative.   There was no
one to whom I could apply for assistance in my
present situation except the captain of this vessel,
and to him I had applied in vain.   My entreaties
were thrown away on him, and even the certainty of
an ample recompense by the British government,
which I had held out to him, had been treated with
contempt.   I had no hopes, therefore, from this
quarter.   Boy had refused to take us to Bonny, asserting that if he could not be paid here he should
not be there, and to go back to Brass town would
be deliberately returning to starvation; my last resource, therefore, was to put the best face on the
business that I could, and as no other plan was left
me, to get away by fair means or foul, and let the
blame fall where it was incurred.

Wednesday, November 24th.—This morning at daybreak I was on the look-out for my brother, and observed him and the people get into the canoe.   They
were no sooner embarked than they all landed again,
which I could account for in no other way, than by
supposing that it was the intention of Boy to keep
them on shore until he had received his goods.   I
was not long in this state of anxiety, for at about
seven o'clock they embarked and were brought on
board.

My brother's journal, which here follows, contains
an account of the events which fell under his notice

at Brass town, and his proceedings during the time
we were absent from each other.

" *Wednesday, November* 17*th.*—This morning my
brother, attended by one of our men, quitted this
town with King Boy and suite, leaving the remainder
of the party and myself behind, as hostages for the
fulfilment of the conditions which we entered into
with him in the Eboe country.   For myself, though
greatly chagrined at this unforeseen arrangement, I
could not from my heart altogether condemn the
framer of it, for it is quite natural to suppose that a
savage should distrust the promises of Europeans,
when he himself is at all times guilty of breach of
faith and trust, not only in his trading transactions
with foreigners, but likewise in familiar intercourse
with his own people.   Forday is the cause of it, and
he displays all the artifice, chicanery, and low cun-
ning of a crafty and corrupt mind.   Therefore, after
a moment's reflection, I was not much surprised at
the step which King Boy has taken, nor can I be very
angry with him ; and I am resolved to wait with
composure his return, and consequently, my release
from this miserable place, though I have begun to
consider with seriousness what will become of us
in the event of Lake's refusal to honour the bill
which we have sent him.   Besides I am rather uneasy on our people's account, for during these two
or three days past they have had scarcely any thing
to eat, and we are now left entirely destitute, nor do
I know where to obtain relief.   The Damuggoo people are with us likewise, and they are interested in
my brother's return equally as much as myself.   Instead of being our guides and protectors, these poor
creatures have shared in our calamity ; their little all
has either been lost or stolen, or else expended in
provisions ; and, like us, they are reduced to great
distress and wretchedness.   They will remain here
in order to receive the few things which we have

promised them and their chief: but, should Lake object to part with his goods, we shall give them a note to the master of any English vessel at Bonny, whither they are destined to go, requesting him to pay the poor strangers their demands.

" *Thursday, November* 18*th*.—After a good deal of solicitation and importunity, we received this morning four small yams from the wives of King Boy, who informed us that the same number of yams will be given us daily. Our people, having nothing else to eat, make a kind of broth of this vegetable; at first, it was of course a most insipid mess, but, with the addition of a little salt, it is rendered more palatable. We sent to King Forday, in the afternoon, for a few plantains, or any thing that could be eaten; but the gloomy old savage shook his head, folded his arms, and refused. All our people complaining this evening of hunger, languor, and indisposition. For myself I am fast recovering.

" *Friday, November* 19*th*.—The man that accompanied my brother to the brig in the river returned this afternoon without him, and gave me the following letter from my brother, which is dated from

" ' *Brass River, November* 18*th*, 1830.

" ' Dear John—You will be surprised to learn that I did not arrive here till this morning; when I came on board, I experienced a very cool reception from Lake, the master. He is apparently in the last stage of fever; but though in so alarming a state, he told me with an oath, after I had made my business known to him, that he would not give a —— flint for any government bill whatever ; as for King Boy, he swore that he would rather send him to the —— than give him any thing. You may guess my emotion on this intelligence ; I knew not what to say or do. I wished to return to Brass with King Boy, and proposed his taking us to Bonny, where I told him that I had no doubt we should be more kindly received;

but Boy answered, that if Lake, who is in his own
river, refuse to pay him, how could he expect to be
paid in a strange country? Therefore he would not
take me from the vessel. In this dilemma I remonstrated earnestly with Lake, who has at length
agreed to tamper with Boy, and promises to enter
into an arrangement with him for the payment of
the debt, as soon as he shall have brought you and
the people in safety to the vessel, but not till then.
Poor Boy looked sullen and disconcerted at this
proposal, though he has agreed to act as desired.
My dear brother, I have little news to tell you from
England, because the captain's manners are uncivil
and repulsive, and I do not like to weary him with
superfluous questions in the present irritable state
of his feelings; I can only learn, and I tell you of
it with deep sorrow, that our good King George is
dead. I herewith send you a piece of beef and a
bottle of rum, which have cost me much pains to
procure, but I know how greatly all of you stood in
need of something, and therefore I have sacrificed my
feelings to necessity. I am sorry that I cannot fulfil
my promise of sending you wearing apparel; a
couple of shirts, which belonged to a seaman who
died lately, is all that I can get. I suppose you will
leave Brass town to-morrow evening; in that case
you will be with me on Saturday, and it is needless
to say I shall wait your arrival here with impatience.
Lake is extremely peevish and ill-tempered; but, as I
have already told you, he is alarmingly ill, and therefore every allowance is to be made for him of course.
His mate and great part of his crew have died of
fever, and the others (except two) are either down
with the same disorder, or slowly recovering from
the effects of it.

" ' I am, &c. &c.—R. LANDER.'

" Nothing could exceed my regret and consternation on the perusal of this letter; and somehow, I

almost dreaded to meet with King Boy. Well know
ing, how much it would influence his behaviour towards us, we had been careful to represent to that
individual the thanks and cheering which he would
receive from our countrymen the moment he should
take us on board the English brig ; that he would
be favoured and caressed beyond measure, and receive plenty of beef, bread, and rum. His face used
to shine with delight on anticipating so luxurious a
treat ; and he had uniformly been in a better humour
after listening to these promises of ours than any
thing else could have made him. The contrast between his actual reception on board the *Thomas*, to
that which his own fancy and our repeated assurances
had taught him to expect, was too dreadful to think
on even a moment ; and for this reason, as much as
any other, I looked forward with something of apprehension and anxiety to an interview with this
savage ; because I knew, that after the cutting disappointment which he had experienced, he would be
under the influence of strongly-excited feelings and
stormy passions, over which he exercises no control. I was convinced, too, that the whole weight
of his resentment, and the fury of his rage, would
fall upon me, for I am completely in his power.

"The interesting moment at length arrived. We
heard King Boy quarrelling with his women, and
afterward walking through their apartments towards
ours, muttering as he went along. He entered it,
and stood still. I was reposing, as I usually do for
the greater part of the day, upon a mat which is
placed on the seat of wet clay ; but on perceiving him,
I lifted my head without arising, and reclined it on
my hand. He looked fixedly upon me, and I returned his glance with the same unshrinking stead-
fastness. But his dark eye was flashing with anger ;
while his upturned lip, which exposed his white teeth,
quivered with passion No face in the world could
convey more forcibly to the mind the feeling of con-

tempt and bitter scorn, than the distorted one before
me. It was dreadfully expressive. Drawing up the
left angle of his mouth on a parallel with his eyes,
he broke silence with a sneering, long-drawn ' Eh !'
and, almost choked with rage, he-cursed me ; and in
a tone and manner which it is infinitely out of my
power to describe, he spoke to the following effect :—
' You are thief man ; English captain no will ! You
assured me, when I took you from the Eboe country, that he would be overjoyed to see me, and give
me plenty of beef and rum ; I received from him
neither the one nor the other. Eh ! English captain
no will. I gave a quantity of goods to free you from
the slavery of Obie ; I took you into my own canoe ; you were hungry, and I gave you yam and
fish ; you were almost naked ; I was sorry to see
you so, because you were white men and strangers ;
and I gave each of you a red cap and a silk handkerchief. But you are no good—you are thief man.
Eh ! English captain no will ; he no will. You also
told me that your countrymen would do this (taking
off his cap and flourishing it in circles over his
head), and cry hurra, hurra, on receiving me on
board their vessel ; you promised my wife a necklace,
and my father four bars But, Eh ! English captain
no will ; he tell me he no will ; yes, I will satisfy
your hunger with plenty more of my fish and yams ;
and your thirst will I quench with rum and palm-
wine. Eh ! you thief man, you are no good ; English captain no will !' He then stamped on the
ground, and gnashing at me with his teeth like a dog,
he cursed me again and again.

" It is true, I did not feel perfectly easy at this
severe rebuke, and under such taunting reproaches ;
but I refrained from giving utterance to a single
thought till after he had concluded his abuse and
anathematizing. Had a spirited person been in my
situation, he might have knocked him down, and
might have had his head taken off for his pains ; but

as for me, all such kind of spirit is gone out of me entirely. Besides, we had unintentionally deceived King Boy, and I also bore in mind the kindness which he had done us in ransoming us from a state of slavery. Most of what he had asserted was most unquestionably true; and in some measure I was deserving his severest reprehension and displeasure.

"The fury of Boy having been somewhat appeased by my silence and submission, as well as by his own extraordinary and violent agitation, I ventured mildly to assure him, on the strength of my brother's letter, that his suspicions were entirely groundless; that Mr. Lake had certainly a *will* or inclination to enter into arrangements with him for the payment of his just demands; and that when he should convey our people and myself to the Thomas, every thing would be settled to his complete satisfaction. He half believed, half mistrusted my words; and shortly afterward quitted the apartment, threatening, however, that we should not leave Brass till it suited his own pleasure and convenience.

"It is really a most humiliating reflection, that we are reduced to the contemptible subterfuges of deceit and falsehood, in order to carry a point which might so easily have been gained by straightforward integrity. But Lake's conduct has left us no alternative; and whatever my opinion of that individual may be, he must surely be destitute of all the manly characteristics of a British seaman, as well as of the more generous feelings of our common nature, to be guilty, on a sick bed, of an action which might, for aught he knew or cared, produce the most serious consequences to his unfortunate countrymen in a savage land, by exposing them to the wretchedness of want and the miseries of slavery;—to mockery, ill-usage, contempt, and scorn; and even to death itself.

"*Saturday, November 20th.*—King Boy has not

visited us to-day, though we have received the customary allowance of four yams from his women.
In addition to which, Addizetta made us a present of
half a dozen this morning, as an acknowledgment
for the benefit she had derived from a dose of lauda-
num which I gave her last night for the purpose of
removing pain from the lower regions of the sto-
mach, a complaint by which she says she is occasionally visited. People are in better spirits this
evening, on account of the increased quantity of
yams received.

" *Sunday, November* 21*st.*—This morning I dis
missed the poor Damuggoo people, with a note to
the master of either of the English vessels lying in
the Bonny river, requesting him to give the bearers
three barrels of gunpowder, and a few muskets, on
the faith of his being paid for the same by his majesty's government. They left Brass in their own
canoe, quite dejected and out of heart; and Antonio,
the young man who volunteered to accompany us
from his Majesty's brig Clinker, at Badágry, went
along with them on his return to his country, from
which he has been absent two or three years. He
is brother to the present and son of the late king of
Bonny.

" *Monday, November* 22*d.*—One or two crafty little
urchins, who are slaves to King Boy, have brought
us a few plantains to-day as a gift. They had been
engaged in pilfering tobacco-leaves from an adjoining apartment, to which our people were witnesse ;
and the juvenile depredators, fearing the consequences of a disclosure, bribed them to secrecy in
the manner already mentioned. Boy's women have
also been guilty, during the temporary absence of
their lord and master, of stealing a quantity of rum
from the store-room, and distributing it among their
friends and acquaintance; and they have resorted to
the same plan as the boys to prevent the exposure
which they dreaded. One of them, who acts as

duenna, is the favourite and confidante of Boy, and
she wears a bunch of keys round her neck in token
of her authority.   She has likewise the care of all
her master's effects; and as a further mark of distinction, she is allowed the privilege of using a walk-
ing-stick with a knob at the end, which is her constant companion.   This woman is exceedingly good-
natured, and indulges our men with a glass or two
of rum every day.

" Last evening King Boy, stripped to the skin, and
having his body most hideously marked, ran about
the town like a maniac, with a spear in his hand,
calling loudly on his *Dju-dju;* and uttering a wild,
frantic cry at every corner.   It appears, that one of
his father's wives had been strongly suspected of
adulterous intercourse with a free man residing in
the town; and that this strange means was adopted,
in pursuance of an ancient custom, to apprize the
inhabitants publicly of the circumstance, and implore
the counsel and assistance of the god at the examination of the parties.   This morning the male ag-
gressor was found dead, having swallowed poison, it
is believed, to avoid a worse kind of death; and the
priest declaring his opinion of the guilt of the sur-
viving party, she was immediately sentenced to be
drowned.   Therefore, this afternoon the ill-fated
woman was tied hand and foot, and conveyed in a
canoe to the main body of the river, into which she
was thrown without hesitation, a weight of some
kind having been fastened to her feet for the purpose
of sinking her.   She met her death with incredible
firmness and resolution.   The superstitious people
believe, that had the deceased been innocent of the
crime laid to her charge, their god would have saved
her life, even after she had been flung into the river;
but because she perished, her guilt is with them unquestionably attested.   The mother of the deceased
is not allowed to display any signs of sorrow or
sadness at the untimely death of her daughter; for

were she to do so, the same dreadful punishment would be inflicted upon her: 'for,' say the Brass people, 'if a parent should mourn and weep over the fate of a child guilty of so heinous a crime, we should pronounce her instantly to be as criminal as her daughter, and to have tolerated her offence. But if, on the contrary, she betray no maternal tender ness, nor bewail her bereavement in tears and groans, we should then conclude her to be entirely ignorant of the whole transaction; she would thus give a tacit acknowledgment to the justice of her sentence, and rejoice to be rid of an object that would only entail disgrace on her as long as she lived.'

"Our people are become heartily tired of their situation, and impatient to be gone. They were re- galed with an extra quantity of rum last evening, by their female friend the duenna; when their grievances appearing to them in a more odious light than ever, they had the courage to go in a body to King Boy, to demand an explanation of his inten- tions towards them. They told him indignantly, either to convey them to the English brig, or sell them for slaves to the Spaniards: for, said they, we would rather lose our liberty than be kept here to die of hunger. Boy returned them an equivocating answer, but treated them much less roughly than I had reason to anticipate. Afterward, I went my- self to the same individual, and with a similar motive; but for some time I had no opportunity of convers- ing with him. It is a kind of holyday here, and most of the Brass people, with their chiefs, are merry with intoxication. As well as I can understand, during the earlier part of the day they were engaged in a solemn religious observance; and since then King Forday has publicly abdicated in favour of Boy, who is his eldest son. I discovered those individuals in a court annexed to the habitation of the former, surrounded by a great number of individuals with bottles, lasses, and decanters at their feet; they

were all in a state of drunkenness, more or less;
and all had their faces and bodies chalked over in
ruJe and various characters. Forday alone sat in
a chair; Boy was at his side; and the others, among
whom was our friend Gun, and a drummer, were
sitting around on blocks of wood, and on the trunk
of a fallen tree. The chairman delivered a long
oration, but he was too tipsy, and perhaps too full
of days, to speak with grace, animation, or power;
therefcre, his eloquence was not very persuasive,
and his nodding hearers, overcome with drowsiness,
listened to him with scarcely any attention. They
smiled, however, and laughed occasionally; but I
could not find out why they did so; I don't think
they themselves could tell. The old chief wore an
English superfine beaver hat, and an old jacket that
once belonged to a private soldier; but the latter
was so small that he was able only to thrust an
arm into one of its sleeves, the other part of the
jacket being thrown upon his left shoulder. These,
with the addition of a cotton handkerchief, which
was tied round the waist, were his only apparel. By
far the most showy and conspicuous object in the
yard was an immense umbrella, made of figured
cotton of different patterns, with a deep fringe of
coloured worsted, which was stuck into the ground.
But even this was tattered and torn, and dirty withal,
having been in Forday's possession for many years,
and it is used only on public and sacred occasions.
I had been sitting among the revellers till the speaker
had finished his harangue, when I embraced the opportunity, as they were about to separate, of en-
treating King Boy to hasten our departure for the
vessel. He was highly excited and elated with
liquor, and, being in an excellent temper, he promised
to take us to-morrow.

   " *Tuesday, November 23d.*—It required little time
to take leave of the few friends we have at Brass,
and we quitted the town, not only without regret

but with emotions of peculiar pleasure—King Boy, with three of his women, and his suite, in a large canoe, and our people and myself in a smaller one. Addizetta would gladly have accompanied her husband to the English vessel, for her desire to see it was naturally excessive; but she was forbidden by old Forday, who expressed some squeamishness about the matter, or rather he was jealous that on her return to her father's house in the Eboe country, she would give too high and favourable an opinion of it to her friends, which might in the end produce consequences highly prejudicial to his interests.

"We stopped awhile at a little fishing village at no great distance from Brass, where we procured a few fish and abundance of young cocoanuts, the milk of which was sweet and refreshing. Continuing our journey on streams and rivulets, intricately winding through mangroves and bramble, which have been already spoken of, we entered the main body of the river in time to see the sun setting behind a glorious sky, directly before us. We were evidently near the sea, because the water was perfectly salt, and we scented also the cool and bracing sea-breeze, with feelings of satisfaction and rapture. However, the wind soon became too stormy for our fragile canoe; the waves leaped into it over the bow, and several times we were in danger of being swamped. Our companion was far before us, and out of sight, so that, for the moment, there was no possibility of receiving assistance, or of lightening the canoe; but happily, in a little while we did not require it, for the violence of the wind abating with the disappearance of the sun, we were enabled to continue on our way without apprehension. About nine o'clock in the evening we overtook the large canoe, and the crews both having partaken of a slight refreshment of fish and plantain together, we passed the ' *Second Brass River*,' which was to the left of us, in company. Here it might have been somewhat more than half a mile in breadth; and though it was dangerously rough for a canoe, with great precaution we reached the opposite side in safety. From thence we could perceive, in the distance, the long-wished-for Atlantic with the moonbeams reposing in peaceful beauty upon its surface, and could also hear the sea breaking and roaring over the sandy bar which stretches across the mouth of the river. The solemn voice of ocean never sounded more melodiously in my ear than it did at that moment; O! it was enchanting as the harp of David. Passing along by the left bank, we presently entered the ' *First Brass River*,' which is the ' *Nun*,' of Europeans, where, at midnight, we could faintly distinguish the masts and rigging of the English brig in the dusky light, which appeared like a dark and ragged cloud above the horizon. To me, however, no sight could be more charming. It was beautiful as the gates of paradise, and my heart fluttered with unspeakable delight, as we landed in silence on the beach opposite the brig, near a few straggling huts, to wait impatiently the dawn of to-morrow.

" *Wednesday, November 24th.*—This was a happy morning, for it restored me to the society of my brother and of my countrymen. The baneful effects of the climate are strongly impressed upon the countenances of the latter, who, instead of their natural healthy hue, have a pale, dejected, and sickly appearance, which is quite distressing to witness. However, the crew of the Spanish schooner look infinitely more wretched: they have little else but their original forms remaining; they crawl about like beings under a curse; they are mere shadows or phantoms of men looking round for their burying-place. No spectacle can be more mortifying to man's pride than this; nothing can give him a more humiliating sense of his own nothingness. It is very much to be wondered at why Europeans in general, and Englishmen in particular, persevere in sending

their fellow-creatures to this *Aceldama* or *Golgotha,*
as the African coast is sometimes not inappropriately
called: they might as well bury them at once at
home, and it is pleasanter far to die there; but interest and the lust of gain, like Aaron's rod, seem
to swallow up every other consideration."

My brother had now joined me, and my station
during the time the canoe was coming from the
shore to the vessel had been by the cannon; it was
the only one on board, but it had been loaded as
Lake had directed, and pointed to the gangway of
the brig, where the Brass people must come.   The
muskets were all ready, lying concealed where Lake
had directed them to be placed, and he repeated the
same orders that he had given me yesterday, respecting the part my people were to take in the business.   Lake received my brother civilly, but immediately expressed his determination to dismiss Boy
without giving him a single article, and to make the
best of his way out of the river.   A short time after
his arrival, a canoe arrived at the beach with Mr.
Spittle, the mate of the brig, as prisoner, who immediately sent a note off to the captain, informing him
that the price of his liberation was the sum demanded
for the pilotage of the vessel over the bar of the
river.   He said further, that he was strictly guarded,
but that notwithstanding this he did not despair of
making his escape if Lake could wait a little for
him.   The vessel had been brought into the river
about three months before, but Lake would never pay
the pilotage, and now all he did was to send Mr.
Spittle a little bread and beef.   The amount demanded was about fifty pounds' worth of goods,
which it was quite out of the question that Lake
would ever pay.

Meanwhile King Boy, full of gloomy forebodings,
had been lingering about the deck.   He had evidently foresight enough to suspect what was to
II.—Y

take place, and he appeared troubled and uneasy,
and bewildered in thought. The poor fellow was
quite an altered person; his habitual haughtiness
had entirely forsaken him, and given place to an
humble and cringing demeanour. A plate of meat
was presented to him, of which he ate sparingly, and
showed clearly that he was thinking more of his
promised goods than his appetite, and a quantity of
rum that was given to him was drunk carelessly,
and without affording any apparent satisfaction.

Knowing how things were likely to terminate,
we endeavoured to get Boy into a good-humour,
by telling him that he should certainly have his
goods some time or other; but it was all to no purpose; the attempt was a complete failure; the present was the only thing in his mind. We really
pitied him, and were grieved to think that our promises could not be fulfilled. How gladly would we
have made any personal sacrifice rather than thus
break our word; for although we had been half-
starved in his hands, yet we felt ourselves indebted
to him for having taken us from the Eboe people and
bringing us to this vessel. I rummaged over the
few things left us from our disaster at Kirree, and
found to my surprise five silver bracelets wrapped
up in a piece of flannel. I was not aware of having
these, therefore I immediately offered them to him,
along with a native sword, which, being a very great
curiosity, we had brought with us from Yarriba with
the intention of taking it to England. Boy accepted
of these, and my brother then offered him his watch,
for which he had a great regard, as it was the gift
of one of his earliest and best friends. This was
refused with disdain, for Boy knew not its value; and
calling one of his men to look at what he said we
wished to impose on him in lieu of his bars, both of
them, with a significant groan, turned from us with
scorn and indignation, nor would they speak to us or
even look at us again. Our mortification was now

complete; but we were helpless, and the fault was not with us.

Boy now ventured to approach Captain Lake on the quarter-deck, and, with an anxious, petitioning countenance, asked for the goods which had been promised him. Prepared for the desperate game he was about to play, it was the object of Lake to gain as much time as possible, that he might get his vessel under way before he came to an open rupture.— Therefore he pretended to be busy in writing, and desired Boy to wait a moment. Becoming impatient with delay, Boy repeated his demand a second and a third time, "Give me my bars."—"I no will!" said Lake, in a voice of thunder, which one could hardly have expected from so emaciated a frame as his. "I no will, I tell you; I won't give you a —— flint. Give me my mate, you black rascal, or I will bring a thousand men-of-war here in a day or two; they shall come and burn down your towns and kill every one of you; bring me my mate!" Terrified by the demeanour of Lake, and the threats and oaths he made use of, poor King Boy suddenly retreated. and seeing men going aloft to loosen the sails, apprehensive of being carried off to sea, he quickly disappeared from the deck of the brig, and was soon observed making his way on shore in his canoe, with the rest of his people; this was the last we saw of him. In a few minutes from the time Boy had left the vessel, the mate, Mr. Spittle, was sent off in a canoe; so terrified were the Brass people that a man-of-war would come and put Lake's threats into execution.

At ten in the morning, the vessel was got under way, and we dropped down the river. At noon the breeze died away, and we were obliged to let go an anchor to prevent our drifting on the western breakers at the mouth of the river. A few minutes more would have been fatal to us, and the vessel was fortunately stopped, although the depth of water where she lay was only five fathoms. The rollers, as the

large high waves are called, which came into the
river over the bar, were so high, that they sometimes
passed nearly over the bow of the vessel, and caused
her to ride very uneasily by her anchor.   We had
been obliged to anchor immediately abreast of the
Pilots' town, and expected every moment that we
should be fired at from their battery.   Time was of the
greatest importance to us; we had made Boy our
enemy, and expected, before we could get out of the
river, he would summon his people and make an attack on us, while our party amounted only to twenty
men, two-thirds of whom were Africans.   The pilot
also, whom Lake had offended so much, is known to be
a bold and treacherous ruffian.   He is the same person who steered the brig Susan among the breakers,
by which that vessel narrowly escaped destruction,
with the loss of her windlass and an anchor and cable.
The fellow had done this merely with the hopes of
obtaining a part of the wreck, as it drifted on shore.
Another vessel, a Liverpool oil-trader, was actually
lost on the bar by the treachery of the same individual, who, having effected his purpose by placing
her in a situation from which she could not escape,
jumped overboard and swam to his canoe, which
was at a short distance.   The treatment of the sur-
vivors of this wreck is shocking to relate: they were
actually stripped of their clothes, and allowed to die
of hunger.   It would be an endless task to enumerate
all the misdeeds that are laid to this fellow's charge,
which have, no doubt, lost nothing by report; but,
after making all reasonable allowances for exaggeration, his character appears in a most revolting light,
and the fact of his running these vessels on the bar
proves him to be a desperate and consummate villain.   This same fellow is infinitely more artful and
intelligent than any of his countrymen, and is one
of the handsomest black men that we have seen.

Not long after we had dropped the anchor, we observed the pilot, with the help of a glass, walking
on the beach and watching us occasionally.   A

multitude of half-naked suspicious-looking fellows were likewise straggling along the shore, while others were seen emerging from a grove of cocoa-trees and the thick bushes near it. These men were all armed, chiefly with muskets, and they sub-sequently assembled in detached groups to the num-ber of several hundreds, and appeared to be consult-ing about attacking the vessel. Nothing less than this, and to be fired at from the battery, was ex-pected by us; and there is no doubt that the strength and loftiness of the brig only deterred them from so doing. The same people were hovering on the beach till very late in the evening, when they dis-persed; many of them could be seen even at mid-night, so that we were obliged to keep a good look-out till the morning.

Thursday, November 25th.—The vessel rode very uneasily all night, in consequence of the long heavy waves which set in from the bar; these are tech-nically called by sailors *ground-swell*, being different from the waves which are raised while the wind blows; the latter generally break at the top, while the former are quite smooth, and roll with great impetuosity in constant succession, forming a deep furrow between them, which, with the force of the wave, is very dangerous to vessels at anchor. Our motions were still closely watched by the natives. About eleven we got under way, but were obliged to anchor again in the afternoon, as the water was not deep enough for the vessel to pass over the bar.— The mate sounded the bar again, and placed a buoy as a mark for the vessel to pass over in the deepest water.

Friday, November 26th.—The wind favouring us this morning, we made another attempt at getting out of the river. We had already made some pro-gress when the wind again died away, and the cur-rent setting us rapidly over to the eastern breakers, we were obliged to let go an anchor to save us from destruction. We could see nothing of the buoy, and have no doubt that it was washed away by the current; our anchorage was in three and a half fathoms water, and the ground-swell, which now set in, heaved the vessel up and down in such a frightful manner, that we expected every moment to see the chain cable break. As soon as we dropped our anchor, the tide rushed past the vessel at the rate of eight miles an hour. After the ebb-tide had ceased running, the swell gradually subsided, and the vessel rode easily.

The mate was again sent to sound the bar, and in about three hours afterward returned with the information that two fathoms and three-quarters was the deepest water he could find. The bar extends across the mouth of the river in the form of a crescent, leaving a very narrow and shallow entrance for vessels in the middle, which is generally concealed by the surf and foam of the adjacent breakers. When the wind is light and the tide high, and the surface of the water smooth, excepting in a few places, the bar is then most dangerous. We observed several fires made by the natives on the beach, which were supposed to be signals for us to return.

Saturday, November 27th.—We passed a restless and most unpleasant night. The captain and the people were much alarmed for the safety of the brig. The heavy ground-swell which set in, increased by the strength of the tide, caused her to pitch and labour so hard, that a man was placed to watch the cable and give notice the moment it complained,—a technical expression, which meant the moment it gave signs of breaking. Daylight had scarcely dawned when the pall of the windlass broke. The purpose of this is to prevent the windlass from turning round on its axis against any strain to which it may be subjected, and consequently it was no sooner broken than the windlass flew round with

incredible velocity, having nothing to resist the strain
of the cable which was passed round it.   The chain-
cable ran out so swiftly, that in half a minute the
windlass was broken to atoms. My brother and I
with our people rendered all the assistance in our
power to prevent the ship from drifting. We succeeded in fastening the cable to ring-bolts in the
deck, until we got sufficient of it clear to go round
the capstan, which we had no sooner effected, than
the ring-bolts were fairly drawn out of the deck by
the strain on the cable.

About eight A. M. a terrific wave, called by sailors
a *sea*, struck the vessel with tremendous force and
broke the chain cable.   " The cable is gone!" shouted
a voice, and the next instant the captain cried out
in a firm, collected tone, " Cut away the kedge !"
which was promptly obeyed, and the vessel was
again stopped from drifting among the breakers.
The man who had been stationed to look out on the
cable came running aft on deck as soon as he had
given notice of the danger, calling out that all was
over.—" Good God !" was the passionate exclamation
of every one, and a slight confusion ensued. But
the captain was prepared for the worst ; he gave his
orders with firmness, and behaved with promptness
and decision.

We were riding by the kedge, a small anchor,
which, however, was the only one left us, and on
which the safety of the brig now depended. The
breakers were close under our stern, and this was
not expected to hold ten minutes,—it was a forlorn
hope—every eye was fixed on the raging surf, and
our hearts thrilled with agitation, expecting every
moment that the vessel would be dashed in pieces.
A few long and awful minutes were passed in this
state, which have left an indelible impression on
our minds. Never shall I forget the chief mate
saying to me, " Now, sir, every one for himself ; a
few minutes will be the last with us." The tumult

uous sea was raging in mountainous waves close by us, their foam dashing against the sides of the brig, which was only prevented from being carried among them by a weak anchor and cable. The natives, from whom we could expect no favour, were busy on shore making large fires, and other signals, for us to desert the brig and land at certain places, expecting, no doubt, every moment to see her a prey to the waves, and those who escaped their fury to fall into their hands. Wretched resource! the sea would have been far more merciful than they.

Such was our perilous situation, when a fine sea-breeze set in, which literally saved us from destruction. The sails were loosened to relieve the anchor from the strain of the vessel, and she rode out the ebb-tide without drifting. At ten A. M. the tide had nearly ceased running out, and the fury of the sea rather abated, but it was quite impossible that the brig could ride out another ebb-tide where she lay, with the kedge anchor alone to hold her: the only chance left us, therefore, was to get to sea, and the captain determined on crossing the bar, although there appeared to be little chance of success. At half-past ten A. M. he manned the boat with two of our men, and two Kroomen belonging to the brig, and sent them to tow, while the anchor was got on board. This had no sooner been done than the wind fell light, and, instead of drifting over to the western breakers as yesterday and the day before, the brig was now set towards those on the eastern side, and again we had a narrow escape. With the assistance of the boat and good management, we at length passed clear over the bar on the edge of the breakers, in a depth of quarter less three fathoms, and made sail to the eastward. Our troubles were now at an end: by the protection of a merciful Providence we had escaped dangers, the very thoughts of which had filled us with horror; and with a grateful heart and tears of joy for all his

mercies, we offered up a silent prayer of thanks for
our deliverance.

The bar extends about four or five miles from the
mouth of the river in a southerly direction, but is
by no means known. This river is by far the best
place on the whole coast at which small vessels may
procure oil, as it is the shortest distance from the
Eboe country, where the best palm-oil is to be had
in any quantity. The Eboe oil is pronounced to be
superior to that of any other part of the country
which is brought to the coast. The river is not
much frequented, owing probably to its being unknown, and the difficulty of crossing the bar; for not
more than five English vessels have been known to
come to it, two of which are stated to have been
lost, and a third to have struck on the bar, but being
a new strong vessel, she beat over it into deep
water. I would recommend the master of any vessel going to the river for palm-oil to provide himself
with two good strong six-oared boats for towing,
and a double complement of Kroomen. The expense
of ten or twelve Kroomen would be trifling, as they
only require a few yams and a little palm-oil to eat,
and they are always ready to perform any laborious
work which may be required of them. If masters
of vessels coming to the river would send a boat
before to sound, and have two good six-oared boats
towing, I think there would be no danger of any being lost, as has been the case with some from being
weakly manned. Vessels are got under way with a
fine breeze, and when they arrive in the most dangerous part it dies away, and if there are no boats
ready for towing, nothing can save them from destruction.

Vessels going out of the river are usually recommended to keep as near as possible to the western
breakers, but I should think this very dangerous, unless there is sufficient wind to keep command of
them. When a vessel leaves her anchorage in the
II.—Z

river, she will be set by the current over to the
western breakers, and when half way to the bar,
will be set over to the eastern, as we were. The
river in the month of December and January would,
I think, be safest, as the rains in the interior will
then be over, and all the extra water will have been
discharged which it has received in the extent of
country through which it runs. When no English
vessels are in the river, the people of Bonny come
and purchase the palm-oil from the Brass people,
probably for the purpose of supplying the ships in
their river, as well as for their own uses.

Sunday, November 28th.—This morning we discovered a strange vessel on our starboard beam,
which directly made sail in chase of us. After firing
a gun to make us stop, or bring us to, as the sailors
expressed it, she sent a boat on board of the brig,
and we found her to be the Black Joke, tender to
the British commodore's ship. We reported ourselves to the lieutenant commanding her, in the
hopes of his taking us on board of his vessel and
landing us at Accra, from whence I thought it would
be easy to find our way by one of his majesty's ships
to Ascension or St. Helena, from either of which
places an opportunity would offer for us to get home
without delay. His orders, however, were to run
down the coast as far as the Congo, and he recommended us to go to Fernando Po, where we should
find every assistance and a vessel about to sail
soon for England. Having obtained from us the intelligence that the Spanish slaver was lying in the
river Nun ready to sail, he immediately altered his
course for that river, for the purpose of captur-
ing her. Captain Lake agreed to land us in his boat
at Fernando Po, as he passed the island on his way
to the river Cameroons, and we again made sail to
the eastward.

Wednesday, December 1st.—The last two days were
employed in making the passage to Fernando Po

and this morning, to our great satisfaction, we discovered the island. We were glad to get out of this vessel, for the unfeeling commander, notwithstanding that our men had rendered him every assistance in getting his brig out of the river, and had done every thing required of them, afterward employed every means he could think of to annoy us and make us uncomfortable while we were with him. At night, while the people were sleeping, he would make his men draw water and throw it over them for mere amusement. There are many commanders as bad as he is on the coast, who seem to vie with each other in acts of cruelty and oppression. The captain of the palm-oil brig Elizabeth, now in the Calebar river, actually whitewashed his crew from head to foot, while they were sick with fever and unable to protect themselves; his cook suffered so much in the operation, that the lime totally deprived him of the sight of one of his eyes, and rendered the other of little service to him.

In the afternoon we were happily landed at Clarence Cove, in the island of Fernando Po, where we were most kindly received by Mr. Becroft, the acting superintendent. This worthy gentleman readily supplied us with changes of linen, and every thing we stood in need of, besides doing all he possibly could to make us comfortable. The kindness and hospitality we received from him, and Dr. Crichton in particular, we shall be grateful for as long as we live.

Accustomed as we had been during the last month to the monotonous sameness of a low, flat country, the banks of the river covered with mangroves overhanging the water, and in many parts, in consequence of its extraordinary height, apparently growing out of it; the lofty summit of Fernando Po, and the still loftier mountains of the Cameroons on the distant mainland, presented a sublime and magnificent appearance. The highest mountain of the

Cameroons is a striking feature on this part of the
coast, being more than thirteen thousand feet high.
The land in its vicinity is low and flat, which renders
the appearance of this mountain still more imposing,
as it towers majestically over the surrounding country in solitary grandeur. It divides the embouchures
of the spacious rivers old Calebar and Del Rey, on
the west, from the equally important one of the
Cameroons on the east. The island of Fernando
Po is detached about twenty miles from the coast,
and appeared to us, when we first saw it, in two lofty
peaks connected by a high ridge of land. The
northern peak is higher than the other, which is
situated in the southern part of the island, and rises
gradually from the sea to the height of ten thousand
seven hundred feet. In clear weather the island can
be seen at the distance of more than a hundred
miles; but this is not always the case, as the summit
is most frequently concealed by clouds and fogs,
which are common at certain seasons of the year.

As we approached the island in fine weather and
with a moderate wind, we had ample time to observe
it. The shore is formed mostly of a dark-coloured
rock, and covered with trees which reach down to
the water's edge. The whole of the lower part of
the island is covered with fine forest trees of various
descriptions, extending about three-fourths up the
sides of the mountain, where they become thinly
scattered, stinted in their growth, and interspersed
with low bushes and a brown dry grass. In various
parts patches of cultivated ground may be seen
along with the huts of the natives, presenting,
with the luxuriant foliage of the trees, a mass of
verdure in the most flourishing condition. Nature
has here done her utmost; the whole appearance of
the island is of the most beautiful description, and
fully justifies its title to the name of *Ilha Formosa*,
signifying "Beautiful Island," which it first received.
As we approached it still nearer, the stupendous pre-

cipices and wide fissures near the summit of the
principal mountain became more distinct by the contrast between their dark recesses and the lights on
the projecting rocks, until, by our proximity to the
shore, the whole became concealed behind the lesser
heights next to the sea.

Until the year 1827, the island lay forsaken and
neglected in its primitive condition, neither the Portuguese nor Spaniards having thought it worth their
consideration. At length the attention of the British
government was directed to it, in consequence of its
favourable position for putting a stop to the slave-
trade in that quarter of Africa. Situated within a
few hours' sail of the coast, in the immediate vicinity
of those rivers, commencing with the Cameroons
on the east, and extending along the whole of the
Gold Coast, where the principal outlets of this un-
lawful traffic are found, Fernando Po presented advantages which were sufficient to authorize a settlement being formed on it; and Captain W. Owen
sailed from England for this purpose in his majesty's
ship Eden, with the appointment of governor, and
with Commander Harrison under his orders. Captain Owen had been previously employed on an extensive and difficult survey of the coasts of Africa
both in the Atlantic and Indian oceans, in which the
shores of this island were included; and therefore,
having visited it before, he was no stranger either
to its nature and resources, or to the climate in which
it is situated. Previous to the arrival of Captain
Owen, the island had been occasionally visited by
some of the ships of war on the African station, for
the purposes of obtaining supplies of vegetables and
water; and perhaps now and then a Liverpool ship
would be seen there waiting for palm-oil, or recovering the health of her crew from fevers obtained
in the rivers on the coast. As the natives reside at
some distance in the interior, the arrival of a ship of
war at the island was announced to them by the

discharge of a cannon on board, which was sufficient
to bring them to the seaside with whatever vegetables, poultry, and other articles they might wish to
sell. The articles most demanded by them in return were pieces of iron hoop, knives, and nails.
At first a piece of iron hoop about six inches long
would purchase a pair of fowls or four yams, so
much value being attached by the natives to iron.

The business of forming a new settlement is a
species of service that requires the exercise of certain qualities of the mind which it is not the good
fortune of every one to possess. In addition to the
pernicious effects of the climate on European con-
stitutions, there were people on the island who, although they might be unable to offer any serious im-
pediment to the progress of the settlement, it was
necessary to conciliate rather than to treat with hos-
tility, and for this no one could have been better
calculated than Captain Owen. Whatever may
have induced him to relinquish the appointment of
governor, no measures for gaining the friendship of
the natives, and thereby securing their good-will towards the colony, could have been better than those
which he adopted, and the chiefs even now frequently
mention his name.

The part selected as the site of the proposed settlement was on the northern side of the island, on
the borders of a small cove formed by a narrow neck
of land projecting out from the shore on the eastern
side of it. This was named " Point William ;" and
the cove, together with the whole establishment, was
called " Clarence," after his most gracious majesty,
who was then Lord High Admiral of Great Britain.
Point Adelaide, with two small islets off it connected
by a sand-bank, forms the western boundary of the
cove, and is distant about half a mile from Point
William. Goderich Bay lies to the east, and Cock-
burn Cove to the west of Clarence Cove. Under
the able directions of Captain Owen, the various

buildings were planned while the operation of clearing the ground was going forward. A flagstaff, which formerly stood on the extremity of Point William, has been removed to the governor's house, and a large commodious building, with a few solitary palm-trees near it, is the first which attracts attention. This building is assigned as the hospital, and is judiciously situated here, as it is the most exposed to the sea-breeze, and stands completely isolated from the rest of the settlement, both which precautions are of no small importance in the climate of Fernando Po. A small round-topped building at a short distance from the hospital, with a few huts near it, and surrounded by stakes, was formerly the magazine; and near it is another large building used as the marine barracks. The officers' quarters and those of the African corps are next in succession, and announce their military character by a piece of artillery mounted close to them, and pointed towards the cove. The governor's house, a large, spacious building, stands eminently conspicuous on the precipice of the shore beneath, which is the landing-place. From hence a fatiguing walk leads immediately to it up an ascent of about one hundred feet. A battery of seven guns were landed for this purpose from his majesty's ship Esk, which are placed in a very commanding situation in front of the governor's house. The house of the mixed commission for the adjudication of captured slave-vessels stands in an unfinished condition at a short distance from the governor's; various other buildings occupy Point William, which are diversified by a few trees, that give it a pleasing and picturesque appearance from the sea. This remark is generally made by those who first visit Clarence Cove, and all are pleased on first seeing it. In addition to the buildings we have enumerated, Mr. Lloyd has a tolerably good house just finished, and the surgeon of the colony, who is a naval officer, has one also assigned for his residence

The Kroomen and free negroes, who amount to about two thousand in number, have a collection of small neat huts at a short distance from government-house, which are constructed of wood and thatched with palm-leaves. They are very careful of them, and have a small garden in the front as well as behind, in which they cultivate Indian corn, bananas and peppers. These huts form two small streets, but they are daily receiving additions from new comers.

The work of clearing the ground is constantly going forward, and is performed by the free negroes, the African troops, and the Kroomen. The principal disease among these people, which arises from accidents in cutting down the trees, is ulcerated legs, and sixteen of them were in the hospital from this cause alone. The Kroomen are a particular race of people, differing entirely from the other African tribes. They inhabit a country called Settra Krou, on the coast near Cape Palmas, their principal employment being of a maritime nature. Their language, as well as their general character, is also different from that of their neighbours. A certain number of these men are always employed on board of the ships of war on the African coast, for the purpose of performing those duties where considerable fatigue and exposure to the sun is experienced. In consequence of their roving employment, they are to be found on all parts of the coast, and are sufficiently acquainted with it to serve as pilots. It is customary with them to establish themselves on various parts of the coast for this purpose, and to leave the elders of the tribes in their own country, unless their presence should be required by any war that might take place. They are said to return to their country after an absence of several years, when they have amassed by their industry sufficient to maintain themselves, and some among them are intelligent and active, but they are not always to be trusted, although they are a very superior class of people in comparison with other African tribes.

Besides a watering-place at a short distance to the right of the governor's house, two small streams, Hay Brook and Horton Brook, run into Goderich Bay, affording plenty of excellent water, and capable of admitting boats. The watering-place above mentioned is generally frequented, from the convenience with which the water is obtained, being conducted to the sea-side by a wooden aqueduct, under which boats may lie and fill their casks very easily without removing them.

Clarence establishment when we arrived consisted of the superintendent, or acting governor, Mr. Becroft, who was generally known by the title of captain; Captain Beattie, the commander of the Portia, colonial schooner; Mr. Crichton, a naval surgeon; Lieutenant Stockwell, with a party of five or six marines; a mulatto ensign of the Royal African corps, with two black troops from Sierra Leone, and some carpenters and sailmakers, besides a mulatto who filled the office of clerk or secretary to Mr. Becroft. An English merchant, by the name of Lloyd, in the employment of Mr. Smith, we also found here, whose residence we have just mentioned.

No place, in point of convenience, could have been better selected for a settlement than that on which Clarence is situated. The bay affords safe anchorage for shipping from the furious tornadoes which are common in this part of the world, and is sufficiently capacious to shelter as many vessels as are likely to visit the island: it abounds with fish, and is free from sunken rocks, and the shore is steep and easy of access to boats. There is another bay, called George's Bay, on the western side of the island, but it has the disadvantage of being open to that quarter, and consequently affords no safety to shipping. The proximity of Clarence Cove to the coast of Africa is also another important point in favour of the object for which the establishment was formed.

The natives of Fernando Po are the filthiest race of people in the whole world. They are different in their manners and appearance from their neighbours on the coast, to whom we have been so much accustomed of late, and possess no single trait of character similar to them, except that of pilfering. In point of civilization, to which the natives of Brass town have scarcely the most distant pretensions, these people have even still less; their language is totally different, and they have no resemblance whatever to them. This in itself affords a tolerable proof of the little intercourse they have had with the world, for while the other islands of the gulf are plentifully stocked with the same race of people as those of the coast, Fernando Po, which is so much nearer to it, is inhabited by a totally different class. They are, generally speaking, a stout, athletic, and well-made race of people, and peculiarly harmless and peaceably inclined in their dispositions, although each individual is generally armed with a spear about eight feet in length, made of a hard wood and barbed at one end. They appear also to be a healthy race of people, for although here and there one or two might be less favoured by nature in their persons, no signs of the diseases so common among the natives of Africa were to be seen among them.

We have said that they are a filthy race, but no words can convey an idea of their disgusting nature. They have long hair, which it is difficult to distinguish, from being matted together with red clay and palm-oil. The clay and oil are so profusely laid on, that it forms an impenetrable shield for the head, and the long tresses, which descend to their shoulders, are generally in a moist condition. Although this covering is a complete safeguard to all inconvenience from without, they still further adorn their heads with a kind of cap made of dried grass, orna-

mented round the border with the feathers of fowls
or any other birds, carefully stuck into it apart from
each other. Some are so vain as to fix the horns
of a ram in front of this cap, which gives them a
most ludicrous and strange appearance. Finally,
the cap with all its ornaments of feathers, horns,
shells, &c., is secured in its place with a piece of
stick, which answers the purpose by being forced
through it on one side and out on the opposite after
passing underneath the hair. Sometimes this elegant pin, as it may be called, is formed of the leg
bone of some small animal, and is pointed at one
end for the purpose of penetrating more easily. The
expression of their countenance, scored and marked
as it is, and surmounted by the cap above described.
is wild and barbarous. They smear their faces entirely over with red clay mixed with palm-oil; sometimes a kind of gray dust is used instead of the clay,
and this preparation, being equally distributed over
their whole persons, renders their presence scarcely
tolerable. It is difficult to find out the colour of
their skin under the filthy covering of oil and clay
by which it is concealed, but we believe it is not so
dark as the African negro, and more resembling a
copper colour.

The natives make use of no other dress than the
cap which they wear on their heads; but a few
leaves, or a bunch of dried grass, are usually secured
round the middle by the people of both sexes, while
the younger, naturally unconscious of indecency,
go entirely naked. The vertebræ of snakes, the
bones of fowls and birds as well as sheep, broken
shells, small beads, and pieces of cocoanut-shell,
are put in requisition by the natives for the ornament of their persons. A profusion of these strung
together hang round the waist, which it seems to
be their principal care to decorate in this manner,
while their necks are scarcely less favoured with a
proportion of these articles. Strings of them are

also fastened round the arms and legs, but not in such quantities as round the waist. The pieces of hoop they have obtained from the ships which have visited the island are formed into rude knives, or polished and worn on the arm in a kind of band made of straw, and are much valued. In their first intercourse with our people, the natives were very shy, and displayed much fear; but this gradually wore off, and they now venture boldly on board, for the purpose of obtaining knives, hatchets, or any thing they can get. They have a few canoes of small dimensions, capable of containing ten or twelve people, but are not very expert in the management of them, although they are so far advanced as to make use of a mast and sail, which latter is constructed of a sort of mat. They seem to be little addicted to the water, and we did not see any among them who could swim. In their fishing excursions the natives are generally very successful, and those who pursue this mode of obtaining their livelihood are compelled to adhere to it, and allowed to have nothing to do with cultivating the island. They exchange their fish for yams, and thus the wants of the fishermen and the cultivators are both supplied.

In the first visits of ships to the island, very considerable aversion was shown by the natives to any of their people attempting to go to their huts, or even to their endeavouring to penetrate into the woods, although only a short distance from the shore, from a fear perhaps of their plantations being plundered.* Their huts, which are of the rudest construction imaginable, may be distinctly seen among the trees in small groups, surrounding a cleared space of ground, in which they cultivate the yam; and are formed of a few stakes driven firmly into the ground, thatched over with the palm leaf, the sides being completed with a sort of wicker-work. They are

---

* They have no such apprehensions now, and allow the colonists to go into any part of the island without molesting them.

about ten or twelve feet long, and half that in breadth, and not more than four or five feet in height. Their only furniture consists of some long flat pieces of wood, raised a few inches from the ground, and slightly hollowed out, to answer the purpose of sleeping in.

Numerous instances have occurred of the thieving propensities of the natives; and it required, at first, a considerable degree of vigilance to prevent them from being successful; but it is due to the chiefs to say, that since the establishment of Clarence, they have invariably taken an active part in putting a stop to it. Whatever may have been their habits previous to the formation of the settlement, they seem to be little improved by their intercourse with the settlers. Their principal chief has received the formidable appellation of Cut-throat from Captain Owen, a name by which he will be known as long as he lives. This fellow is a most determined savage, and seems to have lost none of his natural propensities by communication with the settlers. He has received innumerable presents from the English, of clothes, and a variety of things, which are all thrown away on him, and he goes about, as usual, wearing his little hat, with feathers stuck in it, and the long grass about his waist, disdaining such useless coverings as he imagines them. This is not to be wondered at; for, accustomed as he has been all his lifetime to the unrestrained freedom of his whole person, it would be rather a matter of surprise to see him make use of them, particularly in the climate of Fernando Po, where one almost wishes to follow the example of the natives, excepting in the use of their clay and palm-oil. No doubt Cut-throat thinks this quite a sufficient covering.

The natives pay frequent visits to the colony, and however they may deal out justice among themselves, are by no means backward in seeing it administered among the free negroes and Kroomen of

Clarence. It frequently happens, that in the scarcity of live-stock, some of the former, unable to restrain their desire for more substantial food, and tired of their Indian corn, venture to help themselves to what the natives will not bring them. Parties of these people are accordingly formed, who find their way to the huts of the natives in the interior, and steal their yams, goats, and sheep, or whatever they meet with. These depredations are sure to bring the unfortunate owners to the colony with complaints of their losses, which are laid before the governor. The negroes are then mustered before them, and the native who has been plundered is allowed, if he can do so, to point out the thief. If he should be successful, which is frequently the case, he is allowed to witness the punishment which the offender is sure to receive, and generally gets some recompense for his loss. On the Sunday after our arrival at Clarence, a party of four Kroomen set off into the interior, with a full determination of plunder, let the consequence be what it might. They had not gone far before they met with a goat belonging to a native, which they immediately shot, and returned with it carefully concealed, that they might not be discovered. Their precautions, however, were of little avail, for the owner of the animal, accompanied by a party of his friends, made his appearance at Clarence the next morning, and preferred his complaint in strong terms against the luckless Kroomen, whom, it appeared, he perfectly well knew. The Kroomen were accordingly mustered, and the very four who had gone on this unfortunate expedition were pointed out with exultation by the natives. The law took its course; the Kroomen each received one hundred and fifty lashes from the African drummer usually employed on these occasions, while the natives stood by to see that the punishment was duly performed. This they did to admiration, by counting the number of lashes they each received; and having witnessed the last punished with eyes sparkling with brutal satisfaction at the tortures of the unfortunate sufferers, they went away quite satisfied. The place where this disagreeable operation is performed is in the barrack-yard on Point William, between the officers' house and the hospital. The culprit is tied up to a kind of strong gallows, erected for the purpose. Two stout pieces of timber, about seven or eight feet high, are driven perpendicularly into the ground, about four feet apart from each other; a piece is secured firmly across them at the top, and another at a short distance from the ground. The hands of the man who is to be punished are tied at each end of the upright pieces, and his legs are secured to the same on each side below, in which position he is exposed to the merciless scourge of the drummer, which is a common cat-o'-nine-tails. It is painful even to think of such scenes as these, and when they take place at the mere whim and caprice of the hardened slave-merchant, such a picture is revolting in the extreme. Here however, severe as it may appear, it must be looked on in a different point of view. The punishment is great; but with a certainty of receiving it if discovered, the negro will run the risk of incurring it by what may be termed a breach of the first law of civilized society. In addition to the tendency it has to keep the free blacks in control, such a proceeding convinces the natives of the island that their depredations are not sanctioned by the colony. Were some punishment not instituted to curb the restless, pilfering propensities of these people, no order could be maintained; they would return to a worse condition than that from which they were in at first, and the colony would be no longer secure; for the natives of the island, finding their homes invaded, and their property carried off, unable to obtain redress, would soon take the law into their own hands, and would either murder the colonists or drive them from the island. Therefore, although a severe one, it is a salutary measure, and it has no doubt done much towards keeping the natives themselves honest. What punishment is adopted among the natives we have been unable to ascertain. The chiefs appear to possess considerable authority over them, and it is not improbable that the custom of the settlemen is imitated in some shape or other.

The only weapon used by the natives, excepting the knife before mentioned, is a spear, of about eight feet in length, made of iron-wood, and barbed at one end. The nature of the wood is so hard as not to require the protection of iron at the end, and we did not see any pointed with it. They are very plentiful among the natives, who do not appear to attach any particular value to them. We had no opportunity of witnessing their expertness with them, but they are said to use them for killing monkeys and other animals.

The resources of the island in point of provisions are either exhausted or the natives are determined to reserve what are left for their own purposes.—On the first formation of the establishment, they gladly brought to market all they had to dispose of, in the same manner as they had done to any vessel that chanced to visit the island. These consisted of a few sheep, goats, and fowls, of a very poor quality, and plenty of yams, which were all readily exchanged for pieces of iron hoop, of about six inches long. A piece of hoop of this length would purchase a goat, three or four fowls, or a large bundle of yams, weighing about twenty pounds. As their stock became exhausted, so the iron hoops became less valuable; more were demanded, until the natives could no longer supply the settlement, and had enough to do to provide for themselves, when they discontinued their supplies; and the settlement, not yet able to provide for itself, is depend-

ent on supplies from the Calebar and rivers near
it. Bullocks are stated by the natives to be plentiful on the hills in the interior, but we have not heard
of any having been seen by the people of Clarence,
and they are generally obtained from the Calebar
river. Deer are also said to be on the island, abundance of wild fowl, and a great number of monkeys
—some black and others of a brown colour. Parrots are also innumerable, and the natives are particularly partial to them and monkeys for food.
Turtle have been caught in the bay as well as fish;
but these supplies are uncertain, and therefore not
to be depended on. The island is entirely mountainous, and contains a fine rich soil, capable of producing any thing required of it. Several small moun-
tain-streams fall into the sea, the largest of which
are the two named Hay and Horton, brooks before
mentioned. The principal vegetable cultivated by
the natives is the yam, with which they are particularly successful. The best yams of the island are
said to be those of George's Bay, which are very
large and of uncommonly fine flavour. The supply of these at Clarence is now very limited, and
not to be depended on always, which may probably
be owing to a difference in the season for growing
them. This deficiency has been in some measure
remedied, by the construction of a government
garden, from which some men-of-war have received
supplies, but these are not sufficient to supply the
wants of the colony, and recourse is had for them
to the Calebar river.

Palm-wine at the colony, as well as on the coast,
is the common and favourite drink of the natives.
It is easily procured in any quantity, and is used
either in an unfermented state, when just fresh from
the tree, or after it has been kept some days. It
seems peculiarly intended by a bountiful Providence
for the untutored and destitute Indian, who is unable
to supply himself with those beverages which are

II.—A A

the result of art. The palm-tree affords him a pleasant drink, a valuable oil, a fruit from the nut: and, besides food, it furnishes him with a material to construct his hut, and is always ready for any immediate purpose. The juice, which is called " wine," is obtained by making a hole in the trunk of the tree, and inserting a piece of the leaf into it so as to form a spout ; the liquid flows through this, and is received in a calabash placed beneath it, which probably holds two or three gallons, and will be thus filled in the course of a day. It shortly assumes a milky appearance, and is either used in this state, or preserved till it acquires rather a bitter flavour. The produce of the palm-tree, fish, and yams form the principal food of the natives of Fernando Po, although they do not hesitate to devour monkeys when they can get them.

This method of obtaining the juice of the palm-tree is exactly similar to that which is adopted by the Indians in North America with respect to the maple-tree. A hole is made in the same manner in the trunk of the tree, and a piece of birch bark inserted into it as a spout, which, from its peculiar nature, answers the purpose remarkably well. The juice of the maple, instead of being preserved, is converted into sugar by evaporation. There are various sorts of timber at Fernando Po, among which the African oak is very plentiful, and particularly so in George's Bay, where it grows close to the seaside ; satin-wood, ebony, lignumvitæ, yellow cam-wood, and several sorts of mahogany, besides other wood of a very hard nature, grow in profusion all over the island, and may, probably, hereafter become valuable.

We had the good fortune to arrive at the island during the season of fine weather, but have not yet enjoyed much of the sea-breeze, which, about noon, has sometimes set in from the north-west quarter.—
The harmattan is said to be experienced here, al-

though it extends not to the other islands of the
gulf. This wind, which passes over the sands of
Africa, would be almost insupportable were it not
for the sea-breezes. While the harmattan lasts,
the dryness in the atmosphere produces an unpleasant feeling, although it is said to be not injurious to
health. The atmosphere is filled with a fine light
sand, which prevents objects from being distinctly
seen, the sun loses his brilliancy, and every thing
appears parched and suffering from the want of
moisture. The effect of the harmattan immediately
after the rainy season is said to be most beneficial
in drying up the vapours with which the atmosphere
is loaded; and it has been observed, that on the return of this wind at the end of the rainy season,
the recovery of invalids commences. The harmattan has also the effect of drying up the skin of
the natives in a very extraordinary manner. After
an exposure to it, the skin peels off in white scales
from their whole body, which assumes an appearance as if it were covered over with a white dust.

The islands in the Gulf of Guinea, with the exception of Fernando Po, have each a capital town
of some consequence, and although they produce
sufficient supplies for ships that visit them and
carry on a small trade, it is much to be doubted
whether they are not more indebted for their importance to the slave-trade than any other source.
With respect to Prince's Island and St. Thomas,
they are known to be the receptacles for slaves from
the coast, from whence they are re-embarked and
conveyed away as opportunities offer; and the natives of the small island of Anno-Bon appear to be
living in constant fear of the same, from the effects
of their former treatment by the Spaniards.

The natives of Anno-Bon have a tradition that
they once belonged to the Portuguese, and exhibit
proofs of their having been formerly initiated in the
ceremonies of the Roman Catholic religion. They

are said to be particularly careful, when any stranger
visits their settlement, to let them see their church,
which is appropriately situated for this purpose immediately opposite the landing-place.   At present,
by all accounts, they are living in a state of natural
simplicity and ignorance of the world.   Some idea
may be formed of the condition of their minds by a
story that is currently related of them, in which the
effects of their former tuition are apparent.   The
king once gravely told a visiter, with an idea of im-
pressing him with his importance, that a short time
previous to his arrival he had held a conference with
the Supreme Being, from whom he had learned the
cause of a recent sickness which had visited them,
and also that he had approved of his being the king
of the island.   Other stories equally nonsensical are
told of them, such as might be expected from people
left in this half-informed condition; but the old king's
word was sufficient for his subjects, and this assu-
rance was quite enough to satisfy the harmless inoffensive creatures that he was their legitimate king.
Although Anno-Bon is a healthy island in comparison with any other in the Gulf of Guinea, it is too
far removed from the coast to be of use in putting
down the slave-trade, unless it were made a rendezvous for half a dozen steam vessels, which would do
more than any other class of vessels towards effecting this object.

Favourable as the situation of Clarence is for the
purpose for which it is intended, it is much to be
regretted that it is so unhealthy for Europeans.
During our stay on the island four deaths occurred;
these persons were the sailmaker, one of the carpenters of the colony, a seaman of the Portia colonial schooner, and one of the crew of the Susan, an
English brig that we found here on our first arrival.
The Susan was in the Calebar river waiting for a
cargo, when her crew were attacked with fever,
which quickly carried off her captain, mates, and

eft only one person alive. The vessel, thus reduced, was without her crew to bring her out of the river, much less to complete her cargo, and she might have remained there till the last had died, but for the watchful attention of Mr. Becroft, who brought her to Clarence with a party of men, and after putting a new mast into her, and doing all in his power to set the vessel in order, supplied her with provisions and fresh people, and sent her to sea. We were offered a passage in her to England, but declined accepting it, in consequence of the condition in which she had been. She was afterward obliged to stop at Cape Coast, in consequence of the fever having broken out afresh on board of her. The most melancholy account of the effects of the climate here which came within our knowledge was in the family of Lieutenant Stockwell, the officer commanding the party of marines, whose name we have mentioned before. This gentleman had brought his wife and a large family with him from the island of Ascension, who were residing with his brother officer in a building called the Waterfall House, which had been erected by Captain Owen. Mr. Stockwell successively lost five of his children and five servants, the latter of whom successively died as they came into his service. His brother officer also died, making eleven in number, and Mr. Stockwell and his wife narrowly escaped with their lives. The house was in consequence deserted by them, and has since been occupied by the black people. The fever which attacks Europeans at this island is said to be similar to the yellow fever in the West Indies. The symptoms are the same from the commencement to the end of the disease, and it is equally as summary in its effects. George's Bay is said to be far healthier than Clarence, and being on the western side of the island receives the full benefit of the sea-breeze, while at Clarence this wind is later, and is interrupted by land to the westward of it. In addition

to this, the sea-breeze passes over a long and disagreeable swamp in its progress to Clarence. which
no doubt charges it with all kinds of noxious vapours.   George's Bay, besides having the benefit of
a pure sea-breeze, has a good deal of clear land about
it, and equally as good a soil as Clarence.

It is more than probable, as we have now ascertained, that a water-communication may be carried
on with so extensive a part of the interior of Africa
that a considerable trade will be opened with the
country through which we have passed.   The natives only require to know what is wanted from
them, and to be shown what they will have in return, and much produce that is now lost from neglect will be turned to a considerable account.   The
countries situated on the banks of the Niger will become frequented from all the adjacent parts, and this
magnificent stream will assume an appearance it has
never yet displayed.   The first effect of a trade being opened will be to do away with the monopoly
near the mouth of the river, which has hitherto been
held by the chiefs of the lower countries.   Steam-
boats will penetrate up the river even as far as Lever.
at the time of year in which we came down, and will
defy the efforts of these monopolists to arrest their
progress.   The steam-engine, the grandest invention
of the human mind, will be a fit means of conveying
civilization among these uninformed Africans, who,
incapable of comprehending such a thing, will view
its arrival among them with astonishment and terror, but will gradually learn to appreciate the benefits they will derive, and to hail its arrival with joy.
In this case Fernando Po will become of still greater
consequence, and will no doubt become a depôt of
considerable importance.   It is my opinion, however, that much expense would be saved, and, above
all, many valuable lives, if it were possible to adopt
George's Bay as the place for the principal establishment.   Of the different parts of the coast Accra

is the most healthy, and were it nearer, I should recommend it for such a purpose, the soil being good and clear of underwood for many miles around. But the distance at which it lies from the mouth of the river is too great for such a purpose.

Thursday, December 23d.—The superintendent, Mr. Becroft, invited me to accompany him in the Portia colonial schooner to the Calebar river, whither he was going to procure stock for the use of the colony. The place from which this is obtained is called Ephraim town, where it appears to be very plentiful. Being tired of Fernando Po, I accepted his invitation, to pass away the time that we should yet have to wait before we could get away, notwithstanding all our anxiety to get home with the news of our discovery. My brother, being very ill, was enable to accompany us. I left him at Clarence, and embarked with Mr. Becroft in the evening. We departed from Clarence with a fine breeze, but found it necessary in going out to be particularly careful of being drifted by the tide, either on Point William or on the Adelaide islets at each extremity of the cove, as the tide always sets either towards one or the other. In leaving the cove, it is best to keep as near as possible midway between the two extremes, and not to approach either the one or the other nearer than can possibly be avoided. The currents in the Gulf of Guinea are stated to be very variable. although they are most generally from the westward, obeying the direction of the sea-breeze. The harmattan generally produces a very strong westerly current in direct opposition to this, and the want of knowing it has frequently proved fatal to vessels: the masters of which, imagining that they were under the influence of an easterly current, have been actually drifted many miles to the westward in the course of a single night, and have found themselves on shore the next morning. The violence of the current from the westward, when the sea-breezes are strong, is so great, that it is scarcely possible to believe that a day or two of the harmattan would overcome it; but the effect of this is so powerful, that it is well known to those who have frequented the gulf, that the current produced by the harmattan will even continue against the westerly winds after they may have again set in. A remarkable instance is related of the velocity of the currents in the gulf to the southward of Fernando Po. In the month of June, a vessel performed the passage between Prince's Island and St. Thomas in twenty hours, which generally occupies from eight to ten days. The distance is about ninety-three miles; and the vessel must have averaged 4.6 miles per hour. The harmattan is said not to extend to the southward of Fernando Po, but this has not yet been fully ascertained.

The passage through the gulf from Fernando Po to Sierra Leone is generally extremely long and tedious, owing to the prevalence of calms and the different currents. It is generally made either by running to the southward and getting into the southeast trade, or by keeping in shore as far as Cape Palmas, so as to benefit by the land winds. The former method is generally recommended by the merchant-men, as being safer and quicker; for a vessel adopting the latter is more under the dangerous influence of the currents, besides being obliged to keep close to the shore: it is also adopted by the merchant-men in their homeward voyage. Sometimes vessels, by taking a mean between these two methods, get between two different winds, by which means they lose the benefit of both, and are delayed by calms and rains. This part, I was informed, was at the distance of about sixty miles from the land; so that vessels should pass either far without or else within that distance on leaving Fernando Po.

In this part of the Gulf of Guinea, between Fernando Po and the Calebar river, the rainy season is stated to commence in the month of July, and to be at the worst in August and September, accompanied by tornadoes of a most terrific description. The rains continue during November, and cease in the month of December, but the coast is said to be seldom many days together without a tornado. During the other months of the year, dry hot weather is experienced, excepting about May, when slight rains take place. These rains are looked on as the winter of the natives, and are considered by them equally as cold in their effects as our winters in England are by ourselves. They are equally alive to the change of the seasons as in northern countries, and prepare themselves against the cold weather during the rains, comparatively with as much care as we do against our winter's frost.

The chief peculiarity of this climate, which distinguishes it from all others within the tropics, consists in the furious storms of wind and rain, accompanied by the most terrific thunder and lightning it is possible to imagine. These storms are known by the name of tornadoes; and one would be almost inclined to think that the ancient belief of the torrid zone being of a fiery nature, and too hot for mankind to live in, originated in the exaggerated reports of them which might have gradually found their way into the part of the world then known, and from which they were not very far distant. We have already seen three here, but they were trifling in their effects compared with those which take place in the rainy season. They are described as being most violent, but, happily, of short duration: nothing can withstand the fury of the wind while they last, but they give sufficient indications of their approach, of which the commanders of ships on the coast know how to take advantage. They invariably come from the eastern quarter of the horizon, and last about fifteen or twenty minutes. Their first

314

approach is indicated by a luminous, glaring appearance in the north-east quarter, which in the course of about an hour has shifted gradually to the east and south-east, while the usual sea-breeze from the north-west continues blowing. Having arrived in the south-east quarter, the storm shows its nearer approach by incessant flashes of lightning of a most awful description, accompanied by thunder which is absolutely deafening; the proximity of the lightning contributes not a little to its awful appearance. A short interval of calm now takes place, occasioned probably by the suspension of the sea-breeze, from the advance of the tornado. A small arch may at the same time be perceived near the horizon in the direction of the approaching storm. This, which from the time of its being first seen increases rapidly, being nothing more than the effect of the wind in dispersing the heavy clouds through which it passes. The momentous crisis is now at hand. As soon as the arch has reached about half-way to the zenith, the storm bursts forth with the most impetuous violence, and torrents of rain immediately follow. Ships that happen to be caught in it before they have adopted the necessary precautions for safety by taking in all their sails, are thrown on their side instantly; but happily the warning it gives of its approach is sufficient to enable the experienced navigator, who is ever on the watch for changes in the weather, to reduce the sail from his ship, and put her head in that position in which she is best able to withstand its effects, by running before the wind. This awful period lasts generally about a quarter of an hour—when the wind subsides rather suddenly, while the rain falls incessantly: shortly afterward the wind shifts round by the south to its old quarter, the west, until another tornado comes to disturb it. There are several peculiarities attending the tornadoes, which are rather remarkable. It has been remarked by experienced navigators, that they are much influenced by the different phases of the moon; that they generally commence with the new or full moon, at which time they are the most violent; and that they even come on at the time that the moon sets.   The influence of the moon on the weather in other countries is doubted, but this is an extraordinary fact, relating to the tornadoes, which has been proved by experience.

Saturday, December 25th.—After a pleasant passage we anchored this morning off Ephraim town, in the Calebar river.   The distance from Fernando Po to the north of the Calebar river is about sixty miles; and Ephraim town is distant about fifty miles on the eastern bank.   On our way up the river, my attention was attracted by something of a very extraordinary appearance hanging over the water from the branch of a tree.   My curiosity was excited by it, and I was at a loss to conjecture what it was.   I did not remain long in suspense, for we soon passed sufficiently near it to enable me to discover that it was the body of one of the natives suspended by the middle, with the feet and hands just touching the water.   So barbarous a sight quickly reminded me that I was again among the poor deluded wretches of the coast, although I had seen nothing so bad as this on my way down to the brig Thomas, in the river Nun.   The natives of this place are pagans, in the most depraved condition, and know nothing of Mohammedanism, nor any other creed.   They believe in a good spirit, who they imagine dwells in the water; and sacrifices such as that just mentioned are frequently made to him, with the idea of gaining his favour and protection.   The object selected for this purpose is generally some unfortunate old slave, who may be worn out and incapable of further service, or unfit for the market; and he is thus left to suffer death, either from the effects of the sun, or from the fangs of some hungry alligator or shark, which may chance to find the body.   The circum-

stance of the hands and feet being just allowed to
be immersed in the water is considered by these
deluded people as necessary, and they are thereby
rendered an easier prey.

It is usual with ships on their first arrival in the
river, to be visited by Duke Ephraim, the chief of
the town; a personage who is well known to the
numerous Liverpool traders that frequent the river.
The reason of this visit is, that the duke may receive his present, which consists generally of cloth,
muskets, rum, or any articles of that description;
and he always goes on board in great state in his
canoe for this purpose, previous to which no one is
allowed to leave the ship. This regulation, which
is a method of securing the port-dues, affects those
only who come to the river for the purpose of trade;
and as the Portia was a government vessel, we were
not included. As soon as we had anchored, I accompanied Mr. Becroft on shore, and proceeded
with him to the duke's residence, for the purpose of
paying our respects to him. A walk of about ten
minutes brought us to his house, and we found him
in the palàver square which belongs to it, busily engaged in writing, and surrounded by a great number
of his principal people. It was something unusual
to find a native chief thus employed; but the large
dealings which Duke Ephraim appears to have with
the Liverpool merchants accounts in some measure
for this accomplishment, and the smattering of English he has obtained. His only pretensions to dress
consisted in a smart gold-laced hat, which he wore,
and a handsome piece of silk tied round his loins.
His chief officers, who were next to him, also wore
gold-laced hats, while those next in rank to them
wore silver-lace, and the lower class contented themselves without either. We arrived at council time,
but Mr. Becroft being immediately recognised by
the duke, he received us very cordially, and made
us sit down. Duke Ephraim bears the character of

being always very civil and attentive to the English, and of making himself very active in supplying their wants of live-stock. He has formed a favourable opinion of them from the *fine things* they bring him, but his discernment goes beyond these; for the circumstance of slave vessels having been captured and taken out of the river by the boats of the English ships of war on the station has impressed him with admiration of their boldness and courage, and given him a very exalted opinion of their power. Vessels of war formerly came up the rivers in search of slavers; and he has received their commanders with much kindness, and assisted them all in his power;— a trait in his character which is rather extraordinary, when their object is considered, as he is the principal agent by whom supplies of slaves are furnished from the interior. None, however, are allowed to come up now, in consequence of the deaths which occurred.

After a short time, we were desired to go up-stairs into his best room, and we accordingly ascended about thirty or forty wooden steps, and entered a spacious apartment, when the sight that presented itself was of the most extraordinary description. The room, which was about thirty feet in length by about twenty in breadth, was literally crammed full of all kinds of European furniture, covered with cobwebs and dust about half an inch deep. Elegant tables and chairs, sofas of a magnificent description, splendid looking-glasses, and prints of the principal public characters of England, as well as views of sea and land engagements, set in handsome gilt frames, beautiful cut-glass decanters and glasses, glass chandeliers, and a quantity of other things, too numerous to mention, were all mixed together, in the utmost confusion. A handsome organ attracted our notice, and a large solid brass arm-chair, which an inscription on it announced was the present of Sir John Tobin, of Liverpool. The inscription, or rather raised characters, were these : " Presented by Sir John Tobin of Liverpool, to his friend Duke Ephraim ;". and vain enough is the chief of his present. He exhibits this chair with the rest of his presents to the people, or any stranger who may happen to visit him, and allows them to feast their eyes, as he imagines, on the goodly sight; but such is his care and pride of them, that he will not allow them to be touched by any one; and his attendants are not permitted to approach them, even for the purpose of cleaning off the dust which has accumulated since their first arrival. The whole of this miscellaneous assemblage of goods are presents which have been made to the duke by merchants of Liverpool, as well as French, Spanish, and Portuguese traders, and are the accumulation of a considerable length of time.

Duke town, or Ephraim town, as it is known by both of these appellations, is situated on rather elevated ground, on the left or east bank of the river; and is of considerable size, extending principally along it. From the appearance of it, I should conclude that its inhabitants amount to at least six thousand people. The houses are generally built of clay, like those of the Eboe people. The breadth of the river opposite to it is not quite so wide as the Thames at Waterloo Bridge, and the opposite bank is not so high as that on which the town stands. The houses are built in an irregular manner, leaving very little room for the road between them; which, at this time, is exceedingly wet and dirty. The duke's house is situated in the middle of the town, and, like the rest, is built of clay. It consists of several squares, round each of which is a veranda, similar to the houses in Yarriba. The centre square is occupied by the duke and his wives, the others being the abode of his servants and attendants, which, all together, amount to a considerable number. Immediately opposite to the first square, which forms the entrance to his residence, stands a small tree, profusely decorated with human sculls and bones. This tree is considered by the people as fetísh, or sacred; and is supposed to possess the virtue of preventing the evil spirit from entering the duke's residence. Near the tree stands the house which is inhabited by their priests, a class of beings certainly in the most savage condition of nature that it is possible to imagine. The fetísh priests of Brass town chalked themselves from head to foot, besides dressing after a fashion of their own; but these fellows outdo them by far, and make themselves the most hideous and disgusting objects possible.

Whether it may be with the idea of personifying the evil spirit they are so afraid of, I could not learn, but they go about the town with a human scull fastened over their face, so that they can see through the eye-holes;—this is surmounted by a pair of bullock's horns; their body is covered with net, made of stained grass; and, to complete the whole, and give them an appearance as ridiculous behind as they are hideous before, a bullock's tail protrudes through the dress and hangs down to the ground, rendering them altogether the most uncouth-looking beings imaginable. Sometimes a cocked-hat is substituted for the horns, and the scull of a dog or monkey used, which renders their appearance, if possible, still more grotesque. Thus equipped, they are ready to perform the mysteries of their profession, which I had not sufficient opportunity to inquire into, but which are quite enough to enslave the minds of the people. They seem to believe in a good and evil spirit; that the good spirit dwells in the river, which accounts for their sacrifices being made on it; and that the evil spirit dwells in a tree, which being full of human sculls, keeps him away from them.

Sunday, December 26th.—This morning the duke's principal man came on board the Portia, to receive payment for some bullocks which Mr. Becroft had

purchased.   There was something in his appearance
which attracted my attention, and I fancied that he
seemed to be much dirtier than any I had seen yesterday.   On a nearer inspection, I found his head
and whole body to be covered with ashes, and a very
dirty piece of sackcloth fastened round his loins.
Besides this, he appeared to be suffering great distress of mind, and presented a most woful and
wretched appearance.   I asked him the cause of his
grief, and why he had covered himself with ashes in
such a manner; when he related to me the cause of
all his distress.   It appeared that he had possessed
six wives, one of whom was gifted with a larger
share of personal charms than the rest, the consequence of which was, that she received more attention
from him, and was loved more than any of the others.
This partiality naturally excited the jealousy of the
other ladies; and, mortified by his neglect of them,
they were determined on revenge, and resolved to
get rid of their favoured rival by mixing poison with
her food.   They had just succeeded in effecting their
purpose, which had caused the poor fellow much
distress, and he had not recovered the effects of his
loss this morning when he came on board the Portia.
His tale was simple and ungarnished; and while he
was relating it to me the tears were trickling down
his face.   I never saw a black man feel so much for
the loss of a wife as he did.   This remarkable custom of mourning in sackcloth and ashes appears to
be peculiar to these people; and I find that they do
not cease to cover their persons with them as long
as their sorrow lasts.   They do the same on the
death of a relation; and it is the only instance of the
kind that I have met with in the part of the country
through which I have travelled.

Great uproar and confusion has prevailed in the
town to-day, occasioned by an adventure of the doctor with the duke's most favourite wife, which is
likely to end tragically to the parties concerned.

This person, who is the doctor of the town, it appears, was the bosom friend of the duke, in whom the latter had the greatest confidence, and allowed him to visit his wives professionally as often as he thought proper. The gentleman's visits had lately become so frequent as to excite suspicion, and a look-out was accordingly kept on his movements. The poor doctor was soon caught in the snare; the motive of his visits was found to be of an illegal nature, and the enraged duke has ordered both to be bound hand and foot and thrown into the river to-morrow. There is no doubt that this will be done; for although these men have many wives, still a misdemeanor of this nature is looked on by them with great abhorrence.

We found seven French vessels lying in the river, one Spanish, and two English. One of the latter, named the Caledonia, a ship of five hundred tons burthen, is the property of Sir John Tobin, of Liverpool, which, with the other, the brig Elizabeth, are taking in a cargo of palm-oil.

The river Calebar is very serpentine, and there is scarcely any other tree besides the mangrove to be seen on its banks. The right bank is intersected by numerous creeks, well known to the natives, who frequent them in their canoes; they communicate with all the rivers that fall into the Gulf of Guinea, between this river and that on which Benin is situated. The natives go as far as Benin in their canoes, but there is no communication by water with the Cameroons river, which seems to be totally distinct from the Calebar. The canoes of the natives are the same sort as those of the Eboe people, but not so large. The river is full of crocodiles, which are generally about twelve or fourteen feet long, and are very daring in search of prey. A short time previous to our arrival two deaths had been occasioned by them. Sir John Tobin has a large store close to the river-side, in which palm-oil is kept for

II.—B B

shipment on board the Liverpool vessels, and one evening lately an unfortunate native boy, tired with his day's work, fell asleep on the floor. In the course of the night an alligator attacked him, and he was awoke by finding himself in the jaws of the monster: his struggles and cries were vain; the powerful creature lacerated him in a most dreadful manner, and tore off one of his legs, with which he retreated into the water, and the remains of the unfortunate boy were found the next morning shockingly disfigured, and weltering in blood. The death of the other was occasioned by his losing an arm in a similar manner.

Provisions at present are dear at Duke town, and rather scarce. Bullocks are sold at twenty dollars each, and those not of a very good quality; goats and sheep at three dollars, ducks at half a dollar each, and fowls at half a dollar the pair. Yams are cultivated by the natives very successfully, and are considered the best flavoured and finest of the country. There are no cleared portions of ground on the banks of the river, and their cultivation of the yam and other vegetables is at a distance in the woods.

Thursday, January 20*th.*—Since my first return to Fernando Po from the Calebar river, I have accompanied Mr. Becroft there twice in the Portia. In this interval the Caernarvon, an English vessel, has arrived with government stores from England for the establishment, and as she is going to Rio Janeiro for a cargo to take back, and there seems to be no prospect at present of our getting away from this island by any other means, we have requested Mr. Becroft to conclude an agreement for our passage to that place, from whence we hope to be more successful in finding our way to England. About a week ago the brig Thomas, in which we came from the river Nun, touched at the island on her way home from the Cameroons,—her commander Lake thinking that we should take a passage with him.

We have now been here seven weeks, and would certainly stay seven more rather than put ourselves into his power again. We had experienced quite enough of his care and kindness, and therefore declined his offer of taking us. After waiting three days at the island, he sailed about six o'clock in the morning, and had not got more than a mile from the anchorage, when a large vessel with long raking masts suddenly appeared from behind a part of the island, and was seen in pursuit of him. We observed this vessel fire several guns at him, which at length made him take in sail and wait. We have no doubt that this vessel was a pirate, and our suspicions were confirmed the next day by seeing the two vessels lying becalmed close to each other. There were no signs of them on the next day, and we saw nothing more of the Thomas.*

The commission for the adjudication of slave-vessels is not yet removed from Sierra Leone to this place, and all prizes are taken there for condemnation.

* Since our arrival in England this vessel has never been heard of, and the owners have received an affidavit from us to the above effect. There can be no doubt that the stranger was a pirate, from his suspicious appearance and the firing that we observed; so that we consider it a most providential escape that we did not take our passage in her. This was the general opinion at the settlement; and that when his people had murdered the crew of the Thomas, with their captain, or had compelled them to "walk the plank," as they usually do, that they sunk her, after taking every thing out of her which they might want. "Walking the plank" is literally walking into the sea. A plank is placed across the side of the ship, so that one end projects some distance over it, while the other remains inside. The person condemned by these ruffians to this mode of death, which is generally chosen to avoid one of a more dreadful nature, is placed on the inner end of the plank, and compelled to walk along it till he reaches the outer end, which immediately yields to his weight, and he falls into the sea, never to rise again. To make shorter work of it, he is sometimes loaded with a large shot, which quickly carries him down. These fellows have another method of disposing of any unfortunate vessel that may fall into their hands. After having got rid of the captain and crew as above, they fill her with slaves and send her across the Atlantic. Should the vessel be met with by any ship of war, she escapes examination, as her appearance when in the hands of her own commander was known, and therefore no suspicion is excited

Every thing having been prepared for our departure, we embarked on board of the Caernarvon, —— Garth, commander, for Rio Janeiro. The reception that we have met with at Clarence from the officers of the establishment has been most gratifying, and has far exceeded our expectations. To Mr. Becroft, the superintendent, we are under peculiar obligations, having enjoyed the benefits of his hospitality all the time of our detention here; and the kind attention of this gentleman, as well as that of Mr. Crichton, the naval surgeon, who is one of the most amiable gentlemen we ever met with, and Mr. Beatty, has gone far towards removing the ill effects of the exposure we had undergone on our way down the river. Every thing was supplied us that the place could afford; and it will always be a source of gratification to us to reflect on the time we passed in their company.

At six in the evening, having taken leave of our friends, we embarked and bade adieu to the island of Fernando Po. Mr. Stockwell, the officer of marines, accompanied us on board, having taken his passage, like ourselves, to return to England. Our crew consists of seven European seamen, two free negroes, and one Krooman, besides the commander of the vessel and two mates. Two of the seamen, Owen Williams and Charles Hall, are very ill with fever.

Sunday, January 23d.—The weather has been calm, and we have not lost sight of Fernando Po. At noon, Owen Williams, seaman, died. The funeral service was read over his remains by Lieutenant Stockwell, before they were committed to the sea.

Wednesday, January 26th.— —— Wells, the captain's steward, —— Jones, the second mate, and John Collins, seaman, were taken ill with fever Having been accustomed to perform the office of doctor while in Africa, my services in this line were put in requisition, and I immediately took a large quantity of blood from the two latter and applied blisters, after which Mr. Stockwell gave them medicine. To-day Charles Hall is rather better.

Thursday, January 27th.—John Williams, seaman, was taken ill with fever; I bled him immediately and shaved his head, and Mr. Stockwell gave him medicine. The weather still continues calm, with light winds, and we can still see the island. The fever seems to be making great havoc among us. Those whose fever is intermittent are likely to do well, but the others seem to have no chance of recovery.

Sunday, January 30th.— —— Smith, seaman, was taken ill with fever. This poor fellow, after I had prepared every thing for bleeding him, would not permit me to do it, but I managed to shave his head and put a blister on it. At two P. M. —— Wells, the captain's steward, died, while I was lifting him up in his bed to give him some medicine. The crew are lying in different parts of the vessel ill with fever, in a helpless and most distressing condition. A general panic seems to have taken possession of them all, which is likely to be attended with fatal consequences. We determined on keeping them from knowing of the death of the poor steward, and accordingly at night we carried his remains on deck, and threw them into the sea over the stern of the vessel.

Friday, February 4th.—Captain Garth was taken ill with fever, and John Williams, seaman, died. We still have fine weather, but we are making little progress over to the coast of America.

Sunday, February 6th.—The chief mate taken ill with fever. So much are we reduced now, that the three black men, with my brother and myself, are all who are left to work the vessel, and only one of these, the Krooman, knows how to steer. Mr. Stockwell is constantly employed in attending the sick.

Monday, February 7th.— —— Smith, seaman, died.

In consequence of the sick state of the crew, I have been constantly employed, both day and night, in working the ship. My principal station has been at the helm every night until twelve o'clock, and every morning after four. I manage to get a few minutes to eat my breakfast, and the rest of my time is occupied in attending the sails and looking to the sick. My brother's time is employed in nearly the same manner. In addition to our troubles, the vessel is so completely overrun by rats that it is quite impossible to stay below with any comfort; and as for sleeping there, it is out of the question. The sick are all on the upper deck, in their hammocks, and fortunately, the weather has been hitherto tolerably fine.

Monday, March 14th.—Off Cape Frio. This evening our only Krooman fell into the sea. This poor fellow, whose name was " Yellow Will," called loudly to us for help, and although the vessel was not sailing at a great rate, he missed every thing that we threw overboard to save him. To have altered the ship's course would have endangered the masts and sails, and our small boat was so leaky, that it would not swim. We had no alternative, and were obliged to abandon him to his fate, with the most painful feelings, and heard his cries nearly an hour afterward. There is nothing more distressing than an accident of this nature. To see an unfortunate man grasping in vain at any thing which is thrown to him as the ship passes by him—to see him struggling against his fate as he rises on the distant wave, which frequently conceals him from view, and to be unable to render him the least assistance, while his cries die away in the breeze, raise sensations which it is impossible to describe. This man, in our present condition particularly, was a great loss to us, and was the best among the black people.

Tuesday, March 15th.—This morning the weather was very hazy, which prevented our seeing the land,

Although we knew it to be at no great distance from us. We were becalmed all day, and found, by the decrease of the depth, that we were drifting close on towards the shore. At five in the afternoon the ship was about a quarter of a mile from the land, which we discovered by three large hills of a sugar-loaf appearance being close to us. Finding by pieces of cork and other things which we threw into the water, that we were drifting fast on the breakers, which we could distinctly hear, we made an attempt to get the long-boat out to save ourselves, as we expected the ship would be very soon wrecked, but we found that we could not muster sufficient strength to lift her over the side. At this critical moment a breeze of wind from off the land saved us from destruction, and enabled us to get the vessel under command.

Wednesday, March 16th.—The breeze favoured us, and at 2 P. M. we anchored in the harbour of Rio Janeiro.

Thursday, March 17th.—This morning we went to pay our respects to Admiral Baker, the commander-in-chief on the South American station, and made known to him our situation, and anxiety to return to England. The admiral received us in that kind and hospitable manner which is the peculiar character-istic of a British seaman: he invited us to his table with his officers, and ordered us a passage in the William Harris, a government transport, which is to sail for England in a day or two.

Sunday, March 20th.—We sailed this afternoon for England, in the William Harris. We had scarcely reached the outside of the harbour when the wind failed us, and we were becalmed near one of the islands. As we found the ship drifting fast towards it, we were obliged to come to anchor, and remained so during the first part of the night. About mid-night a strong wind rendered it impossible for the ship to remain longer at anchor, and no time was therefore lost in endeavouring to get her to sea. To get the anchor on board was too long a process; the safety of the ship became endangered by the delay it required, and to save her from drifting on shore, we were under the necessity of cutting the cable, by which we lost about forty-five fathoms of it, besides the anchor. We were then enabled to set sail, and with difficulty cleared the land to leeward of us.

Thursday, June 9th.—We arrived at Portsmouth after a tedious voyage, and gladly landed, with hearts full of gratitude for all our deliverances.

Friday, June 10th.—Having left my brother at Portsmouth, I arrived in London this morning by the mail, and reported our discovery to Lord Goderich, his majesty's colonial secretary.

Note.—The curiosity of the reader will, no doubt, have been excited by the total disregard and apathy displayed by the commander of the brig Thomas, respecting the engagements of Richard Lander, to pay the price for which he and his brother had been ransomed from the hands of the Eboe people. This behaviour, which can be accounted for in no other way than by allowing it to have arisen from a determination not to part with the arms of the vessel, although whatever might have been given would have been replaced at Cape Coast Castle, deeply implicated the good faith of his majesty's government, and must have been attended with a bad effect. It is to be hoped, however, that this has been removed, as, on the return of the Messrs. Lander, orders were immediately sent out to pay the proper demand.—ED.

APPENDIX.

No. I.

Translation of a Letter from the Sultan of Yàoorie in Africa, to his Britannic Majesty, brought to England by Richard Lander and his Brother, in June, 1831.

"Praise be to God, and blessings and salutation be unto that (prophet) since whom there has been no other prophet.

"To our friend in God and his apostle (Mohammed), the prince of the English Christians, salutation and mercy, and blessings of God, be unto you, from your friend the Sultan of Yàoorie, whose name is Mohammed Ebsheer. Perfect salutation be unto you, (and) may God cause your mornings and evenings to be most happy, with multiplied salutations (from us).

"After our salutation unto you, (some) ostrich feathers will reach you (as a present) from the bounty and blessings of God (we have in our country), and we, together with you, thank God (for what he has bestowed). And salutation be unto your hired people (your suite), and peace be unto our people who praise God.

(Signed)   "From the Prince of Yàoorie."

Observation of the Translator.

The original of this is one of the worst of the African papers I have seen, both as to its ungrammatical and its unintelligible character. Indeed, his Yàooric majesty seems to be sadly in need of words to make himself intelligible.

The words between parentheses are not in the original.

Translated, London, 25th June, 1831.
(Signed)   A. V Salame.

E e 2

No. II.

LONDON MILITARY DEPÔT,
1st January, 1830.

*Delivered out of his Majesty's Stores at this Place, by an Order of the
Honourable Board of Ordnance, dated 18th December, 1829, the under-
mentioned Particulars,—to Messrs. Lander, about to proceed on Discovery in Africa.*

	Total.		No.
Cloth, staff sergeants, scarlet....................yds.	50	{ 19¾ in bale	8
		30¼ "	9
Ditto, ditto, blue gray, in lieu of yellow....."	10	"	8
Muslin, striped................................."	47½	"	9
Mirrors..No.	10	{ 4 in pannier	5
		6 "	6
Ditto, inferior quality .... "	100	{ 50 "	3
		50 "	4
Razors, common .... "	50	{ 12 "	3
		12 "	4
		12 "	5
		14 "	6
Scissors, assorted............................pairs	50	{ 10 "	3
		20 "	4
		20 "	6
Knives, clasp, assorted................. .... "	60	{ 5 "	3
		5 "	4
		25 "	5
		25 "	6
Combs, assorted............................... "	100	{ 70 "	5
		30 "	6
Beads, glass ....lbs.	38	{ 10 "	5
		18 "	6
		10 "	7
Boxes, snuff, common........................No.	100	{ 30 "	3
		30 "	5
		40 "	6
Arm-bands, small silver..................... "	64	{ 12 "	3
		12 "	4
		12 "	5
		6 "	6
		22 "	7
	Thous.		
Needles, assorted, 60,000 .... .lbs.	10	{ 10 "	1
		10 "	2
		10 "	3
		10 '	4
		10 "	5
		10 "	6

	Total.		No.
Horns, bugles, with slings	No. 2		in pannier 1
Calico, printed	yds. 88½	{ 60½	in bale 8
		28	" 9
Pipes, German or Dutch	No. 100	{ 60	in pannier 5
		40	" 7
Medals, silver, large size	" 2		" 2
Flints for — Fowling-pieces	" 100	{ 25	" 3
		25	" 4
		25	" 5
		25	" 6
Flints for — Pistols	" 50	{ 12	" 3
		12	" 4
		12	" 5
		14	" 6
Moulds, bullet, cast one ball only	" 3	{ 1	" 3
		1	" 4
		1	" 5
Flasks, powder	" 2		" 2
Belts, shot	" 2		" 2
Shot, for fowling-pieces, in bags of 28 lbs. each	No. 1 lbs. 28		" 6
	" 5 " 56	{ 28 lbs.	" 3
		28	" 4
	" 8 " 28		" 5
Balls, for — Fowling-pieces	No. 250	{ 63	" 3
		62	" 4
		63	" 5
		62	" 6
Balls, for — Pistols	" 150	{ 37	" 3
		37	" 4
		38	" 5
		38	" 6
Powder, gun (rifle), in tin cannisters of 1 lb. each	lbs. 18	{ 4	" 4
		4	" 5
		5	" 6
		1	" 1
		4	" 3
Fowling-pieces, chiefs' guns	No. 2		in case 12
Pistols	brace 2		in pannier 1
Cooking apparatus, or portable kitchen	No. 1		" 1
Tent, circular, complete	" 1	}	in valise 13
Ditto, pins	" 40	}	
Mallets, tent	" 2	}	
Compasses, pocket	" 2		in pannier 2
Thermometers, in brass cases	" 2		" 2
Watch, common silver	" 1		" 7
Stationary	parcel 1		" 10
Mattresses, hammock	" 2	{ 1	" 11
		1	" 1
Soup, portable			"
Tea	lbs. 6		"
Coffee	" 10		" 2
Sugar	" 20		" 2
Padlocks and keys on the medicine panniers	No. 7		
Screw-drivers, common	" 3		" 2

	Total.			*No.*
Rods, cleaning, for fowling-pieces............	No. 2	1 in pannier		3
		1 "		4
Cartridges — Blank, carbine	" 250	60 "		3
		60 "		4
		60 "		5
		70 "		6
Pistol	" 150	30 "		1
		30 "		2
		30 "		4
		30 "		5
		30 "		6
Plates, tin...	No. 6			
Hatchets, hand....................	" 2			
Saws, hand, small...........................	" 1			
Cups, tin drinking, ½ quart....................	" 2			
Tinder-box, complete	" 1			
Thread, whited brown......................	lbs. 1			
Ink-bottle, small........................	No. 1			
Spurs, with leathers.....................pairs 2				
Files, hand, saw	No. 6			
Books, journal, thick quarto	" 2			
Ditto, memorandum	" 2			
Straps, baggage	set 1			
Blankets, single, N. P.......................	No. 2	1 in valise		10
		1 "		11
Sheets, hospital	" 4	2 "		10
		2 "		11
Flems, furriers...	" 6	2 in pannier		1
		1 "		3
		1 "		4
		1 "		5
		1 "		9
Bolsters, hammock, hair.......	" 2	1 "		10
		1 "		11
Water decks, O. P	" 3	2 in bale		8
		1 "		9
Valises	" 3	10, 11, 13		
Panniers, medicine	" 7	No. 1 to 7		
Case, gun	" 1			
Medicines, cases..............................	" 2	No. 15 & 16		

The last five articles as packages.
     (Signed)   G. STACEY.

In addition to the above, the following articles were supplied from
Cape Coast Castle, and presented by the travellers to the King of Ba
dagry '

    40 Muskets.
    12 Signal rockets.
    20 Barrels of ball cartridges

MEDICINAL MIXTURES.

Directions for making one Pint of the Solution of Citric Acid.

Take of Citric Acid.................. 1 oz.
Rain or River Water...... 1 pint.

Mix, and make a solution, which will be equal in strength to Lemon Juice.

To make Saline Effervescent Draughts.

Take of Carbonate of Soda.........25 grains,
Pure Water.............. 3 table-spoonfuls.

Mix, and add one table-spoonful of the Solution of Citric Acid, to be drank *immediately* while in a state of effervescence.

To make Quinine Pills.

Take of Sulphate of Quinine......24 grains,
Conserve of Hips.........a sufficient quantity.

Mix, and divide into 12 pills. One to be taken three times a day.

To make Camphorated Spirits.

Take of Camphor................... 1 oz.
Rectified Spirits of Wine .. 8 oz.

Mix, that the Camphor may be dissolved. To be used as a stimulating embrocation in sprains, bruises, or rheumatic affections of the limbs.

To make Goulard Lotion.

Take of Acetate of Lead (called Sugar of Lead)..1 drachm,
Rain or River Water...................2 pints,
Rectified Spirits of Wine ....2 tea-spoonfuls.

Mix, and make a Lotion; to be applied to inflamed parts, with pledgets of linen, five or six times a day. Is also a good eye-water.

List of Medicines and Surgical Materials to be supplied for the
Africa, with short Directions for their

ARTICLES.	Quantity.	
	lbs.	oz.
Sub-muriate of mercury, or calomel, in 4 bottles	1	..
Compound extract of colocynth, in 2 tins	2	..
Sulphate of magnesia, or Epsom salt................	10	..
Jalap in powder, in 2 bottles	1	..
Seidlitz powders	12 doz.	
Tartarized antimony, or emetic tartar..............	..	1
Ipecacuanha in powder............................	..	4
James's powder....................................	6 packets	
Citric acid, to be used for lemon-juice............	2	..
Carbonate of soda, in 2 bottles, for the same use as carbonate of potash	2	..
Compound powder of ipecacuanha, or Dover's powders, in 2 bottles	1	..
Nitros ether, or sweet spirits of nitre, in 2 bottles ...	1	..
Super-tartrate of potash, or cream of tartar	4	..
Tincture of opium, in half-pints....................	2	..
Opium	1	..
Vitriolic ether, in 2 bottles	..	8
Volatile liquor, or spirits of hartshorn, in 2 bottles ..	1	..
Camphor	..	4
Mercurial pill, or blue pill	..	8
Aromatic confection	..	4

III.

Use of Mr. Lander and his Brother, going on an Expedition to Use an Application.—WOOLWICH, 28 Dec., 1829.

DOSES.	REMARKS.
from 5 to 10 grains.............	a purgative.
from 8 to 15 grains.............	ditto.
from ½ an ounce to an ounce.....	ditto.
from 15 to 30 grains	ditto., with two or three grains of ginger.
....	to be used as before.
from 1 to 3 grains.............	in an oz. of water as an emetic.
from 10 grains to 1 scruple	in an oz. of water as an emetic.
from 4 to 8 grains every four or six hours	to produce perspiration.
1 ounce........................	to be dissolved in a pint of water, the proper strength.
from 10 to 20 grains...........	to make saline draughts, to be taken every two or three hours.
from 10 grains to a scruple in a little cold water.............	to produce perspiration in rheumatism, or in an advanced stage of dysentery at bedtime.
from ½ a drachm to a drachm in a little cold water every 4 hours .	to produce perspiration in colds and fevers without much inflammation.
....	to be used to make acidulated drinks.
from 10 to 30 drops in a little water	as an anodyne, chiefly at bedtime
from 1 to 3 grains	as an anodyne at bedtime.
from ½ a drachm to a drachm in a little water	as a stimulant when necessary.
from ½ a drachm to a drachm and a half in a little water	as a stimulant when necessary.
from 3 to 6 grains made into a pill every six hours.............	as a stimulant in fevers where there is great weakness.
from 5 to 10 grains...........	as a gentle laxative or alterative in bilious diseases.
from 10 to 30 grains in a little peppermint water	as a cordial in cases of great weakness from fever or dysentery, every four hours.

ARTICLES.	Quantity.	
	lbs.	oz.
Ginger root......	..	8
Ditto, in powder	..	8
Oil of cinnamon	..	2
Oil of peppermint....................................	..	2
Compound powder of chalk with opium, in 2 tins ...	..	..
Tincture of catechu................................	..	4
Sulphate of quinine, in 4 bottles	..	4
Blistering plaster....	2	..
Rectified spirits of wine, in half-pints	2	..
Soap liniment, in half-pints	2	.
Acetate of lead, called sugar of lead	1	.
Lint..	..	8
Tape................................... 6 pieces		
Leather .... 2 skins	..	..
Calico rollers.........................12 No.		
Flannel rollers ....12 "		
Sponge................................ 6 pieces		
Pint syringe, &c......... .... 1 No.		
Small syringes .... 2 "		
Small bolus tile....................... 1 "		
Pins .... 6 papers		
Sticking plaster....................... 3 yards		
Lancets .... 1 case		
Aperient pills......................... 1 box		
Pestle and mortar...................... 1 No.		

From Directions given by Sir John Webb, of Woolwich·

DOSES.	REMARKS.
....	to be used at discretion.
from 1 to 2 scruples in a little cold water every six hours, or peppermint water................	as a gentle astringent in an advanced stage of diarrhœa or dysentery
from 1 to 2 drachms in a little peppermint or cinnamon water every six hours	as an astringent in an advanced stage of diarrhœa or dysentery.
from 2 to 5 grains in the form of pills every six hours	as a strengthener after fever or dysentery.
....	to be used at discretion.
....	to be used at discretion.
....	to rub sprains or contusions twice or thrice a day.
....	to make Goulard water as directed.
....	for blisters.

the Remarks were of essential service to us.—R. & J. L.

VOL. II.—F f

THE END.

Lightning Source UK Ltd.
Milton Keynes UK
UKHW021320100522
402722UK00007B/1169

9 781379 220923